Ge Wang

Pains and Gains of Ethnic Multilingual Learners in China

An Ethnographic Case Study

 Springer

Ge Wang
Yunnan University
Kunming, Yunnan
China

ISSN 2213-3208   ISSN 2213-3216 (electronic)
Multilingual Education
ISBN 978-981-10-9222-0   ISBN 978-981-10-0661-6 (eBook)
DOI 10.1007/978-981-10-0661-6

© Springer Science+Business Media Singapore 2016
Softcover reprint of the hardcover 1st edition 2016
This work is subject to copyright. All rights are reserved by the Publisher, whether the whole or part of the material is concerned, specifically the rights of translation, reprinting, reuse of illustrations, recitation, broadcasting, reproduction on microfilms or in any other physical way, and transmission or information storage and retrieval, electronic adaptation, computer software, or by similar or dissimilar methodology now known or hereafter developed.
The use of general descriptive names, registered names, trademarks, service marks, etc. in this publication does not imply, even in the absence of a specific statement, that such names are exempt from the relevant protective laws and regulations and therefore free for general use.
The publisher, the authors and the editors are safe to assume that the advice and information in this book are believed to be true and accurate at the date of publication. Neither the publisher nor the authors or the editors give a warranty, express or implied, with respect to the material contained herein or for any errors or omissions that may have been made.

Printed on acid-free paper

This Springer imprint is published by Springer Nature
The registered company is Springer Science+Business Media Singapore Pte Ltd.

Multilingual Education

Volume 17

Series editors

Andy Kirkpatrick
Department of Languages and Linguistics, Griffith University,
Brisbane, Australia

Bob Adamson
Head, Department of International Education & Lifelong Learning,
Hong Kong Institute of Education

Editorial Board

Jan Blommaert, University of Tilburg, The Netherlands
Feng Anwei, University of Wales at Bangor, UK
Ofelia Garcia, The Graduate Centre, City University of New York, USA
Saran Kaur Gill, Universiti Kebangsaan Malaysia
Gu Yueguo, The Chinese Academy of Social Sciences
Hartmut Haberland, Roskilde University, Denmark
Li Chor Shing David, The Hong Kong Institute of Education
Li Wei, Birkbeck College, University of London, UK
Low Ee-Ling, National Institute of Education, Singapore
Tony Liddicoat, University of South Australia
Ricardo Nolasco, University of the Philippines at Diliman, Manila, The Philippines
Merrill Swain, Ontario Institute of Studies in Education, University of Toronto, Canada
Virginia Yip Choy Yin, Chinese University of Hong Kong

The book series Multilingual Education publishes top quality monographs and edited volumes containing empirical research on multilingual language acquisition, language contact and the respective roles of languages in contexts where the languages are not cognate and where the scripts are often different, in order to be able to better understand the processes and issues involved and to inform governments and language policy makers. The volumes in this series are aimed primarily at researchers in education, especially multilingual education and other related fields, and those who are involved in the education of (language) teachers. Others who will be interested include key stakeholders and policy makers in the field of language policy and education. The editors welcome proposals and ideas for books that fit the series. For more information on how you can submit a proposal, please contact the publishing editor, Jolanda Voogd. E-mail: jolanda.voogd@springer.com

More information about this series at http://www.springer.com/series/8836

This monograph is dedicated to my son, Chujun Wang, as well as all supporting family members and friends. It is also a salute to all colleagues who are engaged in challenging but meaningful multilingual education in the ethnic minority areas in China.

Foreword

This volume marks a welcome advance in research on language policy and language education in China. Ge Wang breaks new ground both methodologically and thematically. By adopting an ethnographic approach to shed light on how policy is interpreted and appropriated by local actors, he not only brings new methodological tools to the study of language policy in China, but also contributes a new case to the ethnography of language policy literature (Hornberger and Johnson 2007; McCarty 2011; Johnson 2013). Likewise, with this volume and his ongoing work (Wang 2011, 2015a, b), Ge Wang joins a small but growing scholarship in China that expands the scope of language education research beyond predominant attention to English language learning to include multilingual education for ethnic minority learners (see also Hu 2012; Yu 2014; Zhou 2000, 2001a, b).

Reflecting on and motivated by his own experiences and successes as ethnic minority learner, teacher, and researcher, Ge Wang here explores the life stories and identities of two ethnic minority learners as they shape and are shaped by global, national, regional, and institutional policy discourses around trilingual ethnic minority education at Yunnan University of Nationalities in southwest China, one of the most ethnically diverse areas of the country–home to 25 of China's 56 officially identified ethnic minority groups, 15 of them unique to Yunnan Province. He writes knowledgeably, comprehensively, and clearly about the demographic and language policy context for ethnic minority multilingual education in China, in Yunnan, and in higher education in particular. He acknowledges and confronts the dilemma of ethnic minority learners' dwindling enthusiasm for learning and keeping their ethnic mother tongues while they see Chinese as a pathway to social mobility and English as a passport to a globalized world—a dilemma exacerbated by China's contradictory policies offering protection to ethnic minority peoples, their languages and cultures, while infusing English language learning ever deeper into the educational curriculum.

Within this policy context, the author situates his case studies of the two learners in the international literature on multicultural education and multilingual learner identity, the institutional context of Yunnan University of Nationalities and its

School of Foreign Languages, and the historical and sociocultural context of their peoples—the Naxi and Hani, respectively. Drawing from his long-term ethnographic study including participant observation in classrooms and off-campus, interview, autobiography, oral narrative, and online chatting, Ge Wang provides in-depth description, analysis, and interpretation of how the two young women, Mammuts and Noma, negotiate multiple identities amidst curricula, examinations, and educational practices that largely ignore or exclude their familiar ways of speaking, learning, knowing, doing, and being. His ethnographic portraits succeed as holistic and emic accounts of the learners' experiences, honoring and respecting the complexity of challenges they confronted and the resiliency with which they met them.

Ge Wang skillfully presents the young women's experiences while also contextualizing them to both Chinese language education policy and the international literature on multilingual education. His work carries implications for ethnic minority multilingual higher education, not only in Yunnan and China, but also around the world. It is both poignant and telling that publication of this work in English affords the latter possibility in ways that publication in Chinese, Naxi, Hani, or his own heritage language Lisu would not.

Though I am not a scholar of China or Chinese languages, it has been my privilege to host a number of Chinese scholars in Educational Linguistics here at the University of Pennsylvania Graduate School of Education over the years, including Ge Wang during his recent Fulbright year. I have been equally honored to visit China several times at the invitation of Chinese colleagues in sociolinguistics and educational linguistics. It is from that vantage point that I welcome Ge Wang's unique and courageous work, powerfully lifting the voice of ethnic minority multilingual learners whose resilience and resourcefulness speak back to marginalizing language policy and education practice.

Philadelphia, USA
January 2016

Nancy H. Hornberger

References

Hornberger, N. H., & Johnson, D. C. (2007). Slicing the onion ethnographically: Layers and spaces in multilingual language education policy and practice. *TESOL Quarterly, 41*(3), 509–532.

Hu, D. (2012). Situation of trilingual education for the ethnic minorities at the border areas of Yunnan China. *Unpublished*.

Johnson, D. C. (2013). Ethnography of language policy: Theory, method and practice. *International Journal of the Sociology of Language, 219*, entire.

McCarty, T. L. (Ed.) (2011). *Ethnography and Language Policy*. New York: Routledge.

Wang, G. (2011). Bilingual education in southwest China: A Yingjiang case. *International Journal of Bilingual Education and Bilingualism, 14*(5), 571–587.

Wang, G. (2015a). Ethnic multilingual education in China: A critical observation. *Working Papers in Educational Linguistics, 30*(2), 51–64.

Wang G. (2015b). Glocalization of Western Pedagogy in China: A Mother Tongue-based Education Project in Jianchuan, China. *Unpublished*.

Yu, Liming (Ed.) (2014) *Educational Linguistics in China*. Shanghai, China: East China Normal University Press.

Zhou, M. (2000). Language policy and illiteracy in ethnic minority communities in China. *Journal of Multilingual and Multicultural Development, 21*(2), 129–148.

Zhou, M. (2001a). Language policy and reforms of writing systems for minority languages in China. *Written Language and Literacy, 4*(1), 31–65.

Zhou, M. (2001b). The politics of bilingual education and educational levels in ethnic minority communities in China. *International Journal of Bilingual Education and Bilingualism, 4*(2), 125–149.

Preface

Existing research on multilingual acquisition indicates that learners confront challenges not only in mastering unfamiliar linguistic forms but also in forming new identities, especially when the languages concerned are socially and linguistically distant from each other. This study shows that ethnic multilingual learners (EMLs) in China face more challenges at universities than the ethnic majority Han, when they choose to study English as their major subject. The textbook written for the majority Han and instructive methods for mainstream students are imposed upon them. The environment is unfamiliar to EMLs, and they are often regarded as "strangers" to the new language learning community. Their problems include the national examination system, the medium of instruction, learning difficulties, psychological issues, and cultural exclusion. In a sense, the current educational policies in China are designed to protect the educational rights of ethnic minorities, but ignore the role of education in promoting ethnic minority cultures. The current university curricula mainly focus on subject knowledge and patriotic education. As a result, the "cultural self-consciousness" or *wenhua zijue* in Chinese and "cultural capital" in English are less emphasized and encouraged. In this study, data are collected on two female ethnic multilingual minority students at Yunnan University of Nationalities (YUN) through ethnographic interviews, autobiography, oral narrative, online chatting, and field observation.

This study provides information at the micro-level on how the two students have successfully navigated the Chinese education system to the tertiary level. They have tried their best to excel in the curricula of YUN by constructing multiple identities. The findings suggest that the informants negotiate their multiple identities through their active engagements, on and off the university campus, as legitimate participants in various "communities of practice." These identities are shaped partly by their own cultural heritage and partly by the present sociopolitical realities in China. Drawing mainly on poststructuralist and multicultural education theories, the study also examines the power relationships exercised in YUN and discusses the impact of these power relationships on the identity formation of the target informants. The national and local policies as well as the curriculum structures of YUN are analyzed to identify the implicit power relationships that cause tensions in the education of EMLs. It is argued that multiculturalism, as a discourse of education, may help to ease the tension between being an ethnic minority and a Chinese national. Multiculturalism may also help reduce the danger of assimilation and marginalization. To achieve the goal of multilingual education based on the notion of multiculturalism, a "collaborative" power relationship, which facilitates the empowerment of EMLs, should be the goal of Chinese higher education. With such a goal, EMLs will be able to act as human resources for raising the productivity of the country, as agents for social transformation and as citizens of the cosmopolitan world.

Acknowledgments

The author of this book would like to thank Dr. MaryJo Benton Lee for her proofreading of the early draft and Prof. Zhenhua Zhang for his comments on the final draft. I would also give my heartfelt gratitude to Prof. Nancy Hornberger for her inspiring lectures on Language Diversity and Education at Graduate School of Education, the University of Pennsylvania and for her generous offer to write a foreword for this monograph. A similar gratitude will be extended to Prof. Minglang Zhou from Maryland University for his writing an afterword for this book.

Parts of the contents were published previously by *The Asia-Pacific Education Researcher* and *Working Papers in Educational Linguistics* in 2012 and 2015, respectively. I would also like to thank for the permissions granted for using Figures and Pictures from Miss Xiaoyu Lin, Mr. Bin Xu, Mr. Yao He, Mr. Baohong Chen, Mr. Ge Wang and the Department of Public Information of the CPC Committee, Yunnan University of Nationalities.

Ge Wang

Contents

1	**The Odyssey**	1
1.1	Journey of Self-Discovery	1
1.2	Previous Professional and Academic Experience	3
1.3	The Choice of the Topic for This Study	4
1.4	Research Design	5
1.5	Summary	7
	References	7
2	**Reconceptualizing Ethnic Multilingual Learners in China**	9
2.1	Ethnic Multilingual Education in China and Yunnan	9
2.2	Multilingual Education Policies in China	10
2.3	Demographic Features and Language Policies in Yunnan	11
2.4	Challenges for Ethnic Minority Higher Education	14
2.5	Policies, Curriculum, and Power Relationships: A Discussion of the Paradox	18
2.6	Summary	23
	References	24
3	**The Study of Multilingual Learners**	27
3.1	Multiculturalism: A Social Trend Around the World	27
	3.1.1 Strategies of Multiculturalism	29
	3.1.2 Assimilation	29
	3.1.3 Integration	30
	3.1.4 Acculturation and Enculturation	30
	3.1.5 Four Acculturation Strategies	30
3.2	Multicultural Education: A Notion of the Twenty-First Century	31
	3.2.1 Multicultural Education in the West	33
	3.2.2 The Configuration of *Duoyuan Yiti* in China	35

	3.3	The Study of Multilingual Acquisition	38
		3.3.1 The Psychological/Cognitive Approach	38
		3.3.2 The Sociocultural Approach	39
		3.3.3 The Post-structuralist Approach	41
	3.4	The Study of the Identity of Multilingual Learners	47
		3.4.1 The Sociocultural Paradigm and Identity Studies	47
		3.4.2 The Post-Structuralist Paradigm to Identities of Multilingual Learners	50
	3.5	The Conceptual Framework of This Study	53
	3.6	Summary	57
	References		57
4	**The Profile of Yunnan University of Nationalities and Methodology**		**69**
	4.1	YUN History	69
	4.2	The History of the School of Foreign Languages	71
	4.3	YUN and SFL Curriculum	72
	4.4	Implications of the SFL Curriculum	74
	4.5	Views of Some SFL Administrators and Teachers	77
	4.6	The Process of Data Collection	83
	4.7	The Choice of the Two Major Informants	87
		4.7.1 The Selection of Mammuts	87
		4.7.2 The Selection of Noma	88
		4.7.3 Data Analysis	89
	4.8	Summary	91
	References		91
5	**The Case of Mammuts**		**93**
	5.1	The Sociocultural Context of the Naxi	94
		5.1.1 Demographic Features of the Naxi	94
		5.1.2 The Naxi Language and Culture	94
		5.1.3 Naxi Education Level and Features	96
	5.2	Studies of the Naxi	97
	5.3	Local Policy and Practice	98
	5.4	The Story of Mammuts	99
		5.4.1 Family and Childhood	99
		5.4.2 School Journey	100
		5.4.3 Language Shift Between Daily Life and Classroom	102
		5.4.4 Tensions with Curriculum	103
		5.4.5 Psychological Problems	107
		5.4.6 Conflict with Parents	108
		5.4.7 Identity Issues	109
		5.4.8 The Enjoyable Off-Campus Life	113
		5.4.9 Happy Vacations	114
		5.4.10 Being a TA in Shane	114

5.4.11 Dae Jang Geum Club . . . 115
5.4.12 Mary Kay Implication. . . . 116
5.5 Discussion and Implications . . . 117
5.5.1 Curriculum and Disempowerment . . . 117
5.5.2 Capital, Agency, and Empowerment. . . . 119
5.6 Summary . . . 122
References . . . 123

6 The Case of Noma . . . 127
6.1 Sociocultural Context of the Hani . . . 127
6.1.1 Demographic Features . . . 127
6.1.2 Characteristics of the Hani People . . . 129
6.1.3 Socioeconomic Development. . . . 130
6.1.4 Hani People's Perception of Education . . . 132
6.1.5 Local Policies to Promote the Education of the Hani . . . 133
6.2 The Story of Noma . . . 134
6.2.1 Family Background . . . 134
6.2.2 Financial Problems. . . . 135
6.2.3 Family Influence . . . 137
6.2.4 Language Shift Between Daily Life and Classroom . . . 139
6.2.5 Learning English as the Third Language . . . 141
6.2.6 Tensions Within the Curriculum. . . . 142
6.2.7 Psychological Problems . . . 144
6.2.8 Culture Shock and Reentry Shock . . . 145
6.2.9 Challenge of Being Class Monitor . . . 147
6.2.10 Thanksgiving Attitude . . . 149
6.2.11 Being Chinese with Hani Characteristics. . . . 151
6.2.12 Dream of Being Noma-Amy . . . 154
6.2.13 Dream, Reality, and Conflict . . . 155
6.3 Discussion and Implications . . . 156
6.3.1 Perception, Policy, and Practice . . . 157
6.3.2 Investment, Legitimacy, and Changing Identity . . . 158
6.3.3 Cultural Heritage, Attitude, and Actions . . . 160
6.4 Summary . . . 162
References . . . 163

7 Discussion and Conclusion . . . 165
7.1 Mammuts and Noma: A Discussion of Contrast. . . . 165
7.1.1 Sociocultural Background, Perception, and School Performance . . . 165
7.1.2 Cultural Awareness . . . 168
7.1.3 Preferential Education Policies. . . . 169
7.1.4 Multilingual Acquisition . . . 170
7.1.5 Psychological Support . . . 171
7.1.6 Identity Issues . . . 171
7.1.7 Investment and Return . . . 175

7.2	Reflections on the Multiple Identities of Ethnic Minority Learners	176
7.3	Suggestions for Further Study	180
7.4	Final Remarks	181
	References	185

Afterword 189

Appendices 193

Index 199

List of Figures

Figure 2.1	The map of Yunnan (Lin 2015)	12
Figure 3.1	The total school environment adapted from Banks (2009)	35
Figure 3.2	Conceptual framework (Wang 2012)	54
Figure 7.1	Multiple roles of Mammuts and Noma (Wang 2012)	172

List of Tables

Table 2.1	The number of ethnic minority students in higher education institutions of the PRC1998–2005 (Tan and Xie 2009).	16
Table 2.2	Higher education in 2006 (MOE)	16
Table 3.1	Berry's four strategies of acculturation.	31
Table 4.1	Courses for English major undergraduates (Wang 2011)	73
Table 4.2	Demographic features of the fourth-year English majors at YUN (2006).	84
Table 4.3	Characteristics of senior ethnic minority students at YUN (2010a, b)	85
Table 4.4	Basic facts about the informants (Wang 2012)	86
Table 4.5	Types of data (Wang 2012).	90
Table 6.1	Education in Mojiang (data from a general introduction to Mojiang Hani Autonomous County of Yunnan Province; A brief history of the Hani people; Chinahani online 2008; Chinese ethnicity and religion online 2010; Pu'er education and information online).	131

List of Pictures

Picture 4.1	The new motto of YUN (2015)	71
Picture 4.2	The "Red Song (Red song in Chinese history refers to patriotic or revolutionary pop songs.) singing contest" at YUN (2015)	74
Picture 4.3	The entrance of the old YUN campus (YUN 2015)	76
Picture 4.4	The entrance of the new YUN campus (YUN 2015)	77
Picture 5.1	The Dongba/Chinese calligraphy (He 2016)	95
Picture 5.2	The memorial arch of Tianyu Liufang (Wang 2011)	96
Picture 5.3	No. 1 Senior Secondary School of Lijiang Ancient City District (© Xu 2011)	100
Picture 5.4	The old library of SSSACD (© Xu 2011)	101
Picture 7.1	The Tusi Mu's Executive Mansion (Wang 2011)	173
Picture 7.2	The Gate of Loyalty and Righteousness (Wang 2011)	174
Picture 7.3	The loyalty bridge (Chen 2015)	175

Abbreviations

BNU	Beijing Normal University
CCTV	Chinese Central TV
CECUS	China Education Center of the University of Sydney
CET	College English Test
CPC	Communist Party of China
DFL	Department of Foreign Languages
EFL	English as a Foreign Language
ELT	English Language Teaching
EML	Ethnic Multilingual Learners
ESL	English as a Second Language
EXPO '99	World Horticultural Exposition in 1999
HKU	The University of Hong Kong
IC	Intercultural Communication
MA	Multilingual Acquisition
MOE	The Ministry of Education
MUC	Minzu University of China
NHEEC	National Higher Education Evaluation Center
PRC	The People's Republic of China
SFL	School of Foreign Languages
SLA	Second Language Acquisition
SSSLAC	Senior Secondary School of Lijiang Ancient City
TEM	Test of English Major
TESOL	Teaching English to the Speakers of Other Languages
YIN	Yunnan Institute of Nationalities
YNU	Yunnan University
YUN	Yunnan University of Nationalities

Chapter 1
The Odyssey

> *I don't feel that it is necessary to know exactly what I am. The main interest in life and work is to become someone else that you were not in the beginning. If you knew when you began a book what you would say at the end, do you think that you would have the courage to write it?*
>
> — Michel Foucault

1.1 Journey of Self-Discovery

I was born in a family of intellectuals of the Lisu (傈僳) and Han Chinese in Hebei Province in northern China. I lost the chance to acquire my native ethnic language and culture for my family spoke Putonghua (Mandarin Chinese). My mother is of Lisu descent, and my father is of Han. Both are natives of Yunnan Province who traveled to Beijing during the early 1950s to pursue higher education. I never understood the true meaning of being a Lisu as this identity was inherited from my mother and, merely a label on my ID card and household registration booklet (*Hukou Bu* 户口簿). I did not know where the Lisu people lived or what their daily life entailed. Actually, I had never thought about that during the first 15 years of my life. I grew up in a city where the Han are the overwhelming majority. I therefore tried to hide my ethnic identity in my school for no one had ever heard of the Lisu. I was quite embarrassed to talk about my ethnic identity because I could neither speak nor write the two characters '傈僳' that represented my ethnicity, either in my native language Lisu or in Chinese script. I remember one of my close secondary schoolmates asked me whether 傈僳 was pronounced as *Luo Luo* (倮倮). I felt very ashamed as I knew Luo Luo was a derogatory term used to address ethnic minorities in a contemptuous tone. As the inquirer was one of my best friends in the secondary school, I quickly forgave his ignorance. Meanwhile, there were even fewer people who knew how to write the word "Lisu" in correct Chinese characters.

No one cared but I did. I cared because I was very embarrassed to find out that I was different from others. Why was I the only ethnic minority in my class? I wanted to be the same as others.

In 1985, I migrated to Yunnan with my parents in my second year of secondary school and settled in Kunming, the provincial capital city. My first challenge was the local Kunming dialect. Although the medium of instruction at school was Putonghua, the classroom and playground were flooded with local Kunming dialect after class. In contrast to showing off my Putonghua during class, I kept silent after class for the first two weeks for the same reason—I did not want to be different from my classmates. After two weeks' silence, I tried to speak with other students in the local Kunming dialect. I picked up this local dialect so quickly that everyone identified me as a local resident a half year later.

One of the reasons that I migrated to Yunnan was that the benchmark for higher education there was not as demanding as in northern China. Furthermore, as a minority student, I could have 20 bonus points in the national matriculation examination. The bonus marks made a dramatic difference for an undergraduate in terms of decent jobs, stable income, and even a good marriage. In the 1980s, a diploma from a university was the access to an "iron bowl" (*Tie Fanwan* 铁饭碗) in China where university graduates were treated as "God's favored guys" (*Tianzhi Jiaozi* 天之骄子).

Personally I did not benefit much from the preferential admission policy,[1] but I did notice the difference in the quality of education between the inland and the frontier provinces like Yunnan. In northern China, my best rank in my class in the secondary school was in the top 18, but when I moved to Yunnan I was one of the top 3 students in my class till I graduated from my university.

I was admitted to an ordinary local normal university in Yunnan though my score was 50 points higher than the enrollment score required for the key university in Yunnan. When I look back, I do not regret my application to the local normal university. Instead, I felt quite happy being a "big fish in a small pond." I had to confess I worked very hard at the university and took the role of a model learner called the "learning representative" (*xuexi weiyuan* 学习委员) in my class. I was a straight A student for four years at my university not only because I was from a professor's family, but also because I wanted my peers who looked down upon the ethnic students to admire me.

Reflecting on my story as a successful "ethnic learner" I often asked myself whether I could have been so "successful" if I were not born into a well-educated

---

[1]The preferential policies include bonus marks in the national matriculation examination, university admissions quotas, flexible admissions conditions and tuition waivers, the *Minkaomin* policy (the national matriculation examinations in particular ethnic minority languages), establishing ethnic minority universities, the *Neidiban* (minority class in inland comprehensive universities), the native language requirement in civil servant selection, bonus marks awarded to applicants who have worked in minority areas for years and wish to be admitted to postgraduate programs, and special arrangements to develop senior specialized minority talents.

middle class family with much better conditions than my kinfolks in the remote mountain areas in Yunnan. If I had not received an excellent education in north China due to the strong government support and much better educational resources, I might have ended up with no more than a junior middle school education and working as either a farmer at hometown or a migrant worker elsewhere.

1.2 Previous Professional and Academic Experience

Before I came to the University of Hong Kong (HKU) to pursue my PhD degree, I had taught English in a tertiary institution in Yunnan for 15 years. I did witness the experiences and difficulties of ethnic multilingual learners, especially the challenges from mastering three languages (the native language, Chinese and English) and negotiating their identities in the mainstream education system. I also observed the tensions between national language policies, local curriculum, and ethnic identities. Although my observation was as an outsider, I did hope to have a better understanding of multilingual learners in Yunnan and voice some advice on the development of a more sensible curriculum integrating English education with multicultural awareness.

With training in English language and literature, my research experience with ethnic minority education was very limited. My first study on ethnic minority education could be traced back to 2001 when I was invited to give a speech on education for ethnic minorities in China at a forum hosted by the China Education Center at the University of Sydney (CECUS). CECUS was the first academic research center in Australia, devoted to Chinese education study. As my supervisor was the director at that time, he asked me to give a talk on ethnic minority education in Yunnan. I was very nervous and worried for I had no knowledge of this area. Thus, I rushed to the Chinese Education Sector of Chinese Consulate in Sydney and found a Green Paper on Chinese Education written in 2000. I was very excited at my discovery and after a few days' work, I wrote an essay on ethnic minority education in China based on the green paper and some other materials from the library and the Internet. My speech was well received, and the paper was published in *CECUS Newsletter*. This presentation made me aware that the educational attainment of ethnic minority learners was very different from that of the majority Han because of the disparities in sociopolitical conditions and socioeconomic development. As a result, the circumstances of ethnic minority education were far from satisfactory.

In 1993, I visited Simao and Xishuangbanna, the communities dominated by the Hani and the Dai. I also took a business trip in 2005 to the three popular tourist cities of Dali, Lijiang, and Shangri-La. The three cities inhabited by the Bai, the Naxi, and the Tibetans are very famous for their landscape and cultural heritage. In Lijiang, I danced with a group of Naxi women for fun and also talked often with a female Tibetan tour guide inquiring about Tibetan customs and rituals. In 2008 and 2009, I did two field studies in Shangri-La and Yingjiang. All these experiences not only triggered my interest in the study of ethnic minorities in Yunnan, but also created a dream. As mentioned before, despite my ethnic minority status, I was often labeled a successful learner with a good education and career prospects. As a multilingual learner with ethnic minority blood, I felt responsible and committed to helping other ethnic minority students master English and become "cultural ambassadors."

1.3 The Choice of the Topic for This Study

The choice of this topic resulted from many rounds of discussion between me and my two supervisors at HKU. I succeeded in applying to the PhD program at HKU with a proposal for studying the learning strategies of ethnic minority students in Yunnan. That topic was, however, my second choice. Before I came to HKU, I had been engaged in the study of intercultural language teaching for five years. As the principal investigator of two provincial grants (2004, 2006) awarded by the Yunnan Educational Committee, I conducted two empirical studies on ethnic multilingual learners in Yunnan. My first study was to develop the intercultural communication competence of English majors through language teaching. The second one was to examine the intercultural teaching competence of in-service teachers.

Based on the findings of the first study, I presented a paper at the first Asia TEFL International Conference in Pusan, Korea in 2003. My presentation drew great interest from the ELT professionals with similar concerns and a paper titled "Task-based Intercultural Language Teaching" was published by the second issue of Journal of Asia TEFL in 2004. This publication was a milestone in my research career. Since then I have become intoxicated with empirical study, and ethnic multilingual learners are my favorite informants. This study not only brought me a second prize for excellent teaching and research in Yunnan (2006) but it further triggered my second round grant application. In 2006, I was successfully funded by the Yunnan Educational Committee again. My study was an extension of my previous work examining the intercultural language teaching competence of in-service teachers. Likewise, a paper on "Intercultural Language Education in China: Problems and Prospect" was first presented at an international conference in Shanghai and later published by a regional journal in 2006. In this paper, I discussed the problems with intercultural language education in China from the perspectives of language planning, teaching methodology, material development, and teacher education. Some questions to be considered as such (Wang and Zhou 2005, p. 89):

- How to achieve cross-cultural understanding? (awareness of one's own culture as well as that of the target culture?)
- How to work harmoniously with people of different nationalities, gender, age and backgrounds?
- How to develop cultural tolerance and behave properly in different cultural contexts?

These questions are not only perplexing to me but they also challenge the current ELT policy and curriculum. To give tentative answers to these questions, I published another book chapter in 2010 entitled "A Reflection on Culture Teaching in an EFL Context". I raised more specific questions as follows (Wang and Liu 2010, p. 453):

- Whose culture should we teach, and what aspects of this culture should we highlight?
- What curriculum and assessments are available or need to be developed?
- What materials on culture teaching should be selected or developed to meet the practical teaching needs?

After completing the two studies, many colleagues asked me about the key to successful grant applications as an inexperienced researcher. At the beginning I did not know how to answer. Good proposals, persistence, and good luck. All of these could be my answers. After a second thought, I found the key to my success were the words in my proposal "ethnic minority students." As a frontier province in Southwest China, the education of ethnic minority learners are less attended and explored. Therefore, in this study, I hope to understand ethnic multilingual learners from both macro and micro perspectives. At the macro level, I expect to understand the policy and practices concerning ethnic minority education in general by examining global, national, regional, and institutional discourses. At micro level, I intend to trace the life stories of the selected informants and discuss the formation of their multiple identities under the given power relationships.

1.4 Research Design

In this study, I am interested in recording the life histories of some ethnic multilingual learners (EMLs) at a tertiary institution in Yunnan. I also would like to report how the EMLs in the case studies negotiate their identities under the pressure of mastering three languages. The tensions resulting from policies and curricula in relation to ethnic minorities, language, and education are also discussed.

Drawing on post-structuralist paradigms to understand identity in a multilingual context, this study aims to investigate multilingual learners in Yunnan through the lens of life histories. The study will answer these questions:

- How are the identities of tertiary ethnic minority learners shaped through the process of multilingual acquisition?
- What factors contribute to the identity construction of ethnic multilingual learners at the tertiary level in Yunnan?
- How do the EMLs in the case study negotiate their identities through trilingual education[2]?

Identity issues of EMLs are not adequately explored in the Asian context. This is quite natural in the Asian collective culture where people try to avoid talking too much about "selves" and "others" (Munro 1969; Mauss 1979). In China's context, individuals are conceived of as social beings that are subordinated to the collective. Pratt (1992, p. 285) argues that:

> The Chinese construction of self emphasizes continuity of family, societal roles, the supremacy of hierarchical relationships, compliance with authority, and maintenance of stability. In Asian culture, harmony and face are important parameters to guide people's communication with each other.

Individuality and diversity often yield to collectivism and unity. Except for limited studies on identity issues of the mainstream Asian students (Lee 2002; Luk 2005; Gao et al. 2007; Chen 2008; Gu 2008), this work is perhaps the first to trace the life history of ethnic multilingual students at the tertiary level in Southwestern China.

In addition to conceptual contributions, it is expected that this study will provide some useful reflections on the current policies in relation to ethnic minorities and multilingual education. Likewise, this study will help stakeholders to make more sensitive policies so as to develop appropriate curricula to meet the needs of multicultural education.

In spite of the study's significance, there are some limitations. First of all, the life histories of the two major informants are among the stories of millions of multilingual learners in China. One may argue that the sample is not big enough, but I believe a case study with thick description and in-depth discussions can help to reveal possible ways the informants nevigate in the Chinese education systems to "promote their positions as a minority *Minzu*" (Hansen 1999, p. 164).

Secondly, I have no proficiency in any ethnic minority languages so all the interviews were conducted in the local Chinese dialect. Although this was not a problem for the main informants, who have acquired high oral Chinese proficiency, misunderstandings in communication and interpretation likely occured when interviewing their parents, who were less proficient Chinese speakers. To fix such possible problems, I decided to collect multiple types of data at various times.

---

[2]Trilingual education in China's context refers to the acquisition of three languages: the native language (it is often the ethnic minority language for ethnic minority groups), Mandarin Chinese (Putonghua), and English or other foreign languages. Chinese is a compulsory subject throughout the curricula at all levels and Putonghua often serves as the medium of instruction in mainstream schools. English has been a compulsory subject since junior secondary school and was introduced into primary school curriculum since 2001.

1.5 Summary

Being a quarter Lisu, I reflected on my personal story of migration with my parents from North China to Southwest China as a top student at the cost of losing my ethnic minority language. I also talked about how my experiences as an English learner first and as a language teacher later helped develop my interest in studying ethnic multilingual learners in Yunnan, how I chose this topic, and how the research was designed.

References

Chen, H. I. (2008). Positioning and repositioning: Linguistic practices and identity negotiation of overseas returning bilinguals in Hong Kong. *Multilingua, 27*(1–2), 57–75.
Gao, Y. H., Zhao, Y., Cheng, Y., & Zhou, Y. (2007). Relationship between English learning motivation types and self-identity changes among Chinese students. *TESOL Quarterly, 41*(1), 133–155.
Gu, M. Y. (2008). Identity construction and investment transformation. *Journal of Asian Pacific Journal, 18*(1), 49–70.
Hansen, M. (1999). *Lessons in being Chinese: Minority education and ethnic identity in southwest China*. Seattle, WA: University of Washington Press.
Lee, J. S. (2002). The Korean language in America: The role of cultural identity in heritage language learning. *Language, Culture and Curriculum, 15*(2), 117–133.
Luk, C. M. J. (2005). Understanding and capitalizing on multiple identities of students in TESL/TEFL: Towards a pedagogy connecting. In S. May., M. Franken, & R. Franker (Eds.), *Proceedings of the 1st International Conference on Language, Education and Diversity* [CD-ROM]. New Zealand: University of Waikato.
Mauss, M. (1979). A category of the human mind: The notion of person; the notion of self. In Brewster, B. (translator). *Sociology and psychology: Essays by Marcel Mauss* (pp. 57–94). London: Routledge and Kegan Paul.
Munro, D. J. (1969). *The concept of man in early China*. Stanford, CA: Stanford University Press.
Pratt, M. L. (1992). *Imperial eyes: Travel writing and transculturation*. London and New York: Routledge.
Wang, G., & Liu, H. Y. (2010). A reflection on culture teaching in an EFL context. In J. P. Chen (Ed.), *The reform and creation of ELT in China: Proceeding of 06' China English Language Education Association Conference* (pp. 452–468). Beijing: Foreign Language Teaching and Research Press.
Wang, G., & Zhou, Z. (2005). Intercultural language education in China: Problems and prospect. *Journal of Communication Practices, 2*(2), 85–97.
Yunnan University of Nationalities. (2006). *Fifty-five Anniversary of Yunnan University of Nationalities*. Kunming: Yunnan Press of Nationalities.

Chapter 2
Reconceptualizing Ethnic Multilingual Learners in China

> *All the people like us are We,*
> *And every one else is They.*
> *And They live over the sea,*
> *While We live over the way,*
> *But-would you believe it?—They look upon We*
> *As only a sort of They!*
>
> –Rudyard Kipling

2.1 Ethnic Multilingual Education in China and Yunnan

The constitution of the People's Republic of China defines China as "a nation of multiethnic" (National People's Congress 1982). This claim is not only a statement concerning a demographic feature of China, but also a political consideration because the designations of the 56 ethnic groups are the "constructs of the state for managing its perceived policy and nationality policy" (Goodman 2004, p. 329). Since the founding of the PRC, the central government has issued a series of top-down laws and policies to legitimize and promote the multilingual competencies of ethnic minority learners. For example, the Constitution of the PRC (1982) declares that "all ethnic minority groups have freedom to develop their languages" (National People's Congress 1982). The 1982 Constitution of China reemphasizes the rights of ethnic minority groups in language use, sociocultural development, and regional autonomy by claiming in Article 4 that:

> All nationalities in the People's Republic of China are equal. The state protects the lawful rights and interests of the minority nationalities and upholds and develops the relationship of equality, unity and mutual assistance among all of China's nationalities. Discrimination against and oppression of any nationality are prohibited; any acts that undermine the unity of the nationalities or instigate their secession are prohibited. The state helps the areas inhabited by minority nationalities speed up their economic and cultural development in accordance with the peculiarities and needs of the different minority nationalities. Regional autonomy is practiced in areas where people of minority nationalities live in compact communities; in these areas organs of self-government are established for the exercise of the right of autonomy. All the national autonomous areas are inalienable parts of the People's Republic of China. The people of all nationalities have the freedom to use and

develop their own spoken and written languages, and to preserve or reform their own ways and customs.

(National People's Congress 1982)

The national constitution establishes the legitimate status of ethnic minority groups in China and paves the way for later bilingual education in ethnic minority areas. The newly issued Outline of China's Mid-long Term Educational Development reiterates that "the right to use and learn native languages and cultures shall be respected and protected" (The State Council of the PRC 2011). At present, the concept of bilingual education has been put into practice within the territory of China and guaranteed by various laws and regulations[1] formulated by central and local governments and legislation. The rights and interests of ethnic minority groups are protected by the granting of regional autonomy to ethnic minority groups, by the creation and reform of ethnic minority scripts, and by the establishment of bilingual education schools, to name just a few.

As a national policy, promoting the prosperity and development of ethnic minority groups has become a sustainable agenda for successive governments in China. For example, ex-Premier Wen Jiabao (2008) stated in the 2008 People's Congress that: "China is a unified, multiethnic country. We must promote unity among all ethnic groups and make a concerted effort to achieve prosperity and development for all."

This observation that China is a state of *Duoyuan Yiti,* "ethnic diversity within national unity" (Fei 1989), suggests that stakeholders at the top level believe national unity and ethnic diversity are the cornerstones of China's socioeconomic development and political stability.

2.2 Multilingual Education Policies in China

Since the founding of the PRC, the Chinese government has proposed and implemented trilingual education policies, except for the short-term suspension during the "Cultural Revolution."[2] As Adamson and Feng (2008) observe, the PRC has initiated educational language policies to "foster trilingualism in ethnic minority areas with three goals: to enhance literacy, to assure internal stability and to allow knowledge transfer in order to strengthen the nation" (p. 9). To achieve these goals,

---

[1] The laws and regulations concerned include the Guidelines for Regional Autonomy for Minority Nationalities in PRC (1952, 1982); Opinions Concerning Improving the Work of Minority Education (1980); The Law of Autonomy of Ethnic Minority Groups, (1984); The Regulation of Illiteracy Elimination, (1988); The Higher Education Law (1999); The General Language and Script Law (2000); The Law of Compulsory Education (2006); Outline of China's Middle and Long Term Educational Development (2010).

[2] The Cultural Revolution Campaign (1966–1976) was a violent, disastrous mass movement, which led to social, political, and economic upheaval in the People's Republic of China. It has been blamed for around 10 years' nationwide chaos and economic disarray and stagnation.

the PRC has issued trilingual policies[3] separately at different historical periods. These policies include promoting Putonghua (Mandarin Chinese) and bilingual education since the 1950s and introducing a third language, English, into the secondary and tertiary curricula in the 1980s.

In 2001, English was introduced into the primary school curriculum, and schools with the necessary conditions are required to teach English starting from primary Grade Three. At present, English is not only a required subject at almost all levels of curricula, but also a yardstick for talent selection and quality evaluation for higher learning institutions. In this sense, being multilingual in China is not only an important personal choice for ethnic multilingual learners (EMLs), but also a reality reflecting the state's political will and national interests.

2.3 Demographic Features and Language Policies in Yunnan

China is a country consisting of 56 officially identified ethnic groups. Yunnan is a frontier province in Southwest China with a great diversity of language, culture, and ethnicity (see Fig. 2.1). With a territory of 3,940,000 km^2 and a population of 45,966,239 (National Bureau of Statistics of China 2011a, b) Yunnan is home to 25 officially identified ethnic minority groups.[4] Among those groups, 15 can be found exclusively in Yunnan and 16 are cross-border ethnic groups.[5] The largest ethnic group, the Han, makes up 66.02 % of the population, while the other 25 ethnic minority groups constitute a combined 33.98 % of the total population of Yunnan. Now Yunnan has 8 autonomous prefectures and 29 autonomous counties. These cover 70.2 % of the territory and are inhabited by 48.08 % of the provincial population.

Yunnan is famous for its ethnic, cultural, and linguistic diversity. The 25 ethnic minority groups in Yunnan speak 26 languages and use 22 scripts (Dao 2005). Here 25 officially identified ethnic minority groups live together in a pattern of "*Dazaju Xiaojuju*"[6] (大杂居、小聚居 big dispersion and small concentration). This

---

[3]English was formally introduced into junior secondary school curricula in 1980. Before that some junior and senior secondary schools in China adopted other influential foreign languages such as Russian or Japanese as school subjects.

[4]These 25 ethnic groups are ethnic minority groups with populations of more than 5000. There are also some ethnic minority groups with small populations that have not been officially identified by the state. Mang People and Kemu People are cases in point.

[5]Although the numbers seem contradictory but they are in fact reasonable for some groups are overlapping. Some ethnic minority groups are exclusive to China and can also be found in the neighboring countries. That is why the sum is not 25. More than 16 ethnic minority groups live in the cross-border areas and have frequent language and economic contact with their friends and relatives on the other side of the border.

[6]According to Zhu and Blatchford's observation (2006), some of China's ethnic minority groups are highly dispersed, whereas others are highly concentrated in certain peripheral areas. The former

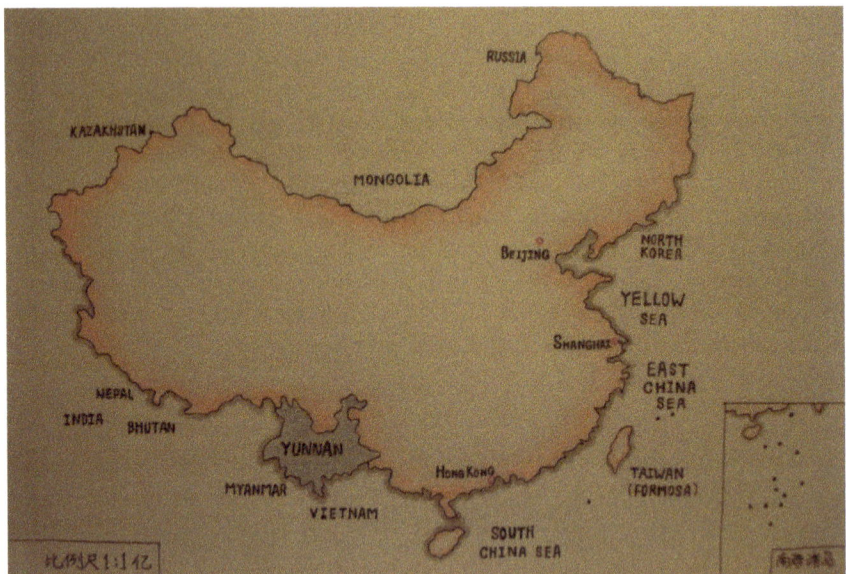

Fig. 2.1 The map of Yunnan and China (Lin 2015)

demographic feature has further contributed to the integration of some ethnic minority groups into the mainstream Han and other neighboring ethnic groups throughout history. Take Yunnan for example. Sixteen ethnic groups live in the cross-border areas where different ethnic people mix, and 22 ethnic groups speak 28 languages[7] (Tsang 2005). This is because some people can speak more than one language due to frequent interethnic contacts.

Given the differences in living environment, population size, community distribution, and socioeconomic development, the language use of ethnic communities is very diversified and complicated. According to the *Records of Ethnic Minority Language and Script, a volume of Record of Yunnan Province*, (Yang 1989), there are four types of language users in Yunnan: monolinguals, who speak the native language with community and non-community members (such as the Lisu, Dai, Tibetans, Jingpo, etc.); bilinguals,[8] who live in the flat lands or cohabit with other ethnic communities (such as the Bai, Naxi, Zhuang, etc.); trilinguals, who have

---

(Footnote 6 continued)

always live with the Han or other ethnic minority groups, whereas the latter usually live together as a community in the frontier areas.

[7]Many cross-border ethnic groups are multilingual due to frequent language contact with the neighboring ethnic communities. Thus, 22 ethnic minority groups can speak 28 languages.

[8]In the ethnic minority areas, bilingual education mainly refers to the instruction of native language and Mandarin Chinese, while in the Han dominated areas, bilingual education usually refers to the instruction of Chinese and English.

frequent contact with neighboring communities (such as the De'ang, Pumi, Bulang, etc.); and transitional language users, who have given up their native languages and adopted new languages (such as the Hui, Man, Shui, etc.). Before the 1990s, the need for trans-ethnic communication was very limited because of geographic isolation and slow socioeconomic development. Therefore, quite a large number of people (about 6.5 million) in Yunnan could not communicate in Putonghua. *The Survey of Language and Script Use in China* (2006) suggested that in Yunnan, only 37.84 % of the provincial population could communicate in Putonghua, which is lower than the national level of 53.06 %. Among the ethnic minority groups, only 12 % can communicate in Putonghua.[9] Take the Dulong for example: 85.99 % of its population does not understand Putonghua at all (Tsang 2005). Therefore, minority people like the Dulong will be at a disadvantage in seeking better education and working opportunities.[10] Thus, bilingual education in the school curriculum is essential as it "contributes to enhanced mutual understanding, respect as well as political and economic equality" (Teng and Wen 2005, p. 268).

To promote the literacy of some ethnic groups in Yunnan, especially those who could not understand Putonghua, in 1995, the Yunnan provincial government issued a transitional bilingual education policy, arguing:

> In minority areas where Chinese [Putonghua] is not understood, instruction in the local language will be vigorously promoted. In primary schools in minority areas where Chinese is not understood and there is a writing system for the local language, textual materials in the local language should be used for the early grades[11] while, at the same time, Chinese should be progressively introduced. For the upper grades,[12] textual materials should be in Chinese, with the local language playing a support role in instruction. In primary schools where Chinese is not understood and there is no writing system for the local language, the local language should be used to explain the texts and play a supporting role in instruction. For middle and primary schools[13] serving ethnic groups that understand Chinese, instruction can generally be carried out in Chinese. In areas where Chinese is understood and there is a writing system for the local language, the wishes of the local people will be respected regarding whether to create local language teaching materials.
> (State Education Commission 1995, as cited in Ma 2007, p. 15)

Echoing the instructions of the provincial government, some prefectural governments have also issued their own bilingual education policies, according to their local needs and special circumstances. For instance, in 1987, the Eighth People's Congress of Dehong Prefecture passed the Regulations of Self-autonomy of the Dai and the Jingpo Nationality. Clause 56 prescribes:

---

[9]They cannot communicate effectively with outsiders in either written or oral Chinese.

[10]A good command of Putonghua has become an essential qualification for migrant workers seeking employment in the nonethnic minority areas. Putonghua is also the dominant medium of instruction at all public educational institutions in China.

[11]The early grades usually refers to K1–K3 in elementary school.

[12]The upper grades usually refers to K4–6 in China.

[13]Primary school in China refers to K1–K6, while middle school refers to K7–12.

Within the autonomous prefecture, the ethnic primary schools which mainly enroll ethnic students should adopt *Shuangyuwen* (bilingual and bi-literacy) education. At the same time, the common language—Putonghua shall be used in schools. The native language courses should be offered for ethnic minority classes in the general secondary schools or technical schools. Within the whole prefecture the native language shall be tested and the score shall be documented in the final scores in the unified examinations.

(Dehong People's Congress 2005)

To sum up, bilingual education in China is a government-led educational campaign and policy, aimed at developing the multilingual competence of ethnic minority learners, improving the overall literacy of ethnic minority students, and achieving progress in national socioeconomic development through the public school curriculum (Wang 2011). The bilingual learning experience will not only help to develop the early literacy of some ethnic groups, but it also will provide them experience in acquiring new languages and access to equal educational opportunities.

2.4 Challenges for Ethnic Minority Higher Education

After over 30 years' reform and opening to the outside world, the transition of China from a planned economy has resulted in differing consequences for China's diverse populations. In particular, the reform in higher education and health care "has exacerbated the negative impact of economic reforms, widening the gap between China's eastern, coastal region and the less-developed western region, between the urban and rural population, and between the Han majority and those living in China's minority areas" (Hill and Zhou 2009, p. 3). The abolition of free higher education and government-guaranteed employment of university undergraduates since the late 1990s has resulted in a stricter screening of talents in an ever more competitive labor market. At the tertiary level, ethnic minority students are expected to master not only generic skills, but also multilingual proficiency at least in the national language—Chinese—and sometimes in English. However, the language, culture and socioeconomic gaps[14] between the majority Han and the minority ethnic groups place the latter at a great disadvantage.

Before 1949, there were no special higher learning institutions for ethnic minorities in China, and the number of students from ethnic groups in higher education was just 1285 (Ha and Teng 2001). Some ethnic groups like the Ji'nuo were unable to receive even basic education. However, since the founding of the

---

[14]Over 30 years prioritized policies for the eastern and coastal China have made these areas more developed. These policies have largely bypassed China's central and western regions inhabited by the largest number of ethnic minority groups. The different socioeconomic development leads to different levels of Putonghua acquisition and some culture gaps. These gaps are partially due to the culture differences and linguistic distance, resulting from the language and education policy imposed on minority groups.

PRC, especially since mass education was introduced in 1998, higher education for ethnic minority groups has developed at a great speed and scale. Now there are 16 minority higher education institutions in China running undergraduate and postgraduate programs. The number of ethnic minority students in ethnic minority universities amounts to more than 200,000 (Lei 2010). The rapid development of ethnic universities can be seen in their enrollment numbers and their efforts to catch up with mainstream institutions in order to be considered "world-class."

Table 2.1 shows that higher education has developed dramatically since 1998, along with ethnic higher education. Currently, higher education in China is in a transitional period from elite education to mass education, from building more universities to building "world-class" universities. It can be seen that from 1998 to 2005, the number of ethnic students at the tertiary level increased by 321 %. However, this figure is lower than the national increase rate of 358 %. On the other hand, the ratio of ethnic students in schools fell from 6.6 % to 6.1 % during the same period, which implies that the chances of ethnic minority students receiving higher education decreased. Zhang's (2008) study of college ethnic minority students in Yunnan also supports this assumption. Zhang's (2008) investigation indicated that the proportion of ethnic minority students in higher educational institutions in 2001 was 19.51 % of the university population, while the ethnic population in Yunnan accounted for 35 % of the provincial population in the same year. At a national level, the population of ethnic students was 5.81 % of the national school population, while the ethnic population was 8.41 % of the national population. The provincial and national figures demonstrate the unequal opportunities for ethnic groups' access to higher education in that the number of ethnic students in various schools is underrepresented in terms of the ethnic population ratio.

For example, the proportion of ethnic minority students at the tertiary level has not increased dramatically with the expansion of higher education. Instead, the proportion of tertiary ethnic students has been decreasing most years. Take Yunnan University of Nationalities (YUN) for example. In the 1950s, the ethnic population accounted for over 90 % of the total enrolled student population, whereas in 2010 the figure was just 41 % (Yunnan University of Nationalities 2011).

Furthermore, among the ethnic minority students themselves, the degree to which they receive public education varies. Tan and Xie's (2009) study showed that there was a gradual decrease in the ethnic population at the postgraduate level, but the population at the undergraduate level was gradually increasing (see Table 2.2). Yang (2009) pointed out that the higher the educational institution, the fewer female students enrolled. At the primary and secondary levels, the decrease in the number of female students is much higher than that of male students.

Choi (2010, p. 170) argues that "economic development and educational reform efforts currently underway in China have altered student demographics and created the potential for dramatic changes in the mission and identity of minority universities." She points out that these challenges are due to the "drastic social, cultural, economic and demographic changes for the ethnic community" (Choi 2010, p. 173). This observation helps to explain the rapid decline in the number of

Table 2.1 The number of ethnic minority students in higher education institutions of the PRC1998–2005 (Tan and Xie 2009)

Year	Number of ethnic tertiary students (10,000)	Number of tertiary students (10,000)	Ratio of ethnic students (%)	Ethnic increase rate (%)	National increase rate (%)
1998	22.63	340.9	6.6	NA	NA
1999	24.77	413.4	6.0	9.5	21.3
2000	31.99	556.1	5.8	29.1	34.5
2001	40.97	719.1	5.7	28.1	29.3
2002	52.39	903.4	5.8	27.9	25.6
2003	65.52	1108.6	5.9	25.1	22.7
2004	75.59	1333.5	5.7	15.4	20.3
2005	95.32	1561.8	6.1	26.1	17.1

NA means the data is not available

Table 2.2 Higher education in 2006 (MOE)

Type	Total tertiary students (10,000)	Ethnic tertiary students (10,000)	Proportion (%)
Postgraduate	110.47	5.14	4.65
Doctoral degree	20.80	0.89	4.26
Master's degree	89.66	4.25	4.74
Bachelor's degree	524.88	107.55	6.19
Associate degree	212.03	64.84	6.87

minority students in minority higher learning institutions and the rapid increase in the number of nonethnic students.

On the one hand, globalization and China's rapid economic rise as a world power call for highly competitive individuals who can make contributions to nation-state building at the global, national, regional, and local levels. To enhance the global competitiveness of the Chinese nation and meet the needs of the "knowledge economy", it is necessary to improve the educational level of the Chinese population, including ethnic minorities. However, the traditional academic strength of ethnic minority universities lies in traditional disciplines such as ethnology, anthropology, sociology, ethnic languages, and culture. With curriculum focusing on ethnic studies, it is difficult for graduates from ethnic higher education institutions to compete with graduates from comprehensive universities who are trained according to the needs of the labor market. Therefore, how to reform the traditional curriculum so as to meet the needs of a market economy is an emergent issue. The state economic transition, first to a market economy and later to a global economy, requires the adjustment of goals in higher education for ethnic minorities.

2.4 Challenges for Ethnic Minority Higher Education

In response to the call for China's higher education reform, a national higher education evaluation system was introduced starting in 2003. The Ministry of Education (MOE) established a five-year cycle system to evaluate regular higher education institutions.

The National Higher Education Evaluation Center (NHEEC) is an organization attached to the MOE. The NHEEC was established with three aims: (1) to improve teaching quality in higher education institutions; (2) to strengthen macroeconomic management and guidance; and (3) to enhance international communication and cooperation.

To achieve the three objectives, the NHEEC has established seven basic standards, an additional unique item, 19 extended standards and 44 observational positions. The results are evaluated according to four categories: "excellent," "good," "qualified," and "unqualified". The guiding principles for higher education evaluation are to "evaluate to enhance improvement" (*Yiping Cujian* 以评促建), "evaluate to facilitate change" (*Yiping Cugai* 以评促改), "evaluate to strengthen management" (*Pingjian Jiehe* 评建结合), and "evaluate to emphasize management" (*Zhongzai Jianshe* 重在建设).

In 2007, Minzu University of China[15] (MUC) received the national undergraduate teaching quality evaluation and was ranked as a "university of excellence." Through the national undergraduate teaching quality evaluation, MUC clarified its thoughts as to future directions, reformed its curriculum and pattern of talent development, highlighted its academic strength, and found its weaknesses.

The MUC case suggests that it is necessary for ethnic minority universities in China to rearticulate and reconceptualize their missions and characteristics for future development. Clothey (2005) argues that higher education in China serves economic and political purposes. The former purpose is to provide professional leaders with high-level technical skills, and the latter is to contribute to ethnic unity, national stability, and patriotism. As for YUN, a representative local university for ethnic groups, questions to be clarified are as follows: Should YUN serve the nation or serve the local population? Should it develop highly skilled professionals or produce agents of social transformation? Should it integrate with mainstream culture or maintain ethnic features? Should it pursue short-term benefits or seek sustainable development? Should it aim to become a world-class comprehensive university or remain a prestigious local university with ethnic features?

Under the national higher education evaluation system, ethnic minority universities face historic opportunities as well as challenges. On the one hand, university infrastructures, such as land, libraries laboratories and the internet access have been improved or newly constructed. More teachers holding high degrees are being developed and recruited. On the other hand, the unified and authoritative evaluation standards, which were mainly designed for comprehensive universities,

---

[15]Minzu University of China refers to what was once known as the Central University of Nationalities. It replaced the term Nationalities with Minzu to highlight the distinctive features of Chinese ethnic groups.

are forcing ethnic higher educational institutions to lose their distinctive features in order to catch up with the mainstream national universities (Bai 2005; Lei 2010; Zhang 2010a, b; Ou 2011).

2.5 Policies, Curriculum, and Power Relationships: A Discussion of the Paradox

Globalization and China's rapid modernization, benefiting from a market-driven economy, has encouraged China's stakeholders to introduce more policies regarding language, culture, ethnicity, education, and socioeconomic development so as to achieve the "great revival of the Chinese nation" (Jiang 2002). Now the wish for a "great revival of the Chinese nation" (*zhonghua minzu de weida fuxing* 中华民族的伟大复兴) is being realized through the policies for socioeconomic development in the whole of China, including the frontier provinces inhabited by ethnic groups. The preferential policies for ethnic minorities not only fit the reality of contemporary China, but also coincide with the international practices concerning ethnic rights and development. For example, the rights to equal access to education are also addressed by such UN documents as the Universal Declaration of Human Rights (1948); the United Nations Convention on the Elimination of All Forms of Discrimination (1979); the Declaration on the Right to Development (1986); the World Declaration for Education for All (1990); the Declaration on the Rights of Persons Belonging to National or Ethnic, Religious and Linguistic Minorities (1992); and the UN International Covenant on Economic, Social and Culture Rights (1994).

According to both international and national laws and conventions, ethnic minority learners in China should have the right to equal education, to enjoyment of the benefits of China's socioeconomic development, and to revitalization of their native languages and cultures. These rights are legitimized by national policies on language, education, ethnicities, and socioeconomic development.

Although some preferential policies, such as bonus marks, do provide ethnic minority students with more opportunities for higher education (Zhang 2008, 2010a, b), the prospects for ethnic minority students are still uncertain. For instance, to ensure that minority learners have fair access to higher education, the central government of the PRC has introduced a variety of preferential policies to lower the "threshold" for entering into higher education for certain ethnic learners and for Han students living in minority areas. For example, Article 8 of the Higher Education Law of the People's Republic of China stipulates that:

> The State, in light of the characteristics and needs of the ethnic groups, assists and supports the development of higher education in regions inhabited by ethnic peoples for the purpose of training senior specialists among them.
>
> (National People's Congress 1999)

2.5 Policies, Curriculum, and Power Relationships: A Discussion of the Paradox

However, the lower "threshold" for access to higher education has not brought about the desired learning outcomes or guaranteed the postgraduation employment of ethnic minority students in the increasingly competitive labor market. Since China has embraced a market economy, its talent selection system has become more and more decentralized. As a result, the national preferential policies on ethnic minorities can function only in governmental sectors and public educational institutions. In other words, it is difficult to persuade state-owned enterprises or private companies to employ ethnic university graduates unless they have high credentials (first-class degrees) or certificates (such as certificates of foreign language proficiency or computer literacy). As Feng and Cheung (2010, p. 257) observed, "The reform from a planned economy to a market economy has fundamentally affected the enforcement of these special policies (preferential policies)."

However, due to the limitations of preuniversity education and poor learning resources, the attainment of ethnic minority students at university is usually lower than that of their Han peers. Thus, it is quite difficult for them to compete with the Han students in the labor market.

Furthermore, the bi/trilingual policies are sound in theory, but are often problematic in their implementation. As for ethnic minority learners, the requirement of mastering three languages is considered critical for their educational and occupational development, and for national security (Lam 2007; Wen 2009). Accordingly, the top stakeholders have tried to adopt a "collaborative policy" (Cummins 2000) to maintain the positive development of bilingual education while strengthening the promotion of Putonghua. For example, in the Law of Autonomy of Ethnic Minority Groups (1984), Article 37 specifies that:

> Schools where most of the students come from minority nationalities should, whenever possible, use textbooks in their own languages and use these languages as the medium of instruction. Classes for the teaching of Chinese (the Han language) shall be opened for senior grades of primary schools or for secondary schools to popularize Putonghua, the common speech based on Beijing pronunciation.
> (National People's Congress 1984)

The spread of English in China and its introduction into all levels of the curriculum, together with the above-mentioned policies on promoting bilingual education, have led to a trilingual education policy for ethnic minority learners.

Current national language policies in China have three goals: to enhance literacy, to assure internal stability, and to acquire scientific knowledge so as to strengthen the nation and withstand foreign aggression (Lam 2007; Adamson and Feng 2008). As a result, ethnic minority learners are expected to acquire three languages: their native language, Chinese, and English. These goals are presented as a collaborative policy (Cummins 2000) in the development of trilingualism. However, the implementation of these policies faces great challenges. For example, at the primary level, the introduction of English to ethnic students is influenced by various factors such as teacher availability, curriculum organization, sustainable financing, technical support, and local attitude. Unlike the policies promoting Putonghua and ethnic minority languages, which are enforced by legislation, the teaching of

English as a compulsory subject at primary school is only a proposal of the MOE (Lam 2005), which is applicable to schools only when the teaching conditions permit. Research shows that the English curriculum at the primary level has not been completely implemented even in some developed areas, such as Zhejiang and Guangdong (Yang 2006a, b; Hu 2008). Therefore, the degree and effect of English education for primary school ethnic learners need further observation and evaluation.

In contrast to students in primary schools, where there is little pressure to learn English, most ethnic minority students in tertiary institutions face real challenges in acquiring English as a third language in comparison to Han students who only need to master two languages (Putonghua and English). These challenges can be detected in minority students' English foundation, impact of negative language transfer, culture shock, tension with the curriculum and psychological problems, to mention just a few. These challenges are further discussed later.

English is a compulsory course for all undergraduates at university. Minority students face more challenges than their Han peers, especially when the minority students' first language is not well developed[16] and their second language is used as the medium of instruction. Starting in the third grade, most minority learners study English in classrooms where Putonghua is the dominant medium of instruction. When teachers explain the difficult language points in Putonghua, students struggle with textbooks that have explanations or translations in standard Chinese. Through the whole process of learning, ethnic minority students have to mentally retranslate the text into their mother tongue (Feng 2005a, b). To some extent, the dominant curriculum, which was developed mainly for the majority Han, marginalizes those ethnic minority learners with poor Chinese language proficiency. Chinese proficiency is considered crucial as a support for learning English in China.

Additionally, the exposure of minority students to the English language comes far later than that of their Han peers, who usually start to learn English at the beginning of or even before primary school. This can be attributed to the lack of resources, which are critical for the development of English proficiency in ethnic minority communities (Feng 2005a, b; Li and Zhou 2005; Yang 2005; Jiang et al. 2007). Moreover, ethnic minority children from the financially disadvantaged families are often absent from school in busy seasons helping their parents with the farm works. As a result, few minority children have any chance to study a foreign language (English) in primary schools, or secondary schools (Ju 2000; Li 2003).

Even if minority students are admitted to tertiary institutions with the support of preferential policies in the matriculation examination, preferential policies terminate at university admission, and the minority students often fall back to a disadvantaged position. For example, after admission to tertiary institutions, except for the

---

[16]Some ethnic minority students leave their hometowns for urban cities for better life opportunities when they are still very young. As a result, their first language (mother tongue) is not well developed due to the limited L1 acquisition at home and less chances of using L1 in the new environment.

2.5 Policies, Curriculum, and Power Relationships: A Discussion of the Paradox

Minkaomin[17] students, all other minority students like their majority Han cohorts are required to sit for the College English Test (CET) or the Test of English Major (TEM), which are compulsory national tests for all university students in China. In order to obtain the CET or TEM certificates, many minority learners take the daunting test again and again, and often become more and more frustrated each time. This causes them to feel increasingly inferior to others (Yu 1997). Ironically, it seems that the "positive discrimination" policy, which lowers the benchmark of admission[18] may end up with "negative discrimination and the loss of sense of worth and identity" (Feng 2005a, b) among those it is intended to help. As a result, EMLs are at a disadvantage in the labor market.

Those universities that enroll minority students also confront big challenges. For instance, minority learners must be admitted to higher learning institutions according to the national policy for ethnic minorities. As a result, these institutions have to enhance the English proficiency of ethnic minority students within two to four years so that they can meet the requirements of the new curriculum and graduate regularly. However, given the gap between the "low threshold" of college admission and the "high threshold" of graduation, both ethnic students and the tertiary institutions are left embarrassed. The well-intentioned affirmative action policy may disappoint both sides.

The gap between the national curriculum and the poor English proficiency of minority students constitutes a big paradox. First of all, as Adamson and Feng (2008) noted, "There are serious social, pedagogical and logistical issues to overcome before a degree of trilingualism can be achieved that matches national policy goals" (p. 2).

Because of the limited social and cultural "capital" of their native language, many minority children, except for those from some large ethnic groups, are losing enthusiasm for learning their mother tongues as they begin to see Chinese as a pathway to social mobility and personal development and English as a passport to the globalized world. For example, Adamson and Feng (2008) reported that some local Zhuang and Yi cadres showed strong resistance to the teaching of their native languages or paid only lip service to native language teaching.

Due to the concern over national stability, some local administrators in Xinjiang have adopted a "coercive policy" of insisting on Putonghua as the primary or sole medium of instruction in primary and secondary schools (Adamson and Feng 2008). These two contradictory mindsets of local cadres and parents toward ethnic minority languages combined with the low social status of some ethnic languages make the promotion and revitalization of ethnic languages a real challenge.

---

[17]*Minkaomin* refers to the ethnic minority students who usually go to minority secondary schools and receive bilingual education before they are admitted to tertiary institutions. These students then continue to study and use their native language after their university enrollment.

[18]Ethnic minority students from groups with very small populations and Han students who live in the frontier area with their parents assigned by the government to offer socioeconomic support in the frontier areas will be awarded 20–30 points in the national matriculation examination.

Furthermore, some ethnic groups have a small population and do not have written scripts, which makes native language teaching an even thornier mission. A case in point is textbook writing. Ma (2007) once pointed out:

> Considering how difficult compiling teaching materials in a minority language was for the Tibetans (a large minority considered very important by the central government), compiling complete sets of such materials for other minorities that were smaller and live dispersed over wide areas would not only be questionable in terms of practicality but would also be problematic with regard to inputs of time and human capital (p. 19).

In addition, trilingual education aims to achieve *Sanyu Jiantong* 三语兼通 (a mastery of three languages) or Duoyu Yitong 多语一通 (multilingual ability with strong competence in only one language) as the general objectives. This notion is based on and developed from the concept of *Minhan Jiantong Xianmin Houhan* 民汉兼通、先民后汉 (a mastery both native language and Chinese at the same time, with the native language being acquired first). However, this slogan raises certain questions. *Minhan Jiantong* is an idealized conception or aspiration that reflects the notion of "perfect bilinguals," who hold "bicultural identities-own minority identity and cultural identification with the Han majority and, more importantly, political allegiance to the nation state" (Feng 2007, p. 259). In reality, *Sanyu Jiantong* (三语兼通 trilingual proficiency) is difficult to realize. First, for most ethnic minority communities in China (except for very few well-educated ethnic groups like the Koreans in Northeast China), their first language is introduced in primary school as a subject in the curriculum. In other words, the mother tongue is just like Math and Social Studies. The ethnic minority learners, if they choose to leave their hometowns for education or employment reasons at a young age, will have a very slim chance later to learn and develop their ethnic minority languages. Even in bilingual schools, in which L1 is used as a medium of instruction, children study their first language for no more than six years unless they are later enrolled in bilingual secondary schools, which are usually few in quantity and poor in quality. Limited L1 learning experiences contribute little to L2 and L3 development and may even exert a negative influence on L2 and L3 learning. This may result in the danger of negative language transfer and ethnic identity loss.

Some scholars in Yunnan have pointed out that the bilingual experiences of ethnic minority learners seem to contribute little to English education. Their research suggests that the English learning outcomes of ethnic minority students are unsatisfactory and that positive attitudes and motivation need to be cultivated (Hu 2007; Yuan 2007). These findings agree with Yang's argument concerning the impact of L2 learning on multilingual learning: "Such a positive second language influence on multilingual learning does not seem to apply to many of China's minority students" (Yang 2005, p. 26). *Sanyu Jiantong* (trilingual proficiency) is even more challenging for EMLs who have to struggle with English acquisition in an EFL context even when their L1 and L2 are not fully developed due to short-term mother tongue education or early migration to nonnative communities. Hu (2007, p. 53) described multilingual learners in Yunnan as follows:

[They] encountered a dilemma that bilingual education has been mainly adopted only in primary schools, and once students are in secondary schools and universities, all learning in their own languages stops. This discontinuity causes minority students to be deficient in both languages.

If Hu and Yang's observations are true, it can be assumed that the inadequate bilingual education in China may not help, but may hinder, multilingual acquisition if EMLs' L1 and L2 literacy are not adequately developed. The argument is also supported by researchers who have studied the negative language transfer of multilingual learners in English classes (Yang 2003; Yang and Song 2006; Hu 2007; Jiang et al. 2007). Hu's assumption is supported by the "Threshold Hypothesis" (Cummins 1999, 2000), which argues that the level of L1 and L2 proficiency of bilingual children may affect their cognitive growth in other domains. However, Cummins' Threshold Theory should be reexamined, for the bilingual superiority only lies in idealized balanced bilinguals. For the less balanced or the limited bilinguals, the advantageous cognitive effect is difficult to achieve.

The gap between the top-down policies and the reality of their implementation also brings multilingual learners in China other challenges such as cultural discontinuity (Ogbu and Simmons 1998; Zhang 2008), identity conflict (Hu 2007; Huang and Yu 2009), and psychological problems (Li 2007), to mention just a few. Therefore, it is necessary to reconceptualize EMLs in the ever dynamic discourses of contemporary China by evaluating current policies and curriculum from a critical perspective.

2.6 Summary

Given the national policies on language, ethnicity, education, and socioeconomic development, it is necessary to reconceptualize ethnic minority learners in the ever changing sociocultural discourse of contemporary China.

At the tertiary level, minority students are required to acquire English as a third language in a mostly Han dominated learning environment. Their teachers usually instruct them in the same way as they do Han students, without considering the difference in linguistic context and distance (Stern 1983; Ytsma 2001). As a result, EMLs have to struggle to negotiate their identities under the tension caused by the highly demanding curriculum and unfamiliar learning environment.

To understand the problems of EMLs in China, it is necessary to deepen the research on them so as to be in an informed position to further develop a curriculum to meet their needs in the twenty-first century. It is argued that the study of EMLs, through and beyond the lens of multilingual education policy and practice, will lead to a better understanding of EMLs' aspirations and experience. Such a study will reveal the strengths, weaknesses, and coping strategies of EMLs in China. This information can make a solid contribution to the design of more relevant language policies, teaching practices, and learning resources. This will help pave the way for future in-depth research.

References

Adamson, B., & Feng, A. W. (2008). A comparison of trilingual education policies for ethnic minorities in China. *Compare: A journal of comparative education, 39*(3), 321–333.

Bai, Y. C. (2005). Higher education for ethnic minorities in the 21st century. In Y. F. Li & Z. X. Xu (Eds.), *A study of the ethnic minority education and development in Yunnan* (pp. 45–52). Kunming: Yunnan Press of Nationalities.

Choi, S. (2010). Globalization, China's drive for world-class universities (211 Project) and the challenges of ethnic minority higher education: The case of Yanbian University. *Asia Pacific Education Review, 11*, 169–178.

Clothey, R. (2005). China's policies for minority nationalities in higher education: Negotiating national values and ethnic identities. *Comparative Education Review, 49*(3), 389–428.

Cummins, J. (1999). Alternative paradigms in bilingual education research: Does theory have a place? *Educational Researcher, 28*(7), 26–32.

Cummins, J. (2000). *Language, power, and pedagogy: Bilingual children in the crossfire.* Clevedon, England: Multilingual Matters.

Dao, F. D. (2005). An analysis of the education for 25 indigenous ethnic minority groups in Yunnan. In Y. F. Li., & Z. X. Xu (Eds.), *A study of the ethnic minority education and development in Yunnan* (pp. 11–20). Kunming: Yunnan Press of Nationalities.

Dehong People's Congress. (2005). *Autonomous regulation of Dehong Dai and Jingpo Autonomous Prefecture.* Retrieved on July 10, 2010, from http://www.seac.gov.cn/gjmw/zcfg/2005-05-10/1170217311843652.htm

Fei, X. T. (1989). Plurality within the organic unity of the Chinese nation. *Journal of Beijing University, 4*, 1–19.

Feng, A. W. (2005a). Bilingualism for the Minor or the Major? An evaluative analysis of parallel conceptions in China. *International Journal of bilingual Education and Bilingualism, 8*(6), 529–551.

Feng, A. W. (2005b). China's minorities learn a difficult language lesson. Guardian Weekly. http://www.theguardian.com/theguardian/2005/feb/11/guardianweekly.guardianweekly13

Feng, A. W. (2007). Intercultural space for bilingual education. In A. W. Feng (Ed.), *Bilingual education in China: Practices, policies, and concepts* (pp. 259–279). Clevedon; Buffalo: Multilingual Matters.

Feng, Y. Y., & Cheung, M. (2010). Public policies affecting ethnic minorities in China. *China Journal of Social Work, 1*(3), 248–265.

Goodman, D. S. G. (2004). The campaign of "Open Up the West": National, provincial-level and local perspectives. *The China Quarterly, 178*, 317–334.

Ha, J. W., & Teng, X. (2001). *A general theory of ethnic minority education.* Beijing: Education and Science Press.

Hill, A. M., &. Zhou, M. L. (2009). Introduction. In A. M. Hill & M. L. Zhou (Eds.), *Affirmative action in China and the U.S.: A dialogue on inequality and minority education* (pp. 1–24). New York: Palgrave Macmillan.

Hu, D. Y. (2007). *Trilingual education of members from ethnic minority nationalities in Yunnan.* Kunming: Yunnan University Press.

Hu, Y. Y. (2008). China's English language policy for primary schools. *World Englishes, 27*(3–4), 516–534.

Huang, C. W., & Yu, A. H. (2009). Acculturation and ethnic identity of minority undergraduates: A case study on Yunnan University of Nationalities. *Journal of Chuxiong Teacher's College, 24*(7), 47–56.

Jiang, Z. M. (2002). *A Reader on the Jiang Zemin's talk on May 13.* Beijing: The CPC University Press.

Jiang, Q. X., Liu, Q. G., Quan, X. H., & Ma, C. Q. (2007). EFL education in ethnic minority areas in northwest China: An investigational study in Gansu Province. In A. W. Feng (Ed.), *Bilingual Education in China: Practices, policies and concepts* (pp. 240–256). Clevedon; Buffalo: Multilingual Matters.

References

Ju, J. N. (2000). An examination of the problems encountered in teaching English to beginning minority students at college. *Nationalities Research in Qinghai, 11*(3), 76–77.

Lam, A. (2005). *Language education in China: Policy and experience from 1949*. Hong Kong: Hong Kong University Press.

Lam, A. (2007). Bilingual or multilingual education in China: Policy and learner experience. In A. Feng (Ed.), *Bilingual education in China: Practices, policies and concepts* (pp. 13–33). Clevedon, UK: Multilingual Matters.

Lei, Z. H. (2010). Some reflections on the strategic development of ethnic minority universities in the new era. *Journal of South-Central University of Nationalities, 30*(3), 160–163.

Li, Y. L. (2003). The study of the special features of ethnic minority students in learning English. *Journal of Southwest University for Nationalities, 24*(8), 334–336.

Li, Y. H. (2007). An analysis of the psychological health and its effect of 4782 freshmen in ethnic minority universities. *Journal of the 4th Military Medical University, (28)*8, 58–760.

Li, S. L., & Zhou, Z. (2005). *Studies on EFL teaching reform in minority ethnic areas*. Kunming: Yunnan University Press.

Ma, R. (2007). Bilingual education for China's ethnic minorities. *Chinese Education & Society, 40*(2), 9–25.

National Bureau of Statistic of China. (2011a). *A report of 2010 national economy and social development of the PRC*. Retrieved on March 25, 2011, from http://www.stats.gov.cn/tjgb/ndtjgb/qgndtjgb/t20110228_402705692.htm

National Bureau of Statistic of China. (2011b). The 6th national population census. Retrieved on August 8, 2011, from http://www.stats.gov.cn/tjgb/rkpcgb/qgrkpcgb/t20110429_402722510.htm

National People's Congress of the PRC. (1982). *Constitution of the People's Republic of China*. Retrieved on August 8, 2015, from http://en.people.cn/constitution/constitution.html

National People's Congress. (1984). *The law of autonomy of ethnic minority groups*. Retrieved on April 3, 2011, from http://english.mofcom.gov.cn/aarticle/lawsdata/chineselaw/200211/20021100050258.html

National People's Congress. (1999). Higher Education law of the People's Republic of China. http://www.moe.edu.cn/publicfiles/business/htmlfiles/moe/moe_2803/200905/48454.html

Ogbu, J., & Simons, H. D. (1998). Voluntary and involuntary minorities: A cultural-ecological theory of school performance with some implications for education. *Anthropology and Education Quarterly, 29*(2), 155–188.

Ou, Y. K. (2011). Coordinated development: Fundamental principles of discipline development with characteristics of ethnic universities. *Journal of Research on Education for Ethnic Minorities, 22*(103), 10–14.

State Education Commission, Office of Ethnic Education. (1995). *Collections of documents for minority education in province, municipality, autonomous regions*. Chengdu: Sichuan Nationality Press.

Stern, H. H. (1983). *Fundamental concepts of language teaching*. Oxford: OUP.

Tan, M., & Xie, Z. Y. (2009). An analysis of ethnic higher education since expansion of higher education in China. *Higher Education Exploration, 2*, 26–31.

Teng, X., & Wen, Y. H. (2005). Bilingualism and bilingual education in China. In N. Ken Shimahara, I. Z. Holowinsky & S. Tomlinson-Clarke (Eds.), *Ethnicity, race, and nationality in education: A global perspective* (pp. 259–278). Mahwah, NJ: Lawrence Erlbaum Associates, Inc.

The State Council of the PRC. (2011). *The outline of China's mid-long term educational development*. Retrieved on November 25, 2010, from http://www.gov.cn/jrzg/2010-07/29/content_1667143.htm

Tsang, M. C., et al. (2005). *Minorities' education in Yunnan: Developments, challenges and policies*. Retrieved on June 5, 2010, from http://www.tc.edu/centers/coce/pdf_files/a11.pdf

Wang, G. (2011). Bilingual education in southwest China: A Yingjiang case. *International Journal of Bilingual Education and Bilingualism, 14*(5), 571–587.

Wen, J. B. (2008). *Report on the work of the government*. Retrieved on May 1, 2008, from http://www.gov.cn/english/official/2008-03/20/content_924600.htm

Wen, Q. F. (2009). Planning China's foreign language education: A scientific development perspective. *Guangming Daily*. Retrieved from http://www.21stcentury.com.cn/story/49159.html

Yang, Y. X. (1989). *Records of ethnic minority language and script: A volume of record of Yunnan Province*. Kunming, China: Yunnan People's Press.

Yang, L. P. (2003). Thoughts on sharing global information and developing Zhuang and English bilingual education. *Journal of Nationalities Education Research, 14*(2), 66–70.

Yang, R. X. (2005). A study on the bilingual education for ethnic minorities in Yunnan. *Education for Ethnic Minorities in China, 2*, 23–25.

Yang, F. Q. (2006a). *The Naxi cultural history*. Kunming: Yunnan University Press.

Yang, J. (2006b). Learners and users of English in China: Just how many millions are there? *English Today, 22*(2), 3–10.

Yang, G. C. (2009). The disparity in socioeconomic development for ethnic groups in southwest frontier regions. *Journal of Yunnan Public Administration Academy, 6*, 134–138.

Yang, Q., & Song, Y. (2006). A survey of English teaching in the Bai-Han bilingual context. *Journal of Dali University, 6*(9), 70–73.

Ytsma, J. (2001). Towards a typology of trilingual primary education. *International Journal of Bilingual Education and Bilingualism, 4*, 11–22.

Yu, J. (1997). Non-intelligence factors in minority students' learning English. *Journal of Nationalities Education Research, 3*, 30–31.

Yuan, Y. C. (2007). *Attitude and motivation for English learning of ethnic minority students in China*. Shanghai: Shanghai Foreign Language Education Press.

Yunnan University of Nationalities. (2011). *Glory of sixty years: A pictorial for the 60th anniversary of Yunnan University of Nationalities* (Unpublished).

Zhang, J. X. (2008). 50-year development and reflection of Yunnan ethnic minority higher education. *Academy, 1*, 62–67.

Zhang, L. J. (2010a). The evolution of the policies of higher education for minority nationality in the thirty-year's reform and open-up. *Education Research Monthly, 8*, 56–60.

Zhang, M. (2010b). A study of the relationship between multicultural ethnic groups in Xinjiang and bilingual education. *Social Sciences in Xinjiang, 3*, 107–110.

Zhu, Y. C., & Blachford, D. Y. (2006). China's fate as a multinational state: A preliminary assessment. *Journal of Contemporary China, 15*(47), 329–348.

Chapter 3
The Study of Multilingual Learners

> *The function of education is to teach one to think intensively and to think critically. Intelligence plus character—that is the goal of true education.*
> —Martin Luther King, Jr.
>
> *Where there is power, there is resistance.*
> —Michel Foucault

3.1 Multiculturalism: A Social Trend Around the World

Since the late 1960s, multiculturalism has been widely discussed among anthropologists, sociologists, and educators due to the global migrant flow. In some countries, multiculturalism has taken the form of official policies designed to achieve unity through diversity. For example, the Canadian government defines the concept as follows:

> Canadian multiculturalism is fundamental to our belief that all citizens are equal. Multiculturalism ensures that all citizens can keep their identities, can take pride in their ancestry and have a sense of belonging. Acceptance gives Canadians a feeling of security and self-confidence, making them more open to and accepting of diverse cultures. The Canadian experience has shown that multiculturalism encourages racial and ethnic harmony and cross cultural understanding, and discourages ghettoization, hatred, discrimination and violence.
> (Citizenship and Immigration Canada 2009 cited from Race 2011)

Despite continuous debate, multiculturalism has been a policy in Canada since 1971, and legislators at various levels are trying their best to implement multicultural policies based on the principle of equal rights.

In Australia, *The People of Australia*, an official multicultural policy (2011), affirms the government's support for a culturally diverse and socially cohesive nation.

> Multiculturalism is in Australia's national interest and speaks to fairness and inclusion. It enhances respect and support for cultural, religious and linguistic diversity. It is about Australia's shared experience and the composition of neighborhoods. It acknowledges the benefits and potential that cultural diversity brings.

Australia's multicultural policy embraces our shared values and cultural traditions. It also allows those who choose to call Australia home the right to practice and share in their cultural traditions and languages within the law and free from discrimination.

Australia will continue to have an ever evolving and ever diversifying population. We will continue to be multicultural. This helps create a strong economy, drives prosperity and builds Australia's future. It will also enable Australia to enjoy the cultural and social benefits that cultural diversity brings. Multiculturalism is our shared future and is central to our national interest.

(Department of Immigration and Citizenship 2011)

In the United States, multiculturalism is seen as a "philosophical position and movement" (Banks and Banks 2007) to be reflected in all of the institutionalized structures of educational institutions. In the UK, multiculturalism is regarded as a perspective on human life with central insights in social construction (Parekh 2000). At present, as a social movement, and a theoretical approach, the notion of multiculturalism has drawn more attention especially after the 7/7[1] and 9/11[2] incidents (Race 2011).

The above perceptions of multiculturalism, as Torres (1998) argued, address the implications of class, race, and gender for identity and the role of the state. The definitions acknowledge cultural diversity within a pluralistic society. Multiculturalism emphasizes the full participation of all ethno-cultural groups in a larger society. It is too idealistic to say multiculturalism is a solution to the ever-increasing problems in a diversified society, because it fails to address the inequality that results from imbalanced power relations between ethnic minorities and the dominant majority.

In the 1990s, critical multiculturalism emerged as a theoretical response to the limitations of liberal multicultural education, such as "the overemphasis on the impact of curriculum changes and the under-emphasis on the impact of structural racism on students' lives" (May and Sleeter 2010). Under liberal multiculturalism, ethnic minorities were labeled according to their characteristics such as ethnicity, race, socioeconomic, and linguistic features. It is pointed out that the key weakness of liberal multiculturalism are "its inability to tackle seriously and systematically these structural inequities, such as racism, institutionalized poverty and discrimination" and its failure to "provide an actual example of transformed and/or emancipatory pedagogy and practice" (May and Sleeter 2010, p. 3).

It is believed that liberal multicultural approaches fail to "see the power-grounded relationships among identity construction, cultural representations and struggles over resources...[for] the most important issues to those who fall outside the white, male, and middle class norm often involve powerlessness, violence and poverty" (Kincheloe and Steinberg 1997, p. 17).

---

[1] 7/7 incident was a series of co-coordinated suicide attacks in London on July 7, 2005, which targeted civilians using the public transport system during the morning rush hour.

[2] 9/11 incidents were terrorist attacks committed in the United States on September 11, 2001, which destroyed the Twin Towers and other landmarks in New York City.

It is argued that critical multiculturalism is aimed at "making links between educational theory, policy and practice, thus potentially providing both a critical and practical account of culturally pluralist forms of teacher education and schooling" (May and Sleeter 2010). Instead of prioritizing culture, critical multiculturalism focuses on analyzing unequal power relationships and the role of institutionalized inequities. The notion of critical multiculturalism will help us understand how power is used and how multiculturalism brings about social transformation. Based on critical multiculturalism, I proposed a conceptual framework for this study and made a structural analysis of the power relationships within educational institutions. I tried to understand how the identities of ethnic minority learners are constructed and negotiated through multilingual education.

3.1.1 Strategies of Multiculturalism

To respond to an ever-diversified society, two strategies are taken by ethnic minorities: an assimilationist strategy or an integrationist strategy. It is believed that the assimilationist strategy can lead to segregation and marginalization, while the integration strategy will bring about multiculturalism (Berry 2005). The four strategies of acculturation will be elaborated and discussed in Table 3.1.

3.1.2 Assimilation

Assimilation, as defined by Coelho (1998) is a "one-way process of absorption whereby minorities abandon, at least publicly, their ethnic identities" (pp. 19–20). Modood (2007) believes that assimilation will cause the least change in the way of doing things by the ethnic majority and the dominating institutions. Race (2011) argues that assimilationist strategy rises to several issues. First, the minority and the oppressed groups may stand up to resist the one-way process. Second, the educational subjects may resist school structures and school curriculum.

Since the end of the Second World War, the USA has been attracting more and more immigrants from all over the world because of its overwhelming economy, military power, democratic system, and promising life opportunities. To pursue the dream of becoming real Americans, some migrants had to give up their ethnic identities such as language and culture in order to achieve the American Dream. The immigrants' memories documented the efforts made by the newly arrived to become "we people of the United States" (Pavlenko and Blackledge 2004).

In the UK, the 1962 Commonwealth Immigration Act also started to control the flow of immigration by setting conditions of the English language and working skills necessary. Later, the British government issued circulars entitled "The Education of Immigrants" to deal with the problems concerned. In a sense, assimilationist policy sees diversity as a problem rather than a value.

3.1.3 Integration

According to Modood (2007, p. 48), the "process of social interaction is seen as two way, and where members of the majority community as well as immigrants and ethnic minorities are required to do something; so the latter cannot alone be blamed for failing to integrate." This process of integration is also called "cultural fusion" (Coelho 1998) in which adaptation and acculturation occur. Jenkins defines integration as "…not a flattening process of uniformity but as cultural diversity coupled with equal opportunity in an atmosphere of mutual tolerance" (Rex 2008, in Eade et al. 2008, p. 32).

3.1.4 Acculturation and Enculturation

Acculturation was first coined by Redfield, Linton, and Herskovits in 1936, referring to the phenomena resulted from the contact of two groups. Berry (2005) sees acculturation as a "dual process of cultural and psychological change" between two or more cultural groups and individual members that involves "various forms of mutual accommodation, leading to some longer-term psychological and sociocultural adaptations between both groups" (p. 699). Berry believes acculturation involves two aspects: cultural adaptation and cultural maintenance. Cultural adaptation means the "gradual adoption of values and mores of a new foreign culture," while cultural maintenance refers to "holding onto the values and mores of one's native or minority culture" (Ruzek et al. 2011, p. 182).

Herskovits (1948) puts forward the concept of enculturation, which is very relevant to the notion of acculturation. According to Herskovits, enculturation is a "process of socialization into and maintenance of the norms of one's minority culture, including its salient ideas, concepts, and values" (Kim et al. 2009, p. 26). Kim sees enculturation as a process of "incorporating and maintaining one's ethnic cultural norms" (Kim 2007, p. 143). In contrast to Berry's emphasis on cultural maintenance, Kim highlights the process of association with the native or minority groups. This argument is supported by Miller (2007) who believes acculturation involves not only the process of ethnic minorities adjusting to adjust to a new culture, but also their socialization into another/host culture.

3.1.5 Four Acculturation Strategies

Berry (2005) argues that when individuals do not wish to maintain their cultural identity but seek daily interaction with the other culture, assimilation will take place (see Table 3.1). On the stage of assimilation, individuals are highly acculturated to the dominant/host culture but no longer adherent to the native/minority culture.

Table 3.1 Berry's four strategies of acculturation

	Cultural maintenance	
	Yes	No
Cultural adoption		
Yes	Integration	Assimilation
No	Separation	Marginalization

If individuals hope to maintain their cultural heritage and avoid interaction with other groups at the same time, separation will occur. On the separation stage, individuals are not acculturated to the dominant/host culture but highly attached to the native/minority culture. If individuals are interested in both maintaining their heritage culture and interaction with other groups, integration will happen. On the stage of integration, individuals are adapted to the values and norms of the new culture and at the same time are able to maintain their native/minority cultural heritage. If individuals have little possibility or interest in maintaining heritage culture and have little intent to interact with other groups, marginalization will take place. On the marginalization stage, individuals are neither acculturated to the new/dominant/host culture nor attached to the native or minority culture.

Berry (2005) points out that the formulation of four acculturation strategies is from the perspective of non-dominant groups. In reality, integration cannot be freely chosen by the non-dominant group unless the dominant society is open and inclusive in its orientation toward cultural diversity. To achieve integration both the non-dominant groups and the dominant society has to be open-minded and flexible toward cultural diversity. On the part of the non-dominant groups they have to adopt the basic values of larger society, while the dominant society has to recognize the fact of culture diversity and adapt the national institutions to meet the needs of individuals living in the plural society. However, Kim (2007) questions whether Berry's concept of cultural maintenance may be applied to individuals who are born in the "foreign culture" or who are generations removed from migration. They have never been fully socialized with their native/minority culture. Therefore, they tend to adopt the values of the host/dominant culture.

3.2 Multicultural Education: A Notion of the Twenty-First Century

Postiglione (2009) summarizes four educational challenges for ethnic minorities in China: (1) How to ensure educational access and equity for the 56 officially identified ethnic groups (2) How to ensure education in view of promoting economic development of its 155 ethnic minority autonomous areas (3) How to make the educational sector in ethnic minority areas function according to the principle of cultural autonomy legitimized by the Chinese constitution (4) How to ensure education to facilitate ethnic unity. Since the founding of the PRC in 1949, the Chinese government has instituted a series of preferential policies to promote ethnic minority education. Wu and Han (2011, p. 238) summarize the five measures taken by the Chinese government to address some of the challenges: (1) autonomous governance of education; (2) priority of financial investment; (3) lowering of university admission standards; (4) cultural aids[3]; and (5) financial aids. I believe Wu and Han's summary responds to at least some of the challenges presented by Postiglione.

With over 30 years of policy implementation, prominent progress has been achieved in ethnic minority education in general. For example, by the end of 2000, the nine-year compulsory education for ethnic minorities was almost accomplished and more and more minority students were being admitted to the mainstream educational institutions from primary to tertiary levels. However, the ethnic minority college students are still under-represented in the overall university-level proportion in comparison to the Han. Minority access to the top tertiary institutions still remains a major challenge (Postiglione 2009).

The current educational policies in China, as Wang (2011) has observed, are designed to protect the rights of ethnic minorities but ignore the role of education in inheriting and developing ethnic cultures. For instance, the university policies and curricula in most Chinese higher learning institutions mainly focus on the professional knowledge building and patriotic education. As a result, the "cultural self-consciousness" 文化自觉 (Fei 2003) and ethnic "cultural capital" (Bourdieu and Passeron 1977) are less emphasized and encouraged. In this sense, the educational policies are not comprehensive in terms of protecting the whole rights of ethnic minorities including use of their native language and preservation of their cultural heritage.

Educators and administrators have to think about this question: Is there any curriculum that will not only benefit the patriotic education and learning outcomes of ethnic minority students, but also at the same time achieve sustainable multicultural development among ethnic communities? To reply to this question, the ever-increasing voice of "multicultural education" in the West and the framework of *Duoyuan Yiti* 多元一体 or ethnic diversity within national unity in English (Fei 1989, 1999) may be a few directions for ethnic minority education in the PRC. In the following section, I will discuss the origin of multicultural education in the West and discuss its implications for ethnic multilingual education in China.

---

[3]Cultural aids (*wenhua yuanzhu*) refers to the partnership relationships between the impoverished counties in the ethnic regions and the developed provinces, cities, and regions, which are established to promote ethnic minority education by providing funding, infrastructure, facilities, advisers, trainers, and teachers or establish in-land classes (*neidiban*) for ethnic minority students especially Uyghurs and Tibetans.

3.2.1 Multicultural Education in the West

Since the movement of ethnic revitalization and civil rights in the 1960s, multicultural education has been widely discussed as an approach to school reform. Due to the ever-increasing ethnic, racial, cultural, linguistic and religious diversity in some nation-states around the world, it is believed that multicultural education should be introduced to the school curriculum to realize "educational equality and social justice" (Banks 2010). Namely, multicultural education aims to assure that all the students will have equal opportunities to learn at all educational levels. However, social inequality has been found in the curriculum, textbooks, teacher attitudes, student-teacher interactions, languages uses and dialect spoken and sanctioned in the schools, and school cultures (Banks 2009). Bennett (2003, p. 16) believes that multicultural education rests on four core values: (1) acceptance and appreciation of cultural diversity; (2) respect for human dignity and universal human rights; (3) responsibility to the world community, and (4) reverence for the earth.

In this sense, teachers are expected to take the responsibility to introduce multicultural knowledge and help both the ethnic majority and minority students develop multicultural awareness so as to become "cosmopolitan citizens" in the cultural, national, civic and global communities. The 9/11 attacks, London bombings and riots in Tibet and Xinjiang have highlighted the significance of producing "responsible" cosmopolitan citizens rather than radical extremists.

Banks (2009) defines multicultural education as "an approach to school reform designed to actualize educational equality for students from diverse racial, ethnic, cultural, social class, and linguistic groups" (p. 13). It seems to him that the "major goal was to reform schools, colleges and universities so that students from diverse groups will have equal opportunities to learn" (p. 13). He talks about the five dimensions of multicultural education: content integration, the knowledge construction process, prejudice reduction, equality pedagogy, and an empowering school culture and structure. He argues that these five dimensions are designed to help educators "understand different aspects of multicultural education and to enable them to implement it comprehensively" (p. 17).

Ethnic minority students are expected to develop their ability to construct and understand all types of knowledge. Banks argues that students should be involved in the debate over knowledge construction from the beginning. In other words, they should be taught how to construct their own interpretations of the past and present, as well as how to identify their own position, interest, ideology, and assumptions. Students should become critical thinkers, who possess the knowledge, skill, attitude, and commitment needed to help their nation and the world close the gap between ideal social justice and the reality of racism, sexism, homophobia, and other 'isms' (Banks 2010).

However, as Banks (2009) points out, the educational institutions can only play limited roles as:

> School is part of the problem and plays a significant role in keeping ethnic groups marginalized. Thus, it is very difficult for the school to empower marginalized groups, because one of its central purposes is to educate students so that they will accept their assigned status in society (Banks 2009, p. 25).

Likewise, some sociologists and international politicians like Barry (2000) and Huntington (2005) criticize the current sociopolitical status quo and challenge the ongoing ignorance of ethnic, cultural, linguistic and religious difference. Torres (1998, p. 446) points out:

> The multitude of tasks confronting multiculturalism is overwhelming. They include the attempt to develop a sensible, theoretically refined, and defensible new meta-theoretical and theoretical territory that would create the foundations for multiculturalism as a paradigm; the attempts to establish its epistemological and logical premise around notions of experience, narrative, voice, agency, and identity; the attempt to pursue empirical research linking culture/power/knowledge with equality/inequality/discrimination; and the need to defend multiculturalism from the conservative Right that has demonized multiculturalism as an unpatriotic movement.

Besides the challenge to multiculturalism from the Right, May (2009) calls for a critical multiculturalism to achieve a significant regulation of the existing social and political circumstances. He also warns about underestimation and ignorance from antiracists and critical educators themselves. For example, Kalantzis and Cope (1999, p. 255) argue:

> Whilst mouthing good intentions about pluralism … this sort of multiculturalism can end up doing nothing either to change the mainstream or to improve the access of those historically denied its power and privileges. It need not change the identity of the dominant culture in such a way that there can be genuine negotiation with the "minorities" about matters social or symbolic or economic. It need not change education in such a way that issues of diversity are on the agenda for all students. It need not change education so that diversity might become a positive resource for access rather than a cultural deficit to be remedied by affirmation of difference alone.

To respond to the limitations of multicultural education in school settings, Banks puts forward a "holistic paradigm," that views the school as an "interrelated whole." He appeals for educational reform as represented by Fig. 3.1

Banks suggests that an appropriate "total school environment" is critical to enhancing multicultural education. This total environment is shaped by the combination of school policy and politics, the formalized curriculum, the medium of instruction, educators' beliefs, instructional materials, teaching strategies, assessment criteria, the hidden curriculum, community support, and counseling programs. Each of these components is indispensable and deserves serious attention. Lee (2001, p. 72) further points out "university structure at the macro level has an impact on student outcomes such as educational goals, academic achievement and empowerment at the micro level." Clothey (2005) argues that schools play dual roles. On the one hand, they "serve economic and political integration needs for nation-states" (p. 389). On the other hand, they "provide a lens to view the relations between national and ethnic identities" (p. 389). It seems to her that the school role can be either supportive or detrimental. When education brings about effective

3.2 Multicultural Education: A Notion of the Twenty-First Century

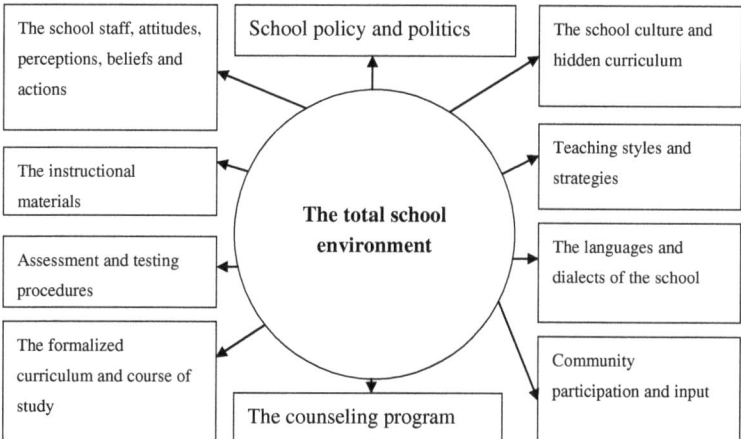

Fig. 3.1 The total school environment adapted from Banks (2009)

participation in the political and economic system, EMLs may support the state. Otherwise, if the school system, due to uneven power structure, reproduces and even enlarges the current inequalities, EMLs will be marginalized and denied effective participation. Hence, they may resist the state policies.

Clothey believes that Chinese ethnic minority policies aim to ensure ethnic stability, national integration, and economic development of minority areas. At the same time these policies have the potential to serve only the dominant majority and exacerbate the tensions between the majority and the minority (Clothey 2005). Bank's framework and the critical multiculturalism theories I mentioned earlier provide us with a lens to observe the power relations playing out in the educational practice. However, it is very interesting to notice that in the West, multicultural education often pays little attention to foreign language education. For example, multilingual policy has been implemented in Australia for more than 30 years, but the curriculum time for second language acquisition for children aged 9–11 in New South Wales is no more than from zero to two per cent. The outcomes of what is called multicultural education have really been the promotion of monolingual education. In contrast, China's multilingual policy promotes only the Han culture in education. Ethnic religion and values do not have so much space in school curriculum. Therefore, I am more interested in Bank's model of the total school environment. I hope to understand how languages and dialects in the school are used when most teachers are monolingual speakers of the Han language.

3.2.2 The Configuration of Duoyuan Yiti in China

In post Mao China, the Communist Party of China (CPC) took *Duoyuan Yiti* 多元一体, or ethnic diversity within national unity in English (Fei 1980, 1989, 1991, 1999), as a political framework and exercised the policies featuring "equality, unity, regional ethnic autonomy and common prosperity for all ethnic groups" (State Council 2009, p. 3). The rights of ethnic minorities are secured by policies on regional autonomy, compulsory education, and higher education.

As a result, impressive measures have been taken in terms of the identification of ethnic minority groups, the creation of new scripts for those ethnic groups who do not have written languages, bilingual education in minority areas, and preferential policies on ethnic minority education. In the past thirty years, ethnic minority education in China has developed dramatically with priority given first to compulsory education and now preschool education. As for tertiary education, more and more ethnic minority students are admitted to universities with the overall expansion of higher education, but the number of such students in the top universities still remains a major challenge (Clothey 2005; Postiglione 2009).

However, the increased number of ethnic minority students does not mean ethnic cultures are strongly promoted in educational institutions. Actually, the previous Hu-Wen[4] administration took a view that ethnic minority culture should develop within the framework of *Hexie Shehui* 和谐社会 (harmonious society). That is to say, national patriotism and ethnic minority culture shall develop synchronically with the pace of the market economy and globalization. Postiglione (2009) argues that the practical challenge for education is "how to make schooling work in the ways that bring ethnic minority culture into the national and global or international spheres with the least amount of dislocation to ethnic communities and ethnic unity" (p. 502).

In China's context, one of the aims of ethnic minority education is to develop ethnic minority talented individuals who can bring about sustainable cultural development in minority areas. The intention of ethnic minority education is to achieve equality and to promote cultural retention, intercultural understanding, cultural adaptation, and mutual respect. One very essential step toward achieving this goal is developing multicultural education curriculum at China's tertiary institutions. Wu and Han (2011, p. 237) point out: "The major issue concerning multicultural education within China is to create equal educational opportunities for minority students, by respecting and preserving the uniqueness of their cultures."

With a similar viewpoint, Teng (2010) proposes a theory of integrative multicultural education. He argues that:

> A nation state takes the responsibility of imparting the common cultural achievements of all human beings. That is to say, a nation state should not only transmit the excellence of the ethnic majority culture but also the cream of ethnic minority culture (p. 51).

Teng (2010) argues that the culture of the ethnic majority should be integrated with that of the ethnic minority. The ethnic minority should learn not only the culture of the ethnic minority, but also the culture of the ethnic majority so as to help the younger ethnic generation adjust to mainstream culture and reach maximum individual development. On the other hand, the ethnic majority should also

---

[4]Hu-Wen refers to President Hu Jintao and Premier Wen Jiabao, the top leaders of the Chinese government from 2003 to 2013.

learn the cream of the ethnic minority culture, so as to promote the egalitarianism of the nationalities and to develop an awareness of the "nationality family" (*Minzu Dajiating* 民族大家庭). Zhang (2010) argues that the model of integrative multicultural education is the only remedy for the conflict between national unity and ethnic plurality in the twenty-first century. Another Zhang, a scholar from Minzu University of China, believes this model is a perfect theoretical framework for the construction of a university of nationalities because it fits Chinese circumstance (Zhang 2011).

I would like to argue here that multiculturalism is not only a western import but can be traced back to the Confucian pedagogical discourse (Wu and Han 2011). By citing numerous dialogues in *Analects*, Wu and Han (2011, p. 226) argue that:

> In the Chinese history, Confucius' way of offering different answers to the same question has left Chinese people a huge space of interpretation for teaching and learning, where diversity and pluralism are appreciated and active construction of meaning is possible. Generations of students can consistently reinterpret, reconstruct and renegotiate the meaning with their evolving cultural identities.

Echoing the western vision of multiculturalism, multicultural education is seen as a means for equity and social justice, benefiting both the ethnic minority and the ethnic majority. Lin (2008) defines multiculturalism both as "a helpful framework" and "a value system," which "seek to empower the disadvantaged and bring the marginalized people from periphery back to the center" (p. 71). Wu and Han's study suggests that the Confucian pedagogical discourse with its openness to multiple perspectives may provide a foundation for Chinese multiculturalism. Confucian ritual hermeneutics also embody pluralism by recognizing differences as the prerequisite of building a harmonious social relationship. Wu and Han believe harmony is the "cosmic vision of diversity and plurality" (Wu and Han 2011, p. 226).

To sum up, given the fact that China is a multiethnic nation with a long history of ethnic contact, integration and peaceful coexistence, there should be a foundation for multilingual education under the framework of critical multiculturalism. This vision of China with ethnic diversity can fit both the Confucius notion of "the good person harmonizes but does not seek sameness" (*Junzi he'er butong* 君子和而不同) as well as the ethnic political framework of "ethnic diversity within national unity." To make *Duoyuan Yiti* happen in a real sense, it must be remembered that the end-product of ethnic multilingual education is not the assimilationist view of "diversity for unity" but the integrative notion of "unity with diversity." In 1988 Fei said *Duoyuan Yiti* was the reality in the history of the nation and its ethnic groups. My concern is how *Duoyuan Yiti* will continue to develop at this crucial time of speedy modernization.

Based on the above literature, I argue that critical multicultural education provides a lens to evaluate the possibility of change in tertiary institutions in China. The total school environment of Banks may act as a very useful analytic tool for my case study, while Teng's proposal may offer a possible solution to the puzzle of *Duoyuan Yiti* in contemporary China.

3.3 The Study of Multilingual Acquisition

In the mid 1990s, Peirce (1995, p. 12) pointed out one of the shortcomings of second language study: multilingual theorists failed to develop "a comprehensive theory of social identity that integrates the language learner and language learning context." Now more than two decades have passed, but this "Utopian theory" is still not available. The language learning context is becoming more complex, as the study of second language acquisition (SLA) is extended from monolingual to multilingual learners in an even more dynamic and diversified learning context (Appadurai 1996; Zuengler and Miller 2006).

During the past thirty years, the studies of multilingual acquisition (MA) have drawn on sociocultural theory (Vygotsky 1979; Lantolf 2000, 2005, 2006; Lave and Wenger 1991; Donato 2000), post-structural theory (Butler 1992; Weedon 1997), social theory (Bakhtin 1981; Dressman 2008), and critical theory (Bourdieu 1977, 1991; Gee 1990; Phillipson 1992; Fairclough 1992, 1995; Cummins 2001; Norton 2000; Pennycook 2001; Norton and Toohey 2004). This chapter mainly discusses multilingual acquisition from a post-structuralist perspective. At the same time, some important notions coined by socioculturalists are discussed. I also talk about power relationships in educational institutions and their effect on the identity construction of ethnic multilingual learners in mainstream Chinese universities.

The literature suggests that interest in multilingual acquisition traces back several centuries (McCarthy 2001). Since the 1960s, scholars have developed frameworks from psychological/cognitive, sociocultural, and post-structural/critical perspectives to examine how a language is learned.

3.3.1 The Psychological/Cognitive Approach

The understanding of multilingual acquisition (MA) has undergone three stages. Before the 1960s, drawing on the theory of structuralism (Bloomfield 1933), the study of MA described the different components in speech production: phonology, morphology, syntax, semantics, and lexicon, to name just a few. This period is called the first generation of psycholinguistics, which aimed to study the "acquisition and processing of discrete units of language" (Lantolf 2006). Under the influence of behaviorism (Skinner 1957) language learning was seen as a cognitive process following the S-R-R (stimuli-response-reinforcement) model. The early 1960s witnessed the second generation of psycholinguistics with the rise of Chomsky's Transformational-Generative (TG) Grammar and Milliner's psychological perspective (Lantolf 2006).

Chomsky's TG Grammar (Chomsky 1957, 1965) challenges behaviorist theory by pointing out the "logic problem" in language acquisition. Chomsky assumes that children are born with an innate capacity called "language faculty," which is "a component of the human mind, physically present in the brain and part of the biological endowment of species" (Chomsky 2002, p. 1).

Lantolf (2006) argues that "neither of the first two generations paid much attention to meaning; neither were they concerned with how language was actually deployed as a tool for communication or for thinking" (p. 694). The cognitive view of multilingual acquisition (MA), as Larsen-Freeman (1991) observes, is trying to describe and explain the process of second language learning (Leontiev 1981; Larsen-Freeman 1991). This process is considered almost unanimously as "an internalized, cognitive process" (Zuengler and Miller 2006, p. 36). Although the psycholinguistic approach pushes MA studies a big step forward, there are many areas still unexplored. For example, the previous studies cannot answer two very important questions: (1) How to use an appropriate language in a given context? (2) Why some L2 learners are more successful than others?

Although the cognitive view of multilingual acquisition has been dominant for decades, it has been challenged recently by many researchers (Bremer et al. 1996; Hall 1995; Rampton 1987; Firth and Wagner 1997). They say this view puts too much emphasis on the individual, is too focused on the internalization of mental processes and sees language learning mainly in terms of the development of grammatical competence (Firth and Wanger 1997; Zuengler and Miller 2006).

3.3.2 The Sociocultural Approach

The birth of Sociocultural Theory (Vygotsky 1962, 1978) was a major breakthrough in MA studies. This theory first appeared in the West in the mid 1980s (Frawley and Lantolf 1984, 1985), was well accepted in the 1990s and still remains popular now (Lantolf 1994, 2006; Lantolf and Appel 1994; Zuengler and Miller 2006).

Different from the cognitive approach which tries to explore the "cake" of MA, socioculturalists attempt to decode the "icing" of MA (Smith 1991). That is to say, they try to understand the development of cognitive processes. Vygotsky once argued, "The social dimension of consciousness [i.e., all mental processes] is primary in time and fact. The individual dimension of consciousness is derivative and secondary" (1979, p. 30). Vygotsky is concerned about individual learners' potential in the process of cognition. His famous conception of the Zone of Proximal Development (ZPD) makes people think about the development of learners' potential (Adair-Hauck and Donato 1994; Aljaafreh and Lantolf 1994; DiCamilla and Anton 1997; Swain and Lapkin 1998; Lantolf 2000, 2006; Donato 2000; Nassaji and Cumming 2000; Ohta 2000; Anton 1999). The key concept in sociocultural theory is the role of interaction in the process of cognition. It is believed that learning is "essentially a social process which is grounded in social cultural learning" (Saville-Troike 2006, p. 111).

Drawing on sociocultural theory, more and more ESL researchers are engaged in studying how learners acquire English in various sociocultural contexts. For example,

Ivanic (2006) uses Activity Theory (Leont'ev 1978) to identify the key elements of social cultural perspectives on language and learning. Donato (2000) reports on how his PhD students draw on their understanding of sociocultural perspectives to carry out eight research projects on classroom-based topics.

There are many other language socialization researchers who identify with Vygotskian approaches to learning. They try to understand the center of learning, learners who are culturally and socially competent members of society (Saville-Troike 2006). Language socialization theory, in contrast to sociocultural theory, attempts to study the language socialization from an anthropological perspective. A great deal of socialization research appeared in the 1980s (Ochs 1988; Schiefflin and Ochs 1986) and the language socialization approach was applied to adult multilingual learners in the 1990s (Poole 1992; Harklau 1994; Duff 1995). However, their findings seem to conflict somewhat with those of other researchers for they see socialization as a "smooth and successful process" (Kanagy 1999; Ohta 1999). Others consider the same process "potentially problematic, tension producing and unsuccessful" (Zuengler and Cole 2005, p. 306).

Situated learning theory (Lave and Wenger 1991) pushes the multilingual acquisition work a step forward. Lave and Wenger (1991) develop two very important notions: "community of practice" and "legitimate peripheral participation." The first notion assumes that learning means participation in the situated practice of skillful practitioners so that individuals are "learning in situated ways—in the trans-formative possibilities of being and becoming complex, full cultural-historical participants in the world" (p. 32). The second notion helps us understand why some language learners fail in their study just because they "take a less empowered position in a community of practice" (Zuengler and Miller 2006, p. 41).

Bakhtin's view of language and the concept of *dialogism* (1981) helps socio-culturalists better their understanding of "situated learning." Bakhtin (1981) claims that "language, for the individual consciousness, lies on the border between oneself and the other" (p. 293). He uses the term *dialogism* to describe language process now and across historical time and space (Dressman 2008). With this in mind, he studies how people borrow others' utterances to form their own language because "an appropriation of words that at one time exist[ing] in other people's mouths before we make them our own" (pp. 293–294). Here, what Bakhtin talks about is not cognitive process but the processes of history, politics and literature (Dressman 2008).

Drawing on Bakhtin's ideas, Hall (2002) argues that an utterance "can only be understood fully by considering its history of use by other people, in other places, for other reasons" (p. 13). Within this framework, Toohey (2000) further sees language learning as a process in which individuals "try on other people's utterances; they take words from other people's mouths; they appropriate these utterances and gradually (but not without conflict) these utterances come to serve their needs and relay their meanings" (p. 13).

To sum up, the sociocultural paradigm emphasizes the process of language acquisition. It addresses how the multilingual learners acquire the new language as "legitimate members" in a "community of practice" such as educational institutions.

This perception of multilingual education triggers new questions in terms of multilingual education: (1) Who are the legitimate members of the "community of practice" and how can they obtain the legitimacy of participation in the process of learning? (2) If some multilingual learners are excluded from "legitimate peripheral participation" will they be marginalized from the mainstream? (3) Who is in the center of a "community of practice" and who is at the periphery? The sociocultural theory also highlights the importance of studying the processes of learning and discourse.

3.3.3 The Post-structuralist Approach

In contrast to the sociocultural paradigm emphasizing meaning as understanding in sociocultural context, the post-structural paradigm focuses on the questioning of meaning. The critical view of multilingual acquisition finds its theoretical support in the "postmodern" critique of the "universal notions of objectivity, progress and reason" (Morgan 2006, p. 1034). The critical perspective drew on Derrida's view (1976) in many cases of binary opposition. It is argued that the two sides are not equal in social and political power (Dressman 2008). Post-structuralism differs from structuralism mainly in its argument that "binaries that structure the social order and our normative sense of reality were not 'natural' but rather the product of historic and cultural inequality" (Dressman 2008). The power of post-structuralism, according to Dressman (2008), lies in "the set of strategies it provides to marginalized groups" such as women; religious minorities; the gay, lesbian, and bi/transsexual community; people of color; the disabled; the colonized; adolescents; and children. In terms of multilingual acquisition, the marginalized groups are those who are labeled as "underachiever," "less proficient English learners," "less talkative, active in group activities," "English speakers with heavy local accent," "poor listeners," and "dumb kids". As for ethnic minority multilingual learners in China, labels include "learners of poor English foundation," "students with poor Chinese proficiency," and "students with low self-esteem."

The role of power in the process of education is deeply influenced by sociologists such as Michel Foucault, Louis Althusser, and Pierre Bourdieu. According to Foucault (1980, 1986), power functions in all activities at all levels, from international corporations to individuals. To him, power operates within "institutional apparatus." He argues that power does not "function in the form of a chain" but through "a net-like organization" (Foucault 1980 p. 98). In other words, power penetrates all levels of social life. Foucault is also concerned about the linkage between knowledge, power, and truth. He believes that knowledge is a form of power and those with power will decide who should possess knowledge and to what extent, knowledge can be true and can be applied.

In multilingual educational settings, power can be traced and detected from the communication between the knowledge-rich and knowledge-poor, the medium of instruction, the school policies, the school curriculum, and the assessment criteria.

Power can achieve both positive and negative effects. As Block (2007) argues, when power "enables and empowers" individuals to act as members of a "community of practice" (Lave and Wenger 1991; Eckert and Mc Connell 1992; Wenger 1998), it works positively; when power "constrains or weakens the capacity to act, it works negatively." As a consequence of the latter case, the issues of "resistance" may arise (Canagarajah 1999).

In terms of multilingual education, Cummins (2009, p. 263) distinguishes two types of power relationships: the coercive power and collaborative power. According to Cummins (2009), a coercive power relationship refers to the "exercise of power by a dominant individual, group, or country," and this relationship is detrimental to the subordinated individual, group, or country. On the other hand, a collaborative power relationship reflects the "sense of the term 'power' that regarding to 'being enabled' or 'empowered' to achieve more" (p. 263). Cummins (2009) argues that "coercive power operates through discourses that position individuals and groups in subordinated relationships" (p. 261).

Drawing on these post-structuralist views, scholars study the power factors in multilingual acquisition. For example, Lam (2007) argues that trilingual education can be an empowerment for ethnic minority learners. This kind of empowerment, as defined by Trueba and Zou (1994), refers to "the capacity to function effectively in a given social setting, with active participation in the cultural, political, and economic institutions, and the possession of full rights and obligations enjoyed by other members of society (1994, pp. 2–3). Lee (2001) views empowerment as an outgrowth of education. Zhao's case study of the Mongolian students suggests trilingual education may help enhance the self-confidence of EMLs, but without structural reforms it can only offer "imagined" empowerment (Zhao 2010, p. 70.).

Throughout my study, I hold this stance: people can acquire knowledge by questioning power and truth. If this assumption is correct, then why cannot EMLs negotiate their identities with the power gained from multilingual education? It is hoped that the newly gained power will become their linguistic, cultural, and social capital, the end products of multilingual and multicultural education.

Foucault (1980) argues that the power to control people's behavior is not realized through direct force but instead through discourses, which establish publicly accepted definitions of sanity and insanity, health and sickness, normative and deviant behavior. As Dressman (2008) observes, these discourses, as part of modern "practices," constitute the structural design of institutions and are established to "discipline the bodies and minds of the mass population" (p. 42). Take educational institutions for example. The modern "practices" are the policies and curriculum that reflect the will of the dominant ethnic majority and aim to achieve "cultural hegemony."

The term "discourse" has been defined and redefined by scholars of the social sciences and humanities. Foucault sees discourse both as "an instrument and an effect of power" for it "transmits and produces power; it reinforces it [the power] but also undermines and exposes it, renders it fragile and makes it possible to thwart it" (Foucault 1978, pp. 100–101). This argument suggests that Foucault sees discourse as both tool and product. It is the origin as well as the end of power

3.3 The Study of Multilingual Acquisition

relationships. Some scholars see discourse both as a language and as a process of language production (DuGay 1995; Layder 1997). Gee (1996) coins the term "Discourses" (with a capital "D" and in plural form) to interpret the broad meaning:

> Discourses are way of being in the world, or form of life which integrate words, acts, values, beliefs, attitudes and social identities, as well as gestures, glances, body positions, and clothes. A discourse is a sort of identity kit which comes complete with the appropriate costume and instructions on how to act, talk and often write so as to take on a particular social role that others will recognize. (Gee 1996, p. 127)

Gee's broad interpretation of discourse as being "certain kind of people" with a capital "D" rather than a lower case "d" (referring to connected stretches of talk or writing) is expanded by Blommaert (2005) who stresses the semiotic role of discourse. He argues that "[d]iscourse …comprise[s] all forms of meaningful semiotic human activity seen in the connection with social, cultural, historical patterns and developments of use" (p. 3). Drawing on the understandings of various scholars, I argue here that D/discourses are important sources of identity construction and reconstruction. I will further elaborate the notion of identity and identity construction later.

To trace the life histories of EMLs, it is necessary to understand discourses in various forms (social, economic, political, ideological, educational) and under various names such as discourses (Foucault 1971, 1978, 1980), communities of practice (Lave and Wenger 1991), cultural communities (Clark 1996), discourse communities (Berkenkotter and Huckin 1995), distributed knowledge or distributed systems (Hutchins 1995), thought collectives (Fleck 1979), practices (Barton and Hamilton 1998; Bourdieu 1998; Heidegger 1962), activity systems (Engestrom 1990; Leont'ev 1978), actor-actant networks (Callon and Latour 1992; Latour 1987), and "forms of life" (Wittgenstein 1958). In Chap. 2, I introduced the various discourses that reconceptulize EMLs in contemporary China. These discourses will be mentioned and discussed further.

Post-structuralists are also interested in the relationship between discourse, ideology and power. Bove (1995) once argued:

> Discourse provides a privileged entry into poststructuralist modes of analysis precisely because it is the organized and regulated, as well as regulating and constituting, functions of language that it studies: its aim is to describe the surface linkages between power, knowledge, institutions, intellectuals, the control of populations, and the modern state as these intersect in systems of thought (pp. 54–55).

Bove's critical conception of discourse is based on Foucault's view of power and resistance (1977). Foucault (1978) believes that power and knowledge are interrelated and that discourse reflects ideology. He asserts that:

> Discourse can be an instrument and effect of power, but also a hindrance, a stumbling block, a point of resistance and a starting point for an opposing strategy. Discourse transmits and produces power; it reinforces it, but it also undermines it and exposes it, renders it fragile and makes it possible to thwart it (p. 101).

Foucault uses the metaphoric term *panopticon* to explain self-surveillance. At present, the *panopticon* can be applied to educational discourse to describe all kinds of disciplinary strategies to keep learning and learners under control. For example, the university code, and the higher education evaluation system mentioned in Chapter Two reinforce the control and surveillance of the ethnic majorities by dominant hegemonic groups.

Drawing on Karl Marx, Louis Althusser (1971) comes up with the notion of "Ideological State Apparatuses" (ISA), which refers to social institutions such as the police, hospitals, the media and schools. Dressman (2008) points out that the ISA's function is to make individuals within the capitalist society employ "interpellation" (Althusser 1971), a discursive process by which the individual is labeled and subjugation is achieved. The concept of "interpellation" may have been influenced by Gramsci's notion of "hegemony" (1988). As one of the units of ISA, educational institutions strive hard to shape their products, to graduate students according to the institutions" needs and standards which facilitate the hegemonic mechanism.

Bourdieu (1977, 1991) put forward the famous notion of habitus after he and Passeron (1977) had made a serious study of Algerian Berber peasants, the French higher education system and the relationship between social class and aesthetic taste in France. Bourdieu defines "habitus" as:

> A set of *dispositions* which incline agents to act and react in certain ways. The dispositions generate practices, perceptions and attitudes which are 'regular' without being consciously coordinated or governed by any 'rule'. The dispositions which constitute the habitus are inculcated, structured, durable, generative and transposable… Dispositions are acquired through a gradual process of *inculcation* in which early childhood experiences are particularly important." (Bourdieu 1991, p. 12, italics in original)

For Bourdieu and his associates, as the product of historical and material forces, *habitus* can guide people to make choices and decisions according to the structuring logic of practice. Morrison (2005) sees habitus as something that is "both a result of social structures and yet also structures; that is, changes and influences, behavior, life-styles and social systems" (p. 313). Thus, the dual nature of habitus as the result of both "structuring structure" and "structured structure" (Bourdieu 1986, p. 170), exerts a dialectical role: promoting creativity and constraining practices. What interests me in this case study is to what extent the habitus of being an ethnic minority (cultural heritage, value system and way of life) will influence the behaviors of EMLs on and off campus. I also hope to know whether the habitus of the EMLs will be extended to the next generation within the ever more sinicizated social practice, which is more and more astray from the ethnic minority culture.[5]

---

[5]In order to achieve social mobility, some ethnic minority groups in China such as the Ji'nuo have decided to embrace Han language and culture at the cost of their own cultural heritage. With the ever-increasing language and cultural contact, as well as the motivation for better life opportunities, motivation has also been created among other ethnic groups to adopt the assimilationist strategy toward the larger society. This process of assimilation (transforming their traditional way of life and adopting more and more Chinese language culture) is referred to as sinicization.

3.3 The Study of Multilingual Acquisition

From the post-structural perspective, if people hope to understand linguistic hegemony, it is necessary to figure out "how power is structured and played out in social, cultural and economic institutions" (Stroud 2002, p. 247).

Bourdieu believes that certain linguistic practices acquire authority, dominance and legitimacy "through a complex historical process, sometimes involving extensive conflict (especially in colonial contexts)" (Thompson 1991, p. 5). If this observation is true, the establishment of a certain linguistic legitimacy will imply the marginalizing of other competing languages. For example, Putonghua and English are gaining more and more popularity in the ethnic minority areas for pragmatic reasons. As a result, the motivation to learn ethnic minority languages is declining. Bourdieu further argues that:

> We learn that the efficacy of a discourse, its power to convince, depends on the authority of the person who utters it, or what amounts to the same thing, on his 'accent' functioning as an index of authority (Bourdieu 1977, p. 653).

The legitimacy of a certain language speaker affects the social, political and economic conditions and status of certain language speakers. Bourdieu (1991) discusses this assumption later in his book *Language and Symbolic Power*. He believes that the labor market will determine linguistic value and that school will provide language learners an access to language required by the market. In contemporary China, the labor market favors people with both Chinese and English proficiency. For instance, if a migrant worker can communicate with others in Putonghua, it will be easy for him/her to find a job in the inland. If he/she has a good command of English, he/she will be competitive in finding a job for which English is required or considered as certain kind of social and cultural capital.

However, Bourdieu's stand on the reproduction of authoritative language is questioned by some western scholars, for this framework fails to explain some exceptional cases. For example, the dominance of Catalan in parts of Spain is a situation making Castilian an authoritative language rather than Spanish, which is promoted in official institutions such as schools and the government. Woollard (1985) wonders if Bourdieu's assumption of a fully integrated linguistic market can be applied to the Spanish case. In this sense, the institutional domination of a language does not necessarily lead to its hegemony.

Swigart (2000) also criticizes Bourdieu's framework because it fails to address the issue of change in linguistic markets and ignores the question of how "the *position* of the legitimate language could itself evolve" (2000 p. 104). Swigart mentions the ascendance of Urban Wolof in Senegal to support his idea of "alternative legitimacy" in the language market.

Haeri (1997) comments that Bourdieu's thinking cannot cope with contradictions between class, language and the state. Citing the position of Arabic in Egypt, she argues that the choice of an official language will be determined by class, religion, institutions and the state.

Another important contribution of Bourdieu is the metaphor of "capital", which provided a framework that Skeggs (1997, 2004) believes will work in the postmodern world. According to Block's interpretation (2007), "economic capital" includes one's financial wealth (income, acquired property and assets). "Cultural capital" as Block (2007) defined are "the right cultural resources and assets" in the form of "behavioral patterns" (e.g. accent and attitude), "association with particular artifacts" (e.g. books and qualifications), and "connection to certain institutions" (university and professional associations). "Social capital" refers to the connection to relations with less or more powerful "others." When the "others" have more cultural capital they will be used to acquire more social capital. "Symbolic capital" refers to "prestige, reputation, fame and is ...the form assumed by [the] different kinds of capital when they are perceived and recognized as legitimate" (Bourdieu 1991, p. 230). Bourdieu's notion of capital brings to mind questions like: Are people born with certain kinds of capital? And if so, how does one activate the dormant capital? Can symbolic capital encourage ethnic minority students to achieve more in their studies or other aspects of life?

Post-structuralist approaches have been applied to the study of the cultural relations between the west and its former colonies (Said 1978; Pratt 1992) and led to the birth of new theories such as Critical Race Theory (Ladson-Billings 1995; Bell 2004) and Actor-Network Theory (Latour 2005).

The critical view of multilingual acquisition comes from the different understandings of the relationship between language learning and social change. Applied linguists tend to perceive language as a "means of expression or communication" (Norton and Toohey 2004) or the "site" in which social and cultural differences are displayed (Morgan 2006). Post-structuralists view language as a "vehicle" through which differences in identity categories are created (Norton and Toohey 2004).

Unlike the sociocultural researchers, who are interested in studying the role of social practice in the process of language learning, post-structuralists are more concerned about the social and power relations and their impact on multilingual learners. In this sense, one must understand the power relationships if one wants to gain a fuller understanding of the process of learning. My hope is that this understanding will lead to social and educational transformations benefiting "disenfranchised groups and individuals" (Zuengler and Miller 2006).

Nowadays, critical approaches have been applied to the study of multilingual acquisition in a range of areas such as the relationship between TESOL, power and inequality (Ibrahim 1999; Goldstein 2004; Frye 1999; Nelson 1999; Benesch 1999; Brutt-Griffler and Samimy 1999; Johnston 1999), TESOL and the global power of English (Cox and Deanis 1999; Lin 1999), re-conceptualization of second language education (Luke 2004; Kubota 2004; Shohamy 2004), identity challenges (Stein 2004; Canagarajah 2004; Starfield 2004; Morgan 2004), critical practices (Brito and Auerbach 2004; Norton and Vanderheyden 2004; Sunderland 2004) and teacher education changes (Lin 2004; Toohey and Waterstone 2004; Goldstein 2004; Pennycook 2004) to name just a few.

In a special issue of *TESOL Quarterly*, Pennycook (1999) introduces three issues that frame critical approaches to TESOL: (a) the domain or area of interest (To what extent do particular domains define a critical approach?), (b) transformative pedagogy (How does a particular approach to education change things?), and (c) a self-reflexive stance on critical theory.

At the beginning of the introductory chapter, Pennycook (1999) says critical approaches can help TESOL professionals better understand the "complex ways the contexts in which TESOL occurs and offer the prospect of change...help us deal with some of the most significant issues of our time" (p. 329).

In 2004, another important book on critical pedagogy was edited by Norton and Toohey. In this collection, a variety of scholars offer their critical views on language education in ever more diversified global settings. All these scholars share a concern with how issues of power affect language learning and language learners. They also discuss the binary relationships between writers and readers, teachers and students, test makers and test takers, teacher educators and student teachers, and researchers and subjects. It is believed that critical language education will not only "open the door to new sources of knowledge and understanding" but also contribute to investigating "whose knowledge has historically been privileged and whose has been disregarded and why" (Norton and Toohey 2004, p. 15.).

Norton and Toohey (2004) summarize four over-lapping themes in this book: (1) re-conceptualizing second language acquisition; (2) challenging identities; (3) researching critical practices and (4) educating teachers for change. Some over-lapping themes that run through the book are seeking critical classroom practices (Brito et al. 2004; Shohamy 2004; Pennycook 2004; Goldstein 2004), creating and adapting materials of critical pedagogies (Brito et al. 2004; Lin 2004; Norton and Vanderheyden 2004; Goldstein 2004; Stein 2004), exploring diverse representations of knowledge (Lin et al. 2004; Shohamy 2004; Stein 2004) and seeking critical research practice (Canagarajah 2004).

Overall, critical applied linguists see post-structuralism as a shift from searching for "universal and invariant laws of humanity to more nuanced, multileveled and ultimately, complicated framings of the world around us" (Block 2007, p. 13). Within this approach, there appears to be more and more research in language learning, language socialization and multilingual practices. It is believed that poststructuralism will offer "an alternative approach to conceptualizing the politics and aesthetics of identity" (Davidson 1996, p. 4)

3.4 The Study of the Identity of Multilingual Learners

3.4.1 *The Sociocultural Paradigm and Identity Studies*

Multilingual acquisition researchers seldom talked about identity issues before the 1990s. As Block (2007) notes, "There was little or no work examining how learners position themselves and are positioned by others depending on where they are and what they are doing" (p. 2). After 1990, identity became a hot topic in MA and applied linguistics as the result of "systematic and extensive borrowing from continuous social science fields of inquiry" (Block 2007, p. 2).

The concept of identity can be traced back to the western European enlightenment and some famous philosophers and social scientists such as Machiavelli, Descartes, Lockes et al. (Taylor 1989; Holstein and Gubrium 1999; Woodward 2002; Bucholtz and Hall 2006; Benwell and Stokoe 2006). Block (2007) summarizes four reasons that made identity study popular. First, the psychology and psychiatry development, led by William James and Sigmund Freud in the late 19th century and early 20th century, caused scholars to make "self" a focus of research. Second, the secularization during the industrialization movement made people pay more attention to the value of life and self-fulfillment. Third, the advancement of human rights in the 20th century in the industrialized nations eroded traditional institutions that had blocked social mobility. And finally, as Giddens (1991), Beck (1992) and Bauman (1992) observe, the ontology of 20th century social scientists was very different from that of previous ages because life in the late modern/postmodern age of globalization had changed a lot more than before.

The basic concept of identity is a certain "kind of person" (Hacking 1983, 1986, 1994, 1995, 1998; Gee 2001). Norton (2000, p. 5) defines identity as "how a person understands his or her relation to the world, how that relationship is constructed across time and space, and how the person understands possibilities for the future." This definition refers to how a "kind of person" is constructed. Gee (2001) comes up with four ways to view identity: the natural perspective (N-identity), the institutional perspective (I-identity), the discursive perspective (D-identity) and the affinity perspective (A-identity). He further acknowledges that those four perspectives are not absolute as "there are many possible approaches to identity" (p. 121). His view of "identity as an analytic lens for research in education" is very thought-provoking. Block (2007) lists seven identity types: (1) ethnic identity; (2) racial identity; (3) national identity; (4) migrant identity; (5) gender identity; (6) social class identity; and (7) language identity. However, he stresses that the different identity types do not "stand independent of one another in the larger general identity of a person (p. 42). Blackledge and Pavlenko (2001, p. 244) even categorize eight domains of identity which they believe are "critical for everyday interactions" namely cultural, ethnic, gender, personal, role, relational, face work and symbolic interaction identities.

Mantero (2007) summarizes three types of identities in the multilingual context: the imposed identity, the assumed identity and negotiable identities. Pavlenko and her associates see the imposed identities as "the ones that individuals cannot resist or contest at a particular time and space" (2004, p. 21). Therefore, they are not negotiable. The assumed identities are often metaphoric "stereotypes" (Mantero 2007), which individuals feel "ease" or "comfortable" with (Pavlenko and Blackledge 2004; Mantero 2007). These kinds of identities are socio-historically acceptable and are legitimized by the dominant social discourse. Negotiable identities in contrast to imposed identities refer to those that can be contested and resisted by individuals or groups (Pavlenko and Blackledge 2004b). Mantero (2007) argues that identity negotiation can also occur when people face resistance or acceptance.

3.4 The Study of the Identity of Multilingual Learners

Anthropologists, sociologists and postmodernists/post-structuralists try to conceptualize the term "identity" from different perspectives. In the field of sociolinguistics, more and more attention is being paid to the construction of identity in relation to language and culture. Kramsch (1998) sees language as "the most sensitive indicator of the relationship between an individual and a given social group" (p. 77). Furthermore, individuals may "assume several collective identities" that are "liable to confront with one another" (p. 67). Through MA people construct "the self" and "the other" (Kramsch 1998). Miller (2000) argues that an individual can construct an identity by learning a new language and establishing membership in a new community. This view of identity as "fluid and constructed in linguistic interaction" (Blackledge and Pavlenko 2001, p. 245) is an ethnographic-oriented sociolinguistic approach. This stand, in contrast to the sociopsychological approach, views identity as stable and unchangeable.

Kellman (2003) points out that "switching the language entails transforming the self...it means constructing a new identity syllable by syllable" (p. xiv). It seems to him that the negotiation of certain kind of "self" or negotiation of one's identity is a given trend in second language acquisition. Multilingual learners attempt to "evoke, assert, define, modify, challenge and/or support their own and others' desired self-images" (Ting-Toomey 1999, p. 40).

At the same time, it is believed that the formation of identity may include the invention of new illiteracies in the second language (Kern 2000). Mantero (2007) argues that "identity formation may involve the creation of linguistic devices and new strategies that help us negotiate meaning." Norton (2000) addresses the role of language "as constitutive of and constituted by a language learner's identity."

Many ESL/EFL researchers (Shen 1989; Feere 2003) reflect on their own or others' personal struggles to create a new identity and ways of self-representing in a second language. It seems to them that their identities as language learners "come to life when they participate in meaning driving discourse in authentic context" (Mantero 2007, p. 9). Peirce (1995) argues that "SLA theory needs to develop a conception of identity that is understood with reference to larger, and frequently inequitable, social structures which are reproduced in day-to-day social interaction" (p. 1). I argue that the above conceptions of identity, from sociocultural perspectives, establish a link between identity theory and language leaning as follows:

1. Identity is shaped by societal and institutional discourses in the process of language learning. However, the construction of identity is always dynamic and flowing.
2. Language switching may be understood as a means of identity negotiation and reconstruction.
3. The newly established identity may help explain the success or failure of ethnic multilingual learners in literacy development and school attainment.

3.4.2 The Post-Structuralist Paradigm to Identities of Multilingual Learners

Many recent studies on identity issues in MA have adopted post-structuralist views on identity. There are three categories of research on the relationship between identity development and multilingual acquisition: (1) theory development; (2) thematic study, and (3) case study of communities.

In terms of theory building, Davies and Harre (2000) discuss how people position themselves in discursive practice. Pavlenko and Lantolf (2000) address SLA as a "(re)construction of selves." Kramsch (1998) investigates social discursive constructions of self in L2 learning. Pomerantz (2002) discusses the relationship of language ideologies and identity construction. Cashman and Williams (2008) describe the conversation analytic approach to bilingual conversation and the sociocultural linguistic approach to the study of identity in interaction. Pavlenko and Norton (2007) propose the notions of "imagined community" (p. 669). They argue that language learners' actual and desired membership in an "imagined community" may influence "learning trajectories, agency, motivation, investment, and resistance in English learning."

The thematic study of identity of L2 learners entails a broad spectrum including topics such as identity negotiation in a multilingual context (Blackledge and Pavlenko 2001; Pavlenko and Blackledge 2004; Kinginger 2004; Block 2007; Swann 2005; Potowski 2007; Gu 2008), teacher identity (Maclure 1993, Li 2007; Liggett 2007; Clarke 2008), identity of migrant English learners (Mckay and Wong 1996; Norton 2000; Lee 2002; Kinginger 2004; Pavlenko and Blackledge 2004; Clark 2007; Harklau 2007; Cook 2008; Wallace 2008), non-American residents in the USA (Bailey 2002; Reyes 2007), overseas returnees of certain ethnicities (Kanno 2003; Miyahira and Petrucci 2007, Chen 2008); code-switching of nonnative speakers in bilingual circumstances (Luk 2005; Chen 2008), textual identity (Lam 2000; Griffin 2006; Charles 2006), politics of identity (Giamapapa 2004), identity and language use (Miller 2003, 2004; Gao 2002, 2007), literacy and social identities (Egbo 2004), cultural identity (Hall 1996; Hall and Gay 1996; Grossberg 1996), positional identities (Holland et al. 1998), and identity investment (Potowski 2007).

There are an increasing number of studies on identity construction through multilingual acquisition. Most of them involve the immigrant children in Europe or North America. For example, Kinginger (2004) reports how Alice, a highly motivated French learner, overcame personal, social, and material obstacles to acquire French successfully as a foreign language (first in America as a part-time and then a full-time college student and later as an exchange student in France). By tracing her learning history through interviews, journals, emails and letters over two years, Kinginger (2004) finds that Alice has been engaged in negotiating many facets of her social, linguistic, gender and class identities through her journey of French acquisition. It seemed that Alice's academic success lies in her persistent effort in gaining access to learning French at home and abroad. With an integration of her personal mission and professional aspirations, Alice makes full use of her "personal experience, talent and resources to upgrade her access to cultural capital" (p. 240). She later becomes a "cultural person" and "share[d] her knowledge with others" (p. 240). Alice's story as a successful French learner resonates with the "investment theory" proposed by Norton (2000) and is supported by the social culture theory in MA. These imply that "one's history, disposition towards learning, access to social cultural world, participation, and imagination together shape the qualities of their achievement" (Kinginger 2004, p. 241).

Drawing on a research involving 36 literate and illiterate rural women in Nigeria, Egbo (2004) examines the interface between literacy and the construction of social, individual and group identities in postcolonial Nigeria. Her findings suggest that literacy is a necessary premise for women to better understand their social, political and material world. Literacy enables women to (re)negotiate their individual and social identities in empowering ways. The literate women are able to enjoy a "comparatively enhanced equality of life and have increased life options as well as some social influence" (p. 252). On the other hand, the lack of literacy reduces the self-image of the non-literate women.

Potowski's longitudinal research on a dual immersion school in Illinois, USA, reports the stories of four Spanish students from Grade five to Grade eight. He (2007) investigates learners' investment using four dimensions: (1) home language use and support for Spanish; (2) students' attitude toward the dual immersion school and toward Spanish; (3) the teachers' positioning of the students; and (4) the student's position within her or his peer group. The findings suggests that the four students maintain personality traits over four years, but some have less enthusiasm than they did in the fifth grade.

Potowski assumes that this reduction of investment is because of the "absence of any eighth-grade classroom-based pressure to perform in Spanish virtually" (p. 199). Based on these findings, he suspects that Norton's (2000) framework of investment, which entails the language learner's identity engagement, is less applicable in the dual immersion school.

Even though there are limited numbers of studies on Asian learners in ESL/EFL contexts, the research available is very informative and valuable. For example, in their two-year investigation, Mckay and Wong (1996) traced four students aged 12–13, in a suburban junior high school in California. These four children come from newly arrived Chinese families of different social economic statuses. By periodic interviewing and assessing English language development, Mckay and Wong (1996) arrive at a "contextualist perspective" to identify the mutual interacting multiple discourses and to trace the participants' negotiations of multiple identities.

Lee (2001) is the first Western scholar who studied tertiary ethnic minority students in Southwest China. She visited Yunnan Normal University many times, first as a foreign teacher and then as a PhD candidate. By studying the life histories of 32 successful minority students at Yunnan Normal University, she documents how these minority students overcame staggering obstacles to achieve educational success. She also talks about the correlation between education, ethnicity and empowerment.

Another Lee (2002) is perhaps the first Asian scholar to study the identity of second generation Korean-American university students. Through qualitative and quantitative analysis of questionnaires distributed to 40 students, he tries to answer three questions: (1) what is the level of heritage language proficiency and language use among these students?; (2) with which culture(s) do these youths identify themselves (Korean or American), and to what extent?; and (3) Is there a relationship between cultural identity and heritage language proficiency? Based on his findings, he concludes that "heritage language proficiency was related to strength of bicultural identification" (p. 117).

By analyzing naturally occurring classroom interaction of adolescent Hong Kong students, Luk (2005) observes the code-switching of Hong Kong adolescents and notes the multiple and contested forms of identity. Based on her research, she proposes a "pedagogy of connection," aimed at developing competent multilingual users. Chen (2008) is also interested in the code-switching of bilinguals. Her study of overseas returning bilinguals in Hong Kong documents how the returnees position and re-position themselves when they are discriminated against as outsiders. She also documents, how they negotiate their ethnic and cultural identities as Hong Kong Chinese.

Clothey (2004, 2005) and Tsung (2010) investigate the *Minkaomin* and *Minkaohan*[6] students at Minzu University of China and Xinjiang University, respectively. These students hold different views of their ethnic languages, cultures, and identities, though both claim to represent their ethnic groups. It seems that given the market economy in China, the ethnic minority learners have to make a decision of assimilation or integration as the mainstream language and culture may bring about better life opportunities and post-graduation employment.

Gu (2008) investigates the identity negotiation and investment transformation of three female university students in China. In light of her findings, she argues that English learning entails complex and intertwined issues of motivation, identity, and culture. In China, the most influential study of the identity of tertiary English learners was made by Gao and her team. After studying 2278 undergraduates, a stratified sample from 30 universities in China, the investigators discuss six categories of self-identity change: self-confidence, subtractive bilingualism, additive bilingualism, productive bilingualism, identity split, and zero change. The findings suggest that English learning exerts a great influence on learners' identities in the Chinese EFL context. Meanwhile, changes in learners' values and communication styles were also observed. The results show that gender, college major, and starting age for English learning have significant effects on certain types of self-identity change. However, as Wang and Gao (2008) observe, "Gao et al.'s study, while illuminating in itself, focuses only on elite Chinese university students with no reference to their ethnic origins, and therefore, the findings are not readily applicable to the understanding of the enormous challenges and difficulties facing thousands of Chinese ethnic and linguistic minority students in learning English" (p. 391).

---

[6]*Minkaohan* refers to the ethnic minority students who go to mainstream school and complete their education in Chinese before they are admitted to tertiary institutions.

One of the prominent problems highlighted by the previous case studies is the issue of identity negotiation of multilingual learners when they try to participate in various communities of practice. The findings resonate with post-structuralist arguments that identity negotiation occurs when certain kind of identity options are "imposed or devalued and others are unavailable or misunderstood" (Pavlenko and Blackledge 2004, p. 22).

The previous case studies on multilingual learners in the West and Asia, though revealing, leave some areas untouched. For example, linguistic minority learners within the dominant culture are less studied. As for China in particular, there are few studies of ethnic multilingual learners in the mainstream education system.

3.5 The Conceptual Framework of This Study

As I have discussed in previous sections, there are various factors contributing to the identity construction of multilingual learners. In this study, I hope to examine the influence of policies (in relation to ethnic minorities, language, and education) and curricula (explicit or hidden) on the experiences of EMLs in China. As can be seen from the figure below, one purpose of this study is to observe how power/knowledge relationships are realized through ethnic multilingual education. A second purpose is to understand what impacts the construction of identity for ethnic multilingual learners in Yunnan. The study will also look at ways that EMLs respond to such impacts.

The framework of this study (Fig. 3.2) is basically built upon Foucault's interpretation of the power/knowledge relationships which Marshall (1990) calls the "analytic grid." Foucault (1980) believes that knowledge is the end product of power relations and is used to legitimize the exercise of power. Ball (1990) comments that "power and knowledge are two sides of a single process. Knowledge does not reflect power relations but [it] is imminent in them" (p. 5).

Figure 3.2 assumes that the power/knowledge relationship in the educational system is affecting the multilingual acquisition (MA) process through which the identities of the ethnic multilingual learners (circle in blue) are formed. Drawing on critical multiculturalism, I see the identities of the EMLs as the end-products of social construction under power relationships. These relationships are "perceptions of knowledge, power, particularly what knowledge is legitimate and should count, what experiences should be celebrated and learned from, and how power can be negotiated among different knowledge and experience" (Torres 1998, p. 436). MA is both the carrier of identity and the process of identity construction for EMLs who are embedded in the sociocultural discourse (circle in red).

In this study, I select discourses about higher learning institutions from various perspectives, and I put the discourses at the center of the discussion for "education systems is a political means of maintaining or modifying the appropriateness of discourses with the knowledge and power they bring with them" (Foucault 1971, p. 46). However, the impacts of other discourses on the EML are also expected.

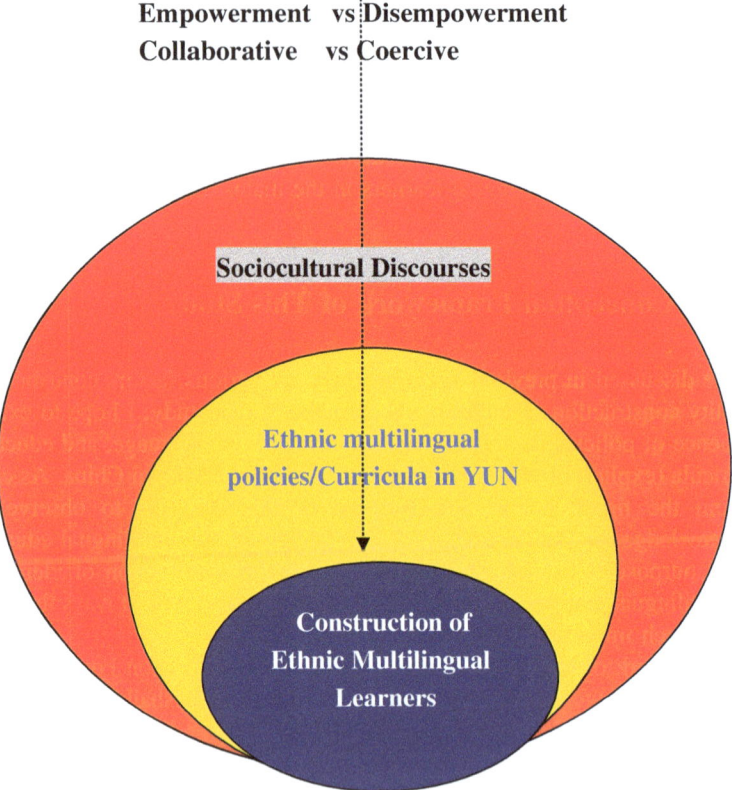

Fig. 3.2 Conceptual framework (Wang 2012)

These come through daily business, media, and personal interactions within their ethnic communities.

The two interactive driving forces (policy/curricula and sociocultural discourses) work together to shape the identities of EMLs. However, these identities are dynamic in time and space. In other words, the nature of these identities, whether imposed or assumed, negotiable or nonnegotiable, may be changeable given various social, historical, and cultural contexts.

The outer layer circle in red refers to the sociocultural discourse in which curricula and policies are made. In addition to the second layer circle in yellow (educational curricula and policies concerned) there are many other components (lying within the red circle), which are crucial for the identity formation of EMLs. These components are historical and geographic factors (migration history, ethnic and language contact, local educational history, and settlement location), level of

3.5 The Conceptual Framework of This Study

integration with the larger society and mainstream culture, the degree of identification with the Chinese education system, religion and the degree of socioeconomic development of the ethnic groups concerned (EMLs'educational level, way of life). I will discuss some of these factors to help the reader understand the context in which EMLs are raised.

In this framework, "knowledge/power" is realized through multilingual education in the sociocultural discourses. According to Foucault, knowledge and power are dialectically related. On the one hand, power is based on knowledge and functions through "a net-like organization" (Foucault 1980, p. 98). On the other hand, knowledge is a form of power. At the same time, knowledge can be acquired by questioning power. Foucault (1986) believes that "individuals are the vehicles of power not [just] its points of application" (p. 234). Wong (2007) observes that the power relationship is "reciprocal." He argues that "individuals have the freedom to make choices" (p. 76). These conceptions of power, knowledge, and individuals suggest the following points of attention for the study:

1. Power is realized through educational institutions, which decide who should have and to what extent they can have knowledge. Power is also implicit in the way knowledge is defined and used in the institutions' discourse and practice.
2. Knowledge is a kind of power and is gained through the negotiation of the multiple realities one experiences with power and truth. Individuals are not the passive receivers of knowledge/power. Actually, they can negotiate their identities by activating their capital through active engagement in different communities.

Educational institutions are just one of the windows reflecting the constructive force of power and knowledge. Educational institutions are a factor in shaping one's identity within the ever-dynamic sociocultural discourses. However, it can exert highly critical roles in developing the prospective talents and agents for social transformation. Deacon (2006, p. 184), examining Foucault's theoretical implications, argues that:

> Universities, like schools, are multifaceted amalgamations of economic, political, judicial and epistemological relations of power, which still reflect the exclusionary and inclusionary binaries of their origins: university campuses are relatively artificial enclaves where students are expected to absorb socially desirable modes of behaviors and forms of knowledge before being recuperated into society.

In reality, the hegemonic status achieved by particular ideologies and forms of capital, along with other factors that constrain and enable identity development, shape the educational institutions. The institutions then shape the identity of EMLs.

The investigator knows quite well that education is just one of the factors influencing the identity construction of EMLs. There are many external factors. For example, the level of political and cultural integration of the ethnic minority groups into the Chinese state, the degree to which people appreciate Chinese school education, local educational history, religion, cross-border ethnic contacts, and economic development (Hansen 1999) may also contribute to the identity construction of EMLs. Therefore, in my case study, some external factors are also considered and discussed. To some extent, I know it is almost impossible to capture every "circle" in the social field, but this model provides a way of viewing social life as contextualized in multiple ways. Relations between factors, within and across different levels, may be characterized by a complex mix of complementarities, conflict, and indifference. This model is very similar to the framework of sociologists Derek Layder and Anthony Giddens, as well as that of critical social linguist, Norman Fairclough. It is also similar to Vygotsky's "genetic" model of individual-social relations.

Throughout the study, I would like to emphasize the significance of examining identity via various discourses. Ball (1990) says "discourses embody meaning and social relationship, they constitute both subjectivity and power relations" (p. 2). It is through the interaction of all kinds of discourses (personal, educational, socioeconomic, sociocultural, historical, political, ideological, educational, and religious) that the identities of multilingual learners are constructed, transformed, and reconstructed. Multilingual acquisition makes it possible for ethnic multilingual students to establish a social membership in new communities of practice (in and out of school). To negotiate the legitimacy of their participation in different "community(s) of practice" (Wenger 1998) they have to struggle to acquire appropriate identities in order to be treated as central or peripheral participants. This transformation of "self" in the new discourses may make them "evoke, assert, define, modify, challenge and/or support their own and others' desired self-images" (Ting-Toomey 1999, p. 40). As discourse can be understood as both language and the process of language production (DuGay 1995; Layder 1997) this study will focus on the process of multilingual acquisition by ethnic minority learners. The study will report how the various discourses interweave and how the distinctive identities of the informants are constructed. This study will also look at how EMLs, by negotiating their identities, struggle for more favorable conditions in and out of their educational institutions.

Multilingual acquisition is still in its infancy in terms of research, but it is becoming more and more common in practice. Previous research on MA suggests that multilingual learners confront constant challenges in mastering new linguistic forms and forming new identities (Cenoz and Jessner 2000; Cenoz et al. 2001; Jordà 2005; Sagin 2006; Potowski 2007). This is all the more so when they have to acquire more than two languages that are quite different in linguistic context and linguistic distance (Stern 1983; Ytsma 2001).

Compared with second language acquisition (SLA), multilingual acquisition (MA) is a more complicated phenomenon, presenting more fluidity and complexity. Cenoz and Jessner (2000) points out that the major differences between SLA and MA can be seen in the order of language acquisition, sociolinguistic factors, and the psychological processes involved. Other scholars believe that MA holds the following defining features (1) nonlinearity; (2) language maintenance; (3) individual variation; (4) interdependence and quality change (Herdina and Jessner 2000).

As for the EMLs in China their personal and local identities may be split between ethnic minority, national Chinese and learners of additional language(s). However, most recent research on the identity issues of multilingual learners is in

European or Anglo-American settings. These studies mainly concern sociolinguistic, psycholinguistic, and educational aspects of multilingual acquisition. In contrast, few studies have been conducted on identity construction, as this relates to multilingual and multicultural development in Asia. This research gap makes the study of EMLs in China meaningful because EMLs are often marginalized in the mainstream education system. As discussed in chapter two, there may also be a need to reconceptualize multilingual learners, given the ever-dynamic and diversified sociocultural discourse in China today.

3.6 Summary

In this chapter, I first reviewed the literature on multicultural education in the West and China. Then I talked about the studies of multilingual acquisition from cognitive, sociocultural, and post-structuralist perspectives. Afterwards, I reviewed the studies of the identities of multilingual learners using sociocultural and post-structuralist paradigms. Finally, I introduced the conceptual framework for this study and explained why this framework was appropriate to answer the research questions. In the next chapter, I will introduce the research design of this study.

References

Adair-Hauck, B., & Donato, R. (1994). Foreign language explanations within the zone of proximal development. *The Canadian Modern Language Review, 50*, 532–555.

Aljaafreh, A., & Lantolf, J. P. (1994). Negative feedback as regulation and second language learning in the zone of proximal development. *The Modern Language Journal, 78*, 465–483.

Althusser, L. (1971). Ideology and ideological state apparatus. In L. Althusser (Ed.), *Lenin and philosophy and other essays by Louis Althusser* (pp. 127–188). London: Monthly Review Press.

Anton, M. (1999). The discourse of a learner-centered classroom: Sociocultural perspectives on teacher-learner interaction in the second language classroom. *The Modern Language Journal, 83*, 303–318.

Appadurai, A. (1996). *Modernity at large: Cultural dimensions of globalization*. Minneapolis: University of Minnesota Press.

Bailey, B. H. (2002). *Language, race, and negotiation of identity: A study of Dominican Americans*. New York: LFB Scholarly Pub.

Bakhtin, M. M. (1981). *The dialogic imagination*. (C. Emerson & M. Holquist, trans.). Austin: University of Texas Press.

Ball, S. (1990). Introducing Monsieur Foucault. In S. J. Ball (Ed.), *Foucault and education: Disciplines and knowledge* (pp. 1–8). London: Routledge.

Banks, J. A. (2009). Multicultural education: Dimensions and paradigms. In J. A. Banks (Ed.), *The Routledge international companion to multicultural education* (pp. 9–32). New York: Routledge.

Banks, J. A. (2010). *Diversity and citizenship education in multicultural nations*. Presentation at Faculty of Education: The University of Hong Kong.

Banks, J. A., & Banks, C. A. M. (2007). *Multicultural education: Issues and perspectives*. Hoboken: Wiley.
Barry, B. (2000). *Culture and equality: An egalitarian critique of multiculturalism*. Cambridge, MA: Harvard University Press.
Barton, D., & Hamilton, M. (1998). *Local literacies: Reading and writing in one community*. London: Routledge.
Bauman, Z. (1992). *Intimations of post modernity*. London: Routledge.
Beck, U. (1992). *Risk society: Towards a new modernity*. (trans. M. Ritter). Thousand Oaks, California: Sage.
Bell, D. A. (2004). *Race, racism and American law*. Gaithersburg, MD: Aspen Publishers.
Benesch, S. (1999). Thinking critically, thinking dialogically. *TESOL Quarterly, 33*(3), 573–579.
Bennett, J. (2003). *Comprehensive multicultural education: Theory and practice*. New York: Allyn & Bacon.
Benwell, B., & Stokoe, E. (2006). *Discourse and identity*. Edinburgh, UK: Edinburgh University Press.
Berkenkotter, C., & Huckin, T. (1995). *Genre knowledge in disciplinary communication: Cognition/culture/power*. Hillsdale, NJ: Lawrence Erlbaum.
Berry, J. W. (2005). Acculturation: Living successfully in two cultures. *International Journal of Intercultural Relations, 25*, 697–712.
Blackledge, A. J., & Pavlenko, A. (2001). Negotiation of identities in multilingual contexts. *International Journal of Bilingualism, 5*(3), 243–258.
Block, D. (2007). *Second language identities*. London: Continuum.
Blommaert, J. (2005). *Discourse*. NY: Cambridge.
Bloomfield, L. (1933). *Language*. New York: Henry Holt.
Bourdieu, P. (1977). Cultural reproduction and social reproduction. In J. Karabel & A. H. Halsey (Eds.), *Power and ideology in education* (pp. 487–511). New York: Oxford University Press.
Bourdieu, P. (1986). The forms of capital (R. Nice, Trans.). In I. C. Richardson (Eds.), *Handbook of theory and research for the sociology of education* (pp. 241– 258). Westport, CT: Greenwood Press.
Bourdieu, P. (1991). *Language and symbolic power*. Cambridge: Polity Press.
Bourdieu, P. (1998). *Practical reason*. Stanford, CA: Stanford University Press.
Bourdieu, P., & Passeron, J. (1977). *Reproduction in education, society and culture*. London & Beverly Hills: Sage.
Bové, P. (1995). Discourse. In F. Lentricchia & T. McLaughlin (Eds.), *Critical terms for literary study* (pp. 50–65). Chicago: University of Chicago Press.
Bremer, K., Roberts, C., Vasseur, M.-T., Simonot, M., & Broeder, P. (1996). *Achieving understanding: Discourse in intercultural encounters*. New York: Longman.
Brito, I., Lima, A., & Auerbach, E. (2004). The logic of nonstandard teaching: A course in Cape Verdean language, culture and history. In B. Norton & K. Toohey (Eds.), *Critical pedagogies and language learning* (pp. 181–200). Cambridge: University Press.
Brutt-Griffler, J., & Samimy, K. K. (1999). Revisiting the colonial in the postcolonial: Critical praxis for nonnative English-speaking teachers in a TESOL program. *TESOL Quarterly, 33*(3), 413–432.
Bucholtz, M., & Hall, K. (2006). Gender, sexuality and language. In K. Brown (Ed.), *Encyclopedia of language and linguistics* (2nd ed., Vol. 4, pp. 756–758). Oxford: Elsevier.
Butler, J. (1992). Contingent foundations: Feminism and the question of "postmodernism.". In J. Butler & J. W. Scott (Eds.), *Feminists theorize the political* (pp. 3–21). New York: Routledge.
Callon, M., & Latour, B. (1992). Don't throw the baby out with the bath school! A reply to Collins and Yearly. In A. Pickering (Ed.), *Science as practice and culture* (pp. 343–368). Chicago: University of Chicago Press.
Canagarajah, S. (1999). *Resisting linguistic imperialism in English teaching*. Oxford, England: Oxford University Press.

References

Canagarajah, S. (2004). Subversive identities, pedagogical safe houses and critical learning. In B. Norton & K. Toohey (Eds.), *Critical pedagogies and language learning* (pp. 116–137). New York, NY: Cambridge University Press.

Cashman, H., & Williams, A. (Eds.). (2008). Accomplishing identity in bilingual interaction, *Multilingua, 27*, 1–2.

Cenoz, J., Hufeisen, B., & Jessner, U. (2001). Toward trilingual education. *International Journal of Bilingual Education and Bilingualism, 4*(1), 1–19.

Cenoz, J., & Jessner, U. (Eds.). (2000). *English in Europe: the acquisition of a third language*. Clevedon: Multilingual Matters.

Charles, M. (2006). Revealing and obscuring the writers' identity: Evidence from a corpus of theses. In R. Kiely, P. R. Dickins, H. Woodfield & G. Clibbon (Eds.), *Language, culture and identity in applied linguistics* (pp. 147–162). London: Equinox Publishing Ltd.

Chen, H. I. (2008). Positioning and repositioning: Linguistic practices and identity negotiation of overseas returning bilinguals in Hong Kong. *Multilingua, 27*(1–2), 57–75.

Chomsky, N. (1957). *Syntactic structures*. La Haye: Mouton.

Chomsky, N. (1965). *Aspects of the theory of syntax*. Cambridge: MIT Press.

Chomsky, N. (2002). *On nature and language*. Cambridge: Cambridge University Press.

Clark, H. H. (1996). *Using language*. Cambridge, England: Cambridge University Press.

Clark, J. B. (2007). Discourse encounters through experiences at school: The notion of Italianita meets the construction of La Francite. In M. Mantero (Ed.), *Identity and second language learning: Culture, inquiry, and dialogic activity in educational contexts* (pp. 93–117). Charlotte, NC: Information Age Publishing.

Clarke, M. (2008). *Language teacher identities: Co-constructing discourse and community*. Clevedon: Multilingual Matters.

Clothey, R. (2004). *Strangers in a strange place: the experience of ethnic minority students in the Central University for Nationalities in Beijing*. Unpublished PhD dissertation, the University of Pittsburgh.

Clothey, R. (2005). China's policies for minority nationalities in higher education: Negotiating national values and ethnic identities. *Comparative Education Review, 49*(3), 389–428.

Coelho, E. (1998). *Teaching and learning in multicultural schools: An integrated approach*. Clevedon: Multilingual Matters.

Cook, K. P. (2008). Navigating identities. *The Americas, 65*(1), 63–79.

Cox, M. I. P., & Deanis Petterson, A. A. (1999). Critical pedagogy in ELT: Images of Brazilian teachers of English. *TESOL Quarterly, 33*(3), 433–452.

Cummins, J. (2001). *Negotiating identities: Education for empowerment in a diverse Society*. Ontario, CA: California Association of Bilingual Education.

Cummins, J. (2009). Pedagogies of choice: Challenging coercive relations of power in classrooms and communities. *International Journal of Bilingual Education and Bilingualism, 12*, 261–272.

Davidson, A. L. (1996). *Making and molding identity in schools: Student narratives on race, gender, and academic achievement*. Albany, NY: State University of New York Press.

Davies, B., & Harré, R. (2000). Positioning: The discursive production of selves. In B. Davies (Ed.), *A body of writing* (pp. 87–106). New York: Altamira.

Deacon, R. (2006). Michel Foucault on education: A preliminary theoretical overview. *South African Journal of Education, 26*(2), 177–187.

Department of Immigration and Citizenship, Australian Government. (2011). *The people of Australia: Australia's multicultural policy*. Retrieved on June 1, 2012 from http://www.immi.gov.au/living-in-australia/a-multicultural-australia/multicultural-policy/.

Derrida, J. (1976). *Of grammatology* (G. Spivak, trans). Baltimore: Johns Hopkins University Press.

DiCamilla, F. J., & Anton, M. (1997). Repetition in the collaborative discourse of L2 learners: A Vygotskian perspective. *The Canadian Modern Language Review, 53*, 609–633.

Donato, R. (2000). Sociocultural contributions to understanding the foreign and second language classroom. In J. P. Lantolf (Ed.), *sociocultural theory and second language learning* (pp. 27–50). Oxford: OUP.

Dressman, M. (2008). *Using social theory in educational research: A practical guide*. London: Routledge.
Duff, P. (1995). Ethnography of communication in immersion classrooms in Hungary. *TESOL Quarterly, 29*, 505–537.
DuGay, P. (1995). *Consumption and identity at work*. London: Sage.
Eade, J., Barrett, M., Flood, C., & Race, R. (Eds.). (2008). *Advancing multiculturalism, post 7/7*. Newcastle upon Tyne: Cambridge Scholars Press.
Eckert, P., & McConnell-Ginet, S. (1992). Think practically and look locally: Language and gender as community–based practice. *Annual Review of Anthropology, 21*, 461–490.
Egbo, B. (2004). Intersections of literacy and the construction of social identities. In A. Blackledge & A. Pavlenko (Eds.), *Negotiation of identities in multilingual contexts* (pp. 243–265). Clevedon, UK: Multilingual Matters.
Engestrom, Y. (1990). *Learning, working and imagining: Twelve studies in activity theory*. Helsinki: Orienta-Konsultit.
Fairclough, N. (1992). *Critical language awareness*. London: Longman.
Fairclough, N. (1995). *Critical discourse analysis*. London: Longman.
Feere, R. (2003). Bilingual in Puerto Rico. In S. G. Kellman (Eds.), *Switching languages: trans-lingual writers reflect on their craft* (pp. ix–xix). Lincoln: University of Nebraska Press.
Fei, X. T. (1980). Ethnic identification in China. *Social Sciences in China, 1*, 97–107.
Fei, X. T. (1989). Plurality within the organic unity of the Chinese nation. *Journal of Beijing University, 4*, 1–19.
Fei, X. T. (1991). *New explorations in China's ethnic studies*. Beijing: Chinese Social Science Press.
Fei, X. T. (Ed.). (1999). *Plurality and unity in the configuration of the Chinese people*. Beijing: Publishing House of Minzu University of China.
Fci, X. T. (2003). Some monologues on culture self-consciousness. *Academic study, 7*, 5–9.
Firth, A., & Wangner, J. (1997). On discourse, communication, and (some) fundamental concepts in SLA research. *The Modern Language Journal, 81*, 285–300.
Fleck, L. (1979). *The genesis and development of a scientific fact*. Chicago: University of Chicago Press.
Foucault, M. (1971). *The archaeology of knowledge and the discourse on language* (A. M. S. Smith, Trans.). New York: Pantheon.
Foucault, M. (1978). *The history of sexuality*. Vol. 1: An introduction (R. Hurley, Trans.). New York: Pantheon Books.
Foucault, M. (1980). *Power/knowledge*. Brighton: Harvester.
Foucault, M. (1986). "Of other spaces", trans. *J. Miskowiec, Diacritics, 16*, 22–27.
Frawley, W., & Lantolf, J. P. (1984). Speaking as self-order: A critique of orthodox L2 research. *Studies in Second Language Acquisition, 6*, 143–159.
Frawley, W., & Lantolf, J. P. (1985). Second language discourse: A Vygotskian perspective. *Applied Linguistics, 6*, 19–44.
Frye, D. (1999). Participatory education as a critical framework for an immigrant women's ESL Class. *TESOL Quarterly, 33*(3), 501–513.
Gao, Y. H. (2002). Productive bilingualism: 1 + 1>2. In W. C. Daniel & G. M. Jones (Eds.), *Education and society in plurilingual contexts* (pp. 143–62). Brussels: VUB Brussels University Press.
Gee, J. P. (1990). *Social linguistics and literacies: Ideology in discourses*. London: Falmer Press.
Gee, J. P. (1996). *Social linguistics and literacies: Ideology in discourses*. London: Taylor & Francis.
Gee, J. P. (2001). Identity as an analytic lens for research in education. *Review of Research in Education, 25*, 99–125.
Giampapa, F. (2004). The politics of identity, representation, and the discourses of self-identification: Negotiating the periphery and the center. In A. Pavlenko & A. Blackledge (Eds.), *Negotiation of identities in multicultural contexts* (pp. 192–218). Clevedon: Multilingual Matters.

References

Giddens, A. (1991). *Modernity and self-identity*. Cambridge: Polity Press.
Goldstein, T. (2004). Performed ethnography for critical language teacher education. In B. Norton & K. Toohey (Eds.), *Critical pedagogies and language learning* (pp. 1–17). Cambridge, MA: Cambridge University Press.
Gramsci, A. (1988). *An Antonio Gramsci Reader: Selected writings, 1916–1935* (Eds.). David Forgacs; NY: Schocken.
Griffin, L. (2006). Who or what is the students' audience? The discoursal construction of audience identity in undergraduate assignments. In R. Kiely, P. R. Dickins, H. Woodfield & G. Clibbon (Eds.), *Language, culture and identity in applied linguistics* (pp. 133–146). London: Equinox Publishing Ltd.
Grossberg, L. (1996). Identity and cultural studies: Is that all there is?". In S. Hall & P. du Gay (Eds.), *Questions of cultural identity* (pp. 87–107). London: Sage.
Gu, M. Y. (2008). Identity construction and investment transformation. *Journal of Asian Pacific Journal, 18*(1), 49–70.
Hacking, I. (1983). *Representing and intervening*. Cambridge: Cambridge University Press.
Hacking, I. (1986). Making up people. In T. C. Heller, M. Sosna, D. E. Wellbery, A. I. Davidson, A. Swidler, & I. Watt (Eds.), *Reconstructing individualism: Autonomy, individuality, and the self in Western thought* (pp. 222–236). Stanford, CA: Stanford University Press.
Hacking, I. (1994). The looping effects of human kinds. In D. Sperber., D. Premack., & A. J. Premack (Eds.), *Causal cognition: A multidisciplinary approach* (pp. 351–383). Oxford, England: Clarendon Press.
Hacking, I. (1995). *Rewriting the soul: Multiple personality and the sciences of memory*. Princeton, NJ: Princeton University Press.
Hacking, I. (1998). *Mad travelers: Reflections on the reality of transient mental illnesses*. Charlottesville: University of Virginia Press.
Haeri, N. (1997). Reproduction of symbolic capital: Language, state and class in Egypt. *Current Anthropology, 38*, 795–816.
Hall, J. K. (1995). (Re) creating our worlds with words: A sociohistorical perspective of face-to-face interaction. *Applied Linguistics, 16*, 206–232.
Hall, S. (1996). The question of cultural identity. In S. Hall, D. Held, D. Hubert & K. Thompson (Eds.), *Modernity: An introduction to modern societies* (pp. 596–634). Oxford: Blackwell.
Hall, J. K. (2002). *Teaching and researching language and culture*. London: Pearson Education.
Hall, S., & du Gay, P. (1996). *Questions of cultural identity*. London: Sage.
Hansen, M. (1999). *Lessons in being Chinese: Minority education and ethnic identity in southwest China*. Seattle, WA: University of Washington Press.
Harklau, L. (1994). ESL versus mainstream classes: Contrasting L2 learning environments. *TESOL Quarterly, 28*, 241–272.
Harklau, L. (2007). The adolescent English language learner: Identities lost and found. In J. Cummins & C. Davison (Eds.), *Handbook of English language teaching* (pp. 639–653). Amsterdam: Kluwer Academic.
Heidegger, M. (1962). *Being and time*. New York: Harper & Row.
Herskovits, M. J. (1948). *Man and his works: The science of cultural anthropology*. New York: Knopf.
Holland, D., Lachicotte, W., Skinner, D., & Cain, C. (1998). *Identity and agency in cultural worlds*. Cambridge, MA: Harvard University Press.
Holstein, J., & Gubrium, J. (1999). *The self we live by: Narrative identity in a postmodern world*. Oxford: Oxford University Press.
Huntington, S. (2005). *Who are we? America's great debate*. New York: Free Press.
Hutchins, E. (1995). *Cognition in the wild*. Cambridge, MA: The MIT Press.
Ibrahim, A. (1999). Becoming black: Rap and hip hop, race, gender, identity and the politics of ESL learning. *TESOL Quarterly, 33*, 349–370.
Ivanic, R. (2006). Language, learning and identification. In R. Kiely, P. Rea-Dickens, H. Woodfield & G. Clibbon (Eds.), *Language, culture and identity in applied linguistics* (pp. 7–29). Equinox.

Johnston, B. (1999). Putting critical pedagogy in its place: A personal account. *TESOL Quarterly, 33*, 557–565.

Jorda, M. P. S. (2005). *Third language learners: Pragmatic production and awareness.* Clevedon, Buffalo: Multilingual Matters.

Kalantzis, M., & Cope, B. (1999). Multicultural education: Transforming the mainstream. In S. May (Ed.), *Critical Multiculturalism: Rethinking multicultural and anti-racist education* (pp. 245–276). London: Routledge Falmer.

Kanagy, R. (1999). Interactional routines as a mechanism for L2 acquisition and socialization in an immersion context. *Journal of Pragmatics, 31*, 1467–1492.

Kanno, Y. (2003). Imagined communities, school visions, and the education of bilingual students in Japan. *Journal of Language, Identity, and Education, 2*, 241–249.

Kellman, S. G. (2003). Preface. In S. G. Kellman (Eds.), *Switching languages: Trans-lingual writers reflect on their craft* (pp. ix–xix). Lincoln: University of Nebraska Press.

Kern, R. (2000). *Literacy and language teaching.* New York: Oxford University Press.

Kim, B. S. K. (2007). Acculturation and enculturation. In F. Leong, A. Inman, A. Ebreo, L. Yang, L. Kinoshita, & M. Fu (Eds.), *Handbook of Asian American psychology* (pp. 141–158), (2nd ed.) Racial and Ethnic Minority Psychology (REMP) Series. Thousand Oaks, CA: Sage.

Kim, B. S. K., Ahn, A. J., & Lam, N. A. (2009). Theories and research on acculturation and enculturation experiences among Asian American families. In N. T. Trinh, Y. C. Rho, F. G. Lu, & K. M. Sanders (Eds.), *Handbook of mental health and acculturation in Asian American families* (pp. 25–43). New York: Humana Press. (10).

Kincheloe, J. L., & Steinberg, S. R. (1997). *Changing multiculturalism.* Philadelphia, PA: Open University Press.

Kinginger, C. (2004). Bilingualism and emotion in the autobiographical works of Nancy Huston. *Journal of Multilingual and Multicultural Development, 25*(2&3), 159–178.

Kramsch, C. (1998). *Language and culture.* Oxford United Kingdom: OPU.

Kubota, R. (2004). Critical multiculturalism and second language education. In B. Norton & K. Toohey (Eds.), *Critical pedagogies and language learning* (pp. 30–52). Cambridge University Press.

Ladson-Billings, G. J. (1995). Toward A critical race theory of education. *Teachers College Record, 97*, 47–68.

Lam, W. S. E. (2000). L2 literacy and the design of the self: A case study of a teenager writing on the internet. *TESOL Quarterly, 34*(3), 457–482.

Lam, A. (2007). Bilingual or multilingual education in China: policy and learner experience. In A. Feng (Ed.), *Bilingual education in China: Practices, policies and concepts* (pp. 13–33). Clevedon, UK: Multilingual Matters.

Lantolf, J. P. (Eds.), (1994). Sociocultural theory and second language learning [Special issue]. *The Modern Language Journal, 78* (4).

Lantolf, J. P. (Ed.). (2000). *Sociocultural theory and second language learning.* Oxford: Oxford University Press.

Lantolf, J. P. (2005). Sociocultural and second language learning research: An exegesis. In E. Hinkel (Ed.), *Handbook of research in second language teaching and learning* (pp. 335–354). Mahwah, NJ: Lawrence Erlbaum.

Lantolf, J. P. (2006). Sociocultural theory: A unified approach to L2 learning and teaching. In J. Cummins & C. Davison (Eds.), *International handbook of education: English language teaching* (Vol. 2, pp. 640–653). Norwell, MA: Springer.

Lantolf, J. P., & Appel, G. (Eds.). (1994). *Vygotskian approaches to second language research.* Norwood, NJ: Ablex.

Larsen-Freeman, D. (1991). Second language acquisition research: Staking out the territory. *TESOL Quarterly, 25*, 315–350.

Latour, B. (1987). *Science in action.* Cambridge, MA: Harvard University Press.

Latour, B. (2005). *Reassembling the social: An introduction to Actor-Network-Theory.* Oxford: Oxford University Press.

Lave, J., & Wenger, E. (1991). *Situated learning: Legitimate peripheral participation*. Cambridge: Cambridge University Press.
Layder, D. (1997). *Modern social theory: Key debates and new directions*. London: UCL Press.
Lee, M. B. (2001). *Ethnicity, education and empowerment: How minority students in Southwest China construct identities*. Aldershot, UK: Ashgate Press.
Lee, J. S. (2002). The Korean language in America: The role of cultural identity in heritage language learning. *Language, Culture and Curriculum, 15*(2), 117–133.
Leont'ev, A. N. (1978). *Activity, consciousness, and personality*. Englewood Cliffs, NJ: Prentice Hall.
Leont'ev, A. N. (1981). *The psychology of language learning*. Oxford: Pergamon.
Li, Y. H. (2007). An analysis of the psychological health and its effect of 4782 freshmen in ethnic minority universities. *Journal of the 4th Military Medical University, (28)*8, 58–760.
Liggett, T. (2007). The alchemy of identity: The role of white racial identity in the teaching and pedagogy of new ESOL teachers. In M. Mantero (Ed.), *Identity and second language learning: Culture, inquiry, and dialogic activity in educational contexts* (pp. 45–70). Charlotte, NC: Information Age Publishing.
Lin, A. M. Y. (1999). Doing-English-lessons in the reproduction or transformation of social worlds? *TESOL Quarterly, 33*(3), 393–412.
Lin, A. M. Y. (2004). Introducing a critical pedagogical curriculum: A feminist, reflexive account. In B. Norton., & K. Toohey (Eds.), *Critical pedagogies and language learning* (pp. 271–290). Cambridge: Cambridge University Press.
Lin, J. (2008). Education and cultural sustainability for the minority people in China: Challenges in the era of economic reform and globalization. In Z. Beckerman & E. Kopelowitz (Eds.), *Cultural education–cultural sustainability* (pp. 69–84). New York and London: Routledge.
Luk, C. M. J. (2005). Understanding and capitalizing on multiple identities of students in TESL/TEFL: Towards a pedagogy connecting. In S. May, M. Franken & R. Franker (Eds.), *Proceedings of the 1st International Conference on Language, Education and Diversity* [CD-ROM]. New Zealand: University of Waikato.
Luke, A. (2004). Twotakeson the critical. In B. Norton & K. Toohey (Eds.), *Critical pedagogies and language learning* (pp. 21–29). Cambridge: Cambridge University Press.
MacLure, M. (1993). Arguing for yourself: Identity as an organizing principle in teachers' jobs and lives. *British Educational Research Journal, 19*(4), 311–322.
Mantero, M. (2007). Toward ecological pedagogy in language education. In M. Mantero (Ed.), *Identity and second language learning: culture, inquiry, and dialogic activity in educational contexts* (pp. 1–11). Charlotte, N.C.: IAP.
Marshall, J. D. (1990). Foucault and educational research. In S. Ball (Ed.), *Foucault and education: Disciplines and knowledge* (pp. 11–28). London: Routledge.
May, S. (2009). Critical multiculturalism and education. In J. A. Banks (Ed.), *The Routledge international companion to multicultural education* (pp. 33–48). New York: Routledge.
May, S., & Sleeter, C. (2010). *Critical multiculturalism: Theory and praxis*. Retrieved on June 7, 2011 from https://researchspace.auckland.ac.nz/bitstream/handle/2292/6217/187502%20AERA-Sym-NZ-2010.pdf?sequence=2
May, S., & Sleeter, C. (2010). *Critical multiculturalism: Theory and praxis*. New York: Routledge.
McCarthy, M. (2001). *Issues in applied linguistics*. Cambridge: Cambridge University Press.
McKay, S. L., & Wong, S. L. C. (1996). Multiple discourses, multiple identities: Investment and agency in second-language learning among Chinese adolescent immigrant students. *Harvard Educational Review, 66*(3), 577–608.
Miller, D. (2000). *Citizenship and national identity*. Cambridge: Polity Press.
Miller, J. (2003). *Audible difference: ESL and social identity in schools*. Clevedon, UK: Multilingual Matters.
Miller, J. (2004). Identity and language use: The politics of speaking ESL in schools. In A. Pavlenko & A. Blackledge (Eds.), *Negotiation of identities in multilingual contexts* (pp. 290–315). Clevedon, UK: Multilingual Matters.

Miller, M. J. (2007). A bilinear multidimensional measurement model of Asian American acculturation and enculturation: Implications for counseling interventions. *Journal of Counseling Psychology, 54*, 118–131.

Miyahira, K., & Petrucci, P. R. (2007). Going home to Okinawa: Perspectives of heritage language speakers studying in the ancestral homeland. In M. Mantero (Ed.), *Identity and second language learning: Culture, inquiry, and dialogic activity in educational contexts* (pp. 257–282). Charlotte, NC: Information Age Publishing.

Modood, T. (2007). *Multiculturalism*. Cambridge: Polity Press.

Morgan, B. (2004). Modals and memories: A grammar lesson on the Quebec referendum on sovereignty. In B. Norton & K. Toohey (Eds.), *Critical pedagogies and language learning* (pp. 158–178). Cambridge: Cambridge University Press.

Morgan, B. (2006). Poststructuralism and applied linguistics: Complementary approaches to identity and culture in ELT. In J. Cummins & C. Davison (Eds.), *Kluwer handbook of English language teaching* (pp. 1034–1052). Dordrecht: Kluwer Academic Publishers.

Morrison, K. (2005). Structuration theory, habitus and complexity theory: Elective affinity or old wine in new bottles? *British Journal of Sociology of Education, 26*(3), 311–326.

Nassaji, H., & Cumming, A. (2000). What's in a ZPD? A case study of a young ESL student and teacher interacting through dialogue journals. *Language Teaching Research, 4*, 95–121.

Nelson, C. D. (1999). Sexual identities in ESL: Queer theory and classroom inquiry. *TESOL Quarterly, 33*(3), 371–391.

Norton, B. (2000). *Identity and language learning: Gender, ethnicity and educational change*. Harlow: Pearson Education Limited.

Norton, B., & Toohey, K. (2004). Introduction. In B. Norton & K. Toohey (Eds.), *Critical pedagogies and language learning* (pp. 1–17). Cambridge, MA: Cambridge University Press.

Norton, B., & Vanderheyden, K. (2004). Comic book culture and second language learners. In B. Norton & K. Toohey (Eds.), *Critical pedagogies and language learning* (pp. 201–221). New York: Cambridge University Press.

Ochs, E. (1988). *Culture and language development*. New York: Cambridge University Press.

Ohta, A. (1999). Interactional routines and the socialization of interactional style in adult learners of Japanese. *Journal of Pragmatics, 31*, 1493–1512.

Ohta, A. S. (2000). Re-thinking interaction in SLA: Developmentally appropriate assistance in the zone of proximal development and the acquisition of L2 grammar. In J. P. Lantolf (Ed.), *Sociocultural theory and second language learning* (pp. 53–80). Oxford, England: Oxford University Press.

Parekh, B. (2000). *Rethinking multiculturalism: Cultural diversity and political theory*. Harvard: Harvard University Press.

Pavlenko, A., & Blackledge, A. (2004). Introduction: New theoretical approaches to the study of negotiation of identities in multilingual contexts. In A. Pavlenko & A. Blackledge (Eds.), *Negotiation of identities in multilingual contexts* (pp. 1–33). Clevedon: Multilingual Matters.

Pavlenko, A., & Lantolf, J. (2000). Second language learning as participation and the (re)construction of selves. In J. P. Lantolf (Ed.), *Sociocultural theory and second language learning* (pp. 155–177). Oxford: Oxford University Press.

Pavlenko, A., & Norton, B. (2007). Imagined communities, identity and English language learning and imagined communities. In J. Cummins & C. Davison (Eds.), *International handbook of education: English language teaching* (Vol. 2, pp. 669–680). Norwell, MA: Springer.

Peirce, B. N. (1995). Social identity, investment, and language learning. *TESOL Quarterly, 29*(1), 9–31.

Pennycook, A. (1999). Introduction: Critical approaches to TESOL. *TESOL Quarterly, 33*, 329–348.

Pennycook, A. (2001). *Critical applied linguistics: A critical introduction*. Mahwah, NJ: Lawrence Erlbaum Associates.

Pennycook, A. (2004). Critical pedagogies and language learning. In B. Norton & K. Toohey (Eds.), *Critical pedagogies and language learning* (pp. 327–345). New York: Cambridge University Press.

Phillipson, R. (1992). *Linguistic imperialism*. Oxford: Oxford University Press.

References

Pomerantz, A. (2002). Language ideologies and the production of identities: Spanish as a resource for participation in a multilingual marketplace. *Multilingua, 21*(2–3), 275–302.

Poole, D. (1992). Language socialization in the second language classroom. *Language Learning, 42,* 593–616.

Postiglione, G. (2009). The education of ethnic and cultural minority groups in Asia and Latin America. In J. A. Banks (Ed.), *The Routledge international companion to multicultural education* (pp. 501–511). New York: Routledge.

Potowski, K. (2007). *Language and identity in a dual immersion school.* Clevedon, England: Multilingual Matters.

Pratt, M. L. (1992). *Imperial eyes: Travel writing and transculturation.* London and New York: Routledge.

Race R. (2011). *Multiculturalism and education.* London/New York: Continuum.

Rampton, B. (1987). Stylistic variability and not speaking "normal" English: Some post-Labovian approaches and their implications for the study of interlanguage. In R. Ellis (Ed.), *Second language acquisition in context* (pp. 47–58). Englewood Cliffs, N J: Prentice-Hall.

Rex, J. (2008). Ethnic-Identity in a multicultural society. In J. Eade, M. Barrett, C. Flood, & R. Race (Eds.), *Advancing multiculturalism, Post 7/7* (pp.29–41). Newscasle-Upon-Tyne: Cambridge Scholars Publishing.

Reyes, A. (2007). *Language, identity, and stereotype among Southeast Asian American youth: The other Asian.* Mahwah, NJ: Lawrence Erlbaum.

Ruzek, N. A., Nguyen, D. Q., & Herzog, D. C. (2011). Acculturation, enculturation, psychological distress and help-seeking preferences among Asian American college students. *Asian American Journal of Psychology, 2*(3), 181–196.

Sagin Simsek, S. C. (2006). *Third language acquisition: Turkish-German bilingual students' acquisition of English word order in a German educational setting.* Munster: Waxmann.

Said, E. (1978). *Orientalism.* New York: Random House.

Saville-Troike, M. (2006). *Introducing second language acquisition.* Cambridge: Cambridge University Press.

Schieffelin, B., & Ochs, E. (Eds.). (1986). *Language socialization across cultures.* Cambridge, England: Cambridge University Press.

Shen, F. (1989). The classroom and the wider culture: Identity as a key to learning English composition. *College Composition and Communication, 40,* 459–466.

Shohamy, E. (2004). Assessment in multicultural societies: Applying democratic principles and practices to language testing. In B. Norton & K. Toohey (Eds.), *Critical pedagogies and language learning* (pp. 72–93). New York/London: Cambridge University Press.

Skeggs, B. (1997). *Formations of class and gender.* London: Sage.

Skeggs, B. (2004). *Class, self, culture.* London: Routledge.

Skinner, B. F. (1957). *Verbal behavior.* New York: Appleton-Century-Crofts.

Smith, A. D. (1991). *National identity.* Harmondsworth: Penguin.

Starfield, S. (2004). Why does this feel empowering: Thesis writing, concordance, and the 'corporatizing' university. In B. Norton & K. Toohey (Eds.), *Critical Pedagogies and language learning* (pp. 138–157). Cambridge: Cambridge University Press.

State Council of the PRC. (2009). China's ethnic policy, common prosperity and development of all ethnic groups. In State Council (Eds.), *White papers of information office of the state council of the People's Republic of China* (pp. 1–153). Beijing: Foreign Languages Press.

Stein, P. (2004). Representation, rights and resources. In B. Norton & K. Toohey (Eds.), *Critical pedagogies and language learning* (pp. 95–115). Cambridge: Cambridge University Press.

Stern, H. H. (1983). *Fundamental concepts of language teaching.* Oxford: OUP.

Stroud, C. (2002). Framing Bourdieu socioculturally: Alternative forms of linguistic legitimacy in postcolonial Mozambique. *Multilingua, 21,* 247–273.

Sunderland, J. (2004). Classroom interaction, gender, and foreign language learning. In B. Norton & K. Toohey (Eds.), *Critical pedagogies and language learning* (pp. 222–241). Cambridge: Cambridge University Press.

Swain, M., & Lapkin, S. (1998). Interaction and second language learning: Two adolescent French immersion students working together. *The Modern Language Journal, 82,* 320–337.

Swann, W. B, Jr. (2005). The self and identity negotiation. *Interaction Studies, 6,* 69–83.

Swigart, L. (2000). The limits of legitimacy: Language ideology and shift in contemporary Senegal. *Journal of Linguistic Anthropology, 10*(1), 90–130.

Taylor, C. (1989). *Sources of the self: The making of the modern identity.* Cambridge: Cambridge University Press.

Teng, X. (2010). Multicultural integration education and reform for fundamental education course. *Journal of Chinese Pedagogy, 1,* 51–52.

Thompson, J. (1991). *Language and symbolic power.* Cambridge, Mass: Harvard University Press.

Ting-Toomey, S. (1999). *Communicating across cultures.* New York: Guilford Press.

Toohey, K. (2000). *Learning English at school: Identity, social relations and classroom practice.* Clevedon, England: Multilingual Matters.

Toohey, K., & Waterstone, B. (2004). Negotiating expertise in an action research community. In B. Norton & K. Toohey (Eds.), *Critical pedagogies and language learning* (pp. 291–310). Cambridge: Cambridge University Press.

Torres, C. (1998). Democracy, education and multiculturalism: Dilemmas of citizenship in a global world. *Comparative Education Review, 42*(4), 421–447.

Trueba, H. T., & Zou, Y. L. (1994). *Power in education: The case of Miao university students and its significance for American culture.* Washington, DC: Falmer.

Tsung, L., & Clarke, M. (2010). Dilemmas of identity, language and culture in higher education in China. *Asia Pacific Journal of Education, 30*(1), 57–69.

Vygotsky, L. S. (1962). *Thought and language.* Cambridge, MA: MIT Press.

Vygotsky, L. S. (1978). *Mind and society: The development of higher mental processes.* Cambridge, MA: Harvard University Press.

Vygotsky, L. S. (1979). Consciousness as a problem in the psychology of behavior. *Soviet Psychology, 17,* 3–35.

Wallance, C. (2008). Literacy and identity: A view from the bridge in two multicultural London schools. *Journal of language, Identity, and Education, 7,* 61–80.

Wang, G. (2011). Bilingual education in southwest China: A Yingjiang case. *International Journal of Bilingual Education and Bilingualism, 14*(5), 571–587.

Wang, W., & Gao, X. (2008). English language education in China: A review of selected research. *Journal of Multilingual and Multicultural Development, 29*(5), 280–299.

Weedon, C. (1997). *Feminist practice and poststructuralist theory* (2nd eds). Oxford: Blackwell.

Wenger, E. (1998). *Communities of practice: Learning, meaning, and identity.* Cambridge: Cambridge University Press.

Wittgenstein, L. (1958). *Philosophical investigations* (G. E. M. Anscombe, Trans.). Oxford, England: Basil Blackwell.

Wong, J. (2007). Paradox of capacity and power: Critical ontology and the developmental model of childhood. In M. A. Peters & T. (A.C.) Belsey (Eds.), *Why Foucault: New directions in educational research* (pp. 72–89). New York: Peter Lang.

Woodward, K. (2002). *Understanding identity.* London: Arnold.

Woolard, K. (1985). Language variation and cultural hegemony: Toward an integration of sociolinguistic and social theory. *American Ethnologist, 12,* 738–748.

Wu, Z. J., & Han, C. Y. (2011). Cultural transformation of educational discourse in China: Perspectives of multiculturalism/interculturalism. In G. Grant & P. Agostino (Eds.), *Intercultural and multicultural education: Enhancing global interconnectedness* (pp. 225–244). New York: Routledge.

Ytsma, J. (2001). Towards a typology of trilingual primary education. *International Journal of Bilingual Education and Bilingualism, 4,* 11–22.

Zhang, L. J. (2010). The evolution of the policies of higher education for minority nationality in the thirty-year's reform and open-up. *Education Research Monthly, 8,* 56–60.

Zhang, J. H. (2011). *University of nationalities through the lens of multiculturalism.* Beijing: Nationality Press.

Zhao, Z. Z. (2010). Trilingual education for ethnic minorities: Toward empowerment? *Chinese Education and Society, 43*(1), 70–81.

Zuengler, J., & Cole, K. M. (2005). Language socialization and L2 learning. In E. Hinkel (Ed.), *Handbook of research in second language teaching and learning* (pp. 301–316). Mahwah, NJ: Lawrence Erlbaum.

Zuengler, J., & Miller, E. R. (2006). Cognitive and sociocultural perspectives: Two parallel SLA worlds? *TESOL Quarterly, 40* (1), 35–58.

Chapter 4
The Profile of Yunnan University of Nationalities and Methodology

Of the nation, of the world.

—By Lu Xun

I chose Yunnan University of Nationalities (hereinafter called YUN) as the site of my main study for ethnographic, pragmatic, and emotional reasons. First, YUN is the only university for ethnic minority groups in Yunnan, and currently around half of its students (49 %) are from rural or ethnic minority areas mainly in Yunnan but also in some other Chinese provinces and autonomous regions. These demographic features make the case study distinctive.

In this chapter, I shall present a detailed history of YUN and its School of Foreign Languages (SFL). Included in this study will be reforms made in recent decades to catch up with mainstream university developments. I will also report on how administrators and teachers concerned reflect on what has been the important losses to the institution, and plans to be considered for the future will also be discussed.

4.1 YUN History

When YUN was established in 1951 it was not a comprehensive university. At that time, it was called the Yunnan Institute of Nationalities (YIN) with a purpose of "train[ing] local minority cadres who could implement government policy in minority areas and future autonomous regions" (Hansen 1999, p. 22). The YIN curriculum emphasized socialism, patriotism, unity of all nationalities, the Communist Party policy, and Chinese language education. At that time students were recruited from among local religious leaders, local aristocracies, and secondary schools (Hansen 1999). Starting in 1979, the enrollment in YIN was determined by the national matriculation examination, and common university subjects were introduced into the curriculum. In the spring of 2004, YIN was renamed the Yunnan University of

Nationalities. The renaming signaled the transition of YIN from a small-scale liberal arts college to a modern multidisciplinary comprehensive university.

In 2006, the YUN administration repositioned the university as a teaching and research comprehensive university giving priority to undergraduate, continuing, vocational and international education. In its Tenth Five-year Plan (2001–2005), YUN intended to develop into a key university for ethnic groups in Western China. Its goal was to produce more qualified tertiary students who could help social and economic development of Yunnan's ethnic groups.

On January 4, 2006, with the support of the Yunnan Provincial Government, a working conference was held to set the direction of YUN development. It was planned that by 2020, YUN would become a comprehensive modern teaching–research university of nationalities, first class in China and well known in the world (YUN 2011a, b, p. 156).

At the entrance of the old campus, one can see the previous motto of "Unity, Nobility, Knowledge and Creativity." It was expected that this motto would reflect the features of YUN and inspire students and staff to make a better university (YUN 2006, p. 27). Attempts to interpret the motto are as follows:

> Unity is the most prominent feature of YUN. Unity signifies politics, national unity and friendship, harmonious co-existence, teamwork, and cooperative spirit. Nobility fits for the requirement in ideal, moral, and virtue. Knowledge is compulsory for national development and social progress. And creativity is the pathway to breakthrough and quality education. Creativity is the soul and mission of YUN (p. 221).

Due to the concerted effort of its staff and students, YUN was awarded the title of "Model Unit for the National Solidarity and Progress" (民族团结进步模范单位) in 1999, 2005, and 2009, respectively.

It was quite interesting that since January 14, 2008, YUN changed its motto into *Gezhi Mingde, Hongdao Zhishan* 格致明德、弘道至善, (see Picture 4.1) suggesting the pursuit of academic and moral perfectness. The new motto, as the periodical for the 60th anniversary interpreted it is:

> To acquire the truth by constant exploration of the principles of things so that all inborn virtues in humans can be reflected; to achieve ultimate virtue and beauty by persistent scientific, culture, ideological and moral transmission and innovation (YUN 2011a, b, pp. 1–2).

To ensure that students from the remote boarder areas and ethnic minority groups get access to higher education, YUN made special policies in favor of them. For example, besides the bonus point policies in enrollment at the provincial level, some ethnic groups were given 10–30 points deducted from the benchmark for university admission. Similarly, applicants from 12 minority groups[1] and from the countryside would be admitted with priority. At the same time, a "preparatory

---

[1]The 12 designated ethnic groups with enrollment priority are the Miao, Yao, Lisu, Jingpo, De'ang, Nu, Ji'nuo, Bulang, Lahu, Pumi, Dulong, and Mosuo.

Picture 4.1 The new motto of YUN (2015)

program"[2] (预科课程) was established to help ethnic students with weak academic foundations to achieve admission to the undergraduate program (YUN 2011a, b). So far, the "preparatory division" (*Yukebu* 预科部) of YUN has sent more than 8000 ethnic minority students (EMS) to tertiary institutions all over China. About 1800 of these students were from minority groups in Yunnan.

4.2 The History of the School of Foreign Languages

The School of Foreign Languages (SFL) was developed from the Department of Foreign Languages (DFL), which was established in 1982 as one of the earliest faculties of English education among all the ethnic minority universities in China. The establishment of DFL in an ethnic minority university was an unprecedented event in Yunnan higher education history. This department is the second oldest in English education among the 14 ethnic minority universities in China.

---

[2]YUN started a preparatory program in 1980 with an aim of enhancing the academic foundation of the ethnic minority students by offering some remedial courses in mathematics, Chinese, English and other subjects. Some ethnic minority learners are required to spend one year strengthening their high school knowledge before they can be enrolled to the undergraduate courses. The preparatory program is believed to be a solution, allowing ethnic minority students to catch up in the formal university program. It usually takes five years for these ethnic minority students to finish their university program.

In 2002, the SFL was established. It consists of an English Department, a College English Teaching and Research Division, a Postgraduate English Teaching and Research Division, and three research centers (in English teaching and assessment, in foreign literature and in Canadian study).

SFL website (2009a, b) boasts "SFL is a faculty with a long history, big scale, certain reputation and bright prospect in Yunnan" (SFL online). SFL is labeled as a "teaching and research" faculty, aimed at developing talented scholars with high foreign language proficiency and professional qualities. With "open and cooperative, distinctive and down-to-earth specialty features," SFL intends to "set foot on Yunnan, face China and look at the world" (Ma 2010).

My strong attachment to YUN could be traced back to one of my uncles' involvement as the first dean of the English Department. He was the founder of the English faculty in 1982 and thus witnessed the development of English education for ethnic minority learners. In his personal memoir titled *A Half Century Career in English Education*, he documented his life and his work (Wang 2004). Furthermore, I have fellow alumni and friends who work at YUN as teachers and administrators. These connections have made my data collection at YUN easier. These networks became very helpful as they provided me with a relative ease of access to the research sites and individuals concerned.

4.3 YUN and SFL Curriculum

The demanding curriculum brought the EMLs their greatest challenges. Like most English major students in China, they were expected to pass the national English proficiency test in the second and the fourth years. Although the poor English foundations of ethnic minority learners were well acknowledged by administrators and teachers, no remedial courses were provided in the regular curriculum. Instead, the English faculty aimed to become "a first-class discipline in Yunnan and well known in China" (SFL 2009a, b, online).

To achieve such high aims, the SFL of YUN offered over 40 courses of six types: (1) required public subjects (RPS); (2) basic discipline subjects (BDS); (3) required major subjects (RMS); (4) selective major subjects (SMS); (5) general education subjects (GES); and (6) internship practice training (IPT) (see Table 4.1).

Table 4.1 lists the courses provided for YUN English major undergraduates for 2009–2010 academic year. I categorize these courses into five domains according to their nature and characteristics.

The first domain mainly focuses on English knowledge and skill development, and 17 subjects are offered to promote students' language proficiency. There are also general education courses and major-related internship practice to reinforce these objectives. The second domain contains five subjects, which provide knowledge about Chinese language, culture, history, and current politics. The purpose of these courses is to improve the students' Chinese proficiency, arouse patriotism, and strengthen their identification with China as a "united multiethnic

4.3 YUN and SFL Curriculum

Table 4.1 Courses for English major undergraduates (Wang 2011)

Course area	RPS	BDS	RMS	SMS	GES	IPT	Sum
English knowledge and skills		8	2	3		✓	13
English literature and culture			2	1	✓		3
English linguistics and rhetoric			1	1	✓		2
English education				3	✓		3
Foreign trade				1	✓		1
World politics and economy					✓		
Chinese language, history, and culture	1		1	2			4
Current China's situation and policy	1						1
A survey of ASEAN countries		1					
Some facts of ASEAN cultures		1					
ASEAN languages		5					
The 2nd foreign language			1				1
Foundation of computer science and information technology	4						4
Political ideology	2						2
Moral and law	1						1
Physical education and military training	1					✓	1
Ethnic theory and policy	3						1
Social science study				1	✓	✓	1
Major-related internship practice						✓	

nation" with a long history and splendid civilization. These courses, combined with those subjects on political ideology and law, aim to develop civic citizens with socialist morality and politically correct mentality.

The third domain is designed to provide the fundamental knowledge about computer science and information technology. Therefore, four compulsory courses are offered. The university aims to pay close attention to the teaching of basic and applied courses such as computer science and information technology. Emphasis is placed on practicing their skills.

The fourth domain includes courses on English teacher education. The SFL offers courses such as English teaching methodology, applied linguistics, pedagogy, and educational psychology. Teacher education has been a traditional objective of SFL. In the 2008 enrollment pamphlet, it was stated clearly that "in aiming for an all-round development (*Suzhi Jiaoyu* 素质教育), the English department intends to develop comprehensive English talents and English teachers with a solid foundation of English phonetics, broad cultural knowledge, political integrity and professional competence" (School of Foreign Languages 2008).

The fifth domain aims to introduce the language and culture of Southeast Asian Nations. For example, two public general education courses are offered to present the basic facts and culture of ASEAN countries. Similarly, five basic language courses of ASEAN countries are provided: Thai, Burmese, Vietnamese, Laotian, and Cambodian.

4.4 Implications of the SFL Curriculum

By analyzing the SFL curriculum, it can be seen that the ultimate goal is to develop English major students with professional knowledge and skills. The courses focus on English knowledge and skill development, political education, information technology, and the national policy on Southeast Asian countries. This curriculum represents the traditional, ideologically correct concept of higher education in China: to turn out "red" (politically correct) and "professional" talents 又红又专的人才 (see Picture 4.2). In a book to commemorate the 60th anniversary of YUN, education for ethnic unity was highlighted as one of the features of YUN.

> To strengthen ethnic unity and maintain the national unification is the responsibility of YUN and the special mission and requirement endowed by the CPC and the state. In the operation of YUN, the administration has always emphasized the education of ethnic unity and national unification, and has always integrated the education of ethnic unity to the implementation of all missions in daily life. YUN has developed a large number of talents, who firmly maintain ethnic unity and national unification devoting to the development of ethnic areas, ethnic unity and progress (Yunnan University of Nationalities 2011a, b, p. 101).

However, the courses to enhance YNU students' Chinese proficiency and multicultural awareness are very inadequate. Throughout the 4 years, only one compulsory

Picture 4.2 The "Red Song (Red song in Chinese history refers to patriotic or revolutionary pop songs) singing contest" at YUN (2015)

course—College Chinese—was offered at the university level, and very few courses on ethnic minority topics were provided for the nonethnic major students.

In reviewing this documentary data, it is found that YUN seems to be of no difference from other comprehensive universities in China in terms of its training plan and teaching objectives. Although the current number of EMS accounts for around 50 % of all students, it is difficult to say that YUN is a place that successfully integrates ethnic cultures into the curriculum. Take the courses of English majors, for example: they neither show the features of YUN nor highlight the multicultural context. Some critical terms such as "nationalities," "ethnic minorities," and "cultural diversity" were not mentioned at all in the 2010 Guidance of YUN Undergraduate Program Training Plan, which was used to develop teaching objectives. It remains unknown whether these words are intentionally avoided to understate the diversity of the institution or whether it is an attempt to bridge the gap between YUN and mainstream comprehensive universities.

The following is the "guiding principle" of YUN, which emphasizes "Strengthening the foundation, broadening disciplinary study, enhancing quality and developing ability" (Yunnan University of Nationalities 2010a, b, p. 21). This guiding principle seems to apply equally to all the universities. It does not address any special policy to accommodate the diversity of ethnic groups and students of different cultural backgrounds. Ethnic identity and diversity seem to be ignored and become invisible within the academic environment.

Apart from examining written documents, I also studied the university entrances of the old and new campuses. I found the entrance designs of the old and new campuses disclose the perceptions of YUN administrators. The entrance of the old YUN campus of (see Picture 4.3) was designed by the Kunming Garden Planning Institute. It was built in 1997 in the west district of Kunming along 12.1 Street. The site of the old campus was designed in the 1950s by Sicheng Liang,[3] a world famous architect in contemporary China (Yunnan University of Nationalities 2011a, b). 12.1 Street was named after the "12.1 Movement," an important student protest occurring in Kunming. 12.1 Street is the home to four prestigious universities. The main entrance of the old campus is of traditional Chinese style, with golden glazed tiles and four upturned eaves. Above the university entrance, one can see the name of YUN in red paint in Mao's calligraphy.[4] Red was a popular color during the Cultural Revolution suggesting revolutionary spirit.

---

[3]As the son of Qichao Liang (梁启超), a well-known Chinese thinker in the late Qing Dynasty, Sicheng Liang is the author of China's first modern history on Chinese architecture and founder of the Architecture Department of Northeast University in 1928 and Tsinghua University in 1946. He was the first Chinese representative in the Design Board, which designed the United Nations headquarters in New York, and was recognized as the "Father of Modern Chinese Architecture".

[4]Mao Zedong is not only one of the founders of communist China but also has great reputation as a statesman, military leader, poet and calligrapher. His calligraphy is praised for its traditional style and revolutionary overtones. During the "Cultural Revolution" campaign, Mao's calligraphy was often inscribed on the plates of universities. Peking University's entrance is a case in point.

Picture 4.3 The entrance of the old YUN campus (YUN 2015)

Mao style calligraphy was widely used in public spaces. From the outside one can read "unity and progress" inscribed on the YUN wall. In the front of the main building of the old campus there is a stone wall engraved "Unity, Nobility, Knowledge and Creativity." During holidays, one may see students in their traditional ethnic dress holding parties or celebrations.

The old campus of YUN was built in the early 1950s. With the expansion of higher education, YUN, together with seven other local universities, moved in 2009 to new campuses in Chenggong. Chenggong is a university town as well as the new administrative center of Kunming City. To show their distinctive features, these universities constructed their new campuses in varying colors and architectural styles. The main color theme of the new YUN campus is a series of red brick buildings similar to those found in western universities.

The new campus of YUN (see Picture 4.4) was designed by the Architectural Design and Research Institute of Tongji University. The campus displays less traditional features but more modern styles popular in western universities. A noticeable change is that the new campus has no university gate or wall. The university name is inscribed on a granite stile in black paint. It is very interesting that the new campus maintains the sign with Mao's calligraphy, but also provides an English translation.

The change of architecture signifies the change in YUN administrators' perceptions. That is to say, transforming YUN from a single local ethnic minority college to a world-class comprehensive modern university. When the university wall was removed and the bilingual title was adopted, the YUN campus became more open. On the other hand, the maintenance of Mao's calligraphy implies a wish to maintain ideological correctness.

4.4 Implications of the SFL Curriculum

Picture 4.4 The entrance of the new YUN campus (YUN 2015)

These findings also suggest that, as a university of nationalities, YUN has urgent needs and rich resources to develop a multicultural educational curriculum. A multicultural curriculum, as Parekh (1986) put it, will "expose children and students to other societies and culture, develop imagination and critical faculties" (p. 22).

4.5 Views of Some SFL Administrators and Teachers

Responding to a request for higher education reform and designing to build a "first-class ethnic minority university in China" makes YUN want to compete with other comprehensive local universities. I am happy to say, some SFL administrators and teachers have realized that the school should display its own features in terms of curriculum design and course development. What is to be most appreciated is that the head of SFL and a large number of teachers prefer to see "integration" emphasized rather than "assimilation." The former approach, while it encourages a modification of the minority culture through cultural contact, at the same time, tries to maintain the essence of culture. The latter sees diversity as a problem and encourages the ethnic minorities to abandon their identities and join the mainstream for better life chances. Berry (2003) sees integration as "a selective adoption of new behaviors from the larger society and retention of valued features of one's heritage culture" (p. 31). Assimilationist policies try to eliminate the cultural differences completely and assume that the minority will acquire the dominant culture. Berry

(2003) regards "assimilation as the yield of the acculturating person to the behavioral norms of the dominant group" (p. 31).

At SFL in 2009, a course called intercultural communication (IC) was introduced into the English curriculum. The course aims to develop students' cultural awareness and IC competence. This course has been successful and has become very popular. In 2011, the course was awarded an excellent course designation in the YUN teaching contest. However, the effort to incorporate the course into a bilingual university program failed, for some administrators said if it were taught in English, not many students would understand it.

Another positive change in the YUN curriculum is that now students have more options to learn about ethnic minority cultures. Before 2010, Marxist Ethnic Theory and Policy was the only course offered for English majors. Since 2010, the new curriculum provides courses for science and humanity students. These courses include (1) Marxist Ethnic Theory and Ethnic Policy; (2) Ethnology; and (3) History of Chinese Minorities.

Marxist Ethnic Theory and Ethnic Policy is a compulsory general education course in which all YUN undergraduates have to enroll. It was introduced into the YUN newly recruited teachers training program in 2011. The purpose of this course is to introduce Marxist nationality theory and CPC nationality policy. Ethnology introduces the basic principles of cultural anthropology and research methods. The History of Chinese Minorities focuses on events involving nationalities in the Northeast, North, and Northwest China during different periods. This course will:

> help students master the basic clues of Chinese minorities; be familiar with the basic facts and research of these minority groups and as a result enhance the self-confidence and unity of ethnic minority students. And in the long run, it will help students to analyze and study the history of ethnic minorities from specific perspectives (YUN 2010a, b).

Therefore, at the university level, it seems that students now have more options to gain multicultural and world knowledge. However, the effects of these courses need further observation.

Take the course, Marxist Ethnic Theory and Ethnic Policy, for example. This course is part of the ideological curriculum of YUN, which focuses on introducing the CPC's policies on minority issues in China. In the latest Introduction to General Education Courses of YUN, the objective of the course is explained as follows:

> After taking this course, students are expected to understand and master the fundamental perspectives of Marxist ethnic theory, systematically comprehend and command the main contents of the CPC's guiding principles, policies and measures to solve problems of Chinese nationalities, enhance students' theoretic levels in understanding ethnic theory and policies, and improve students' ability to analyze and solve practical problems based on the CPC's nationality policies. In short, by enrolling in this course, students are expected to establish Marxist perception on nationality, religion and the state (YUN 2010a, b, p. 19).

At SFL, Marxist Ethnic Theory and Ethnic Policy is offered as a compulsory course for all English majors. But Professor Qiang pointed out that although it was a course considered as "one of the important components" in ethnic students' development, the effect of this course remains unexamined. What role would this

4.5 Views of Some SFL Administrators and Teachers

course play in students' education and development remains unknown. Besides, there is no reflection of cultural diversity in the curriculum. This is shown in Qiang's remark:

> Is there a kind of mechanism, (which can be used to examine) the teaching quality of this course …em, (to find out if) it is one of the important components in cultivating students…, but, whether (it) plays such a role. This is a question worth further study. This is one aspect. Another aspect I feel that the greatest deficiency is that in the two large modules of language and culture education, in the curriculum, there is not much reflection of "multi-culturalism." Regarding the multicultural education, if this is not taken as a major premise, the mainstream, then you can't talk further about developing students' awareness of intercultural communication.
> (Teacher YUN, Qiang, Interview, November 30, 2010)

Noma, a Hani female student looked at the course from a quite different way. She argued that the teacher can deal with the content in his own way, although the content could be fixed. She told me she liked the course very much because she met a very good teacher.

> The course instructor had very rich knowledge about this topic. When he talked about an ethnic group he would tell us something very interesting about this nationality so I am very interested in his lesson. A course on theory could have been much abstract but he used some concrete examples to explain. I think it is very interesting.
> (Noma, Interview, March 30, 2010)

At the faculty level, there is not yet any visible plan to integrate multicultural education into the English curriculum. For instance, except for the university public education subjects, no special course on multicultural education is offered at the school level, and no multicultural content is highlighted in the instructional material, medium of instruction, assessment criteria, or teaching process. As mentioned before, the features of multiethnicity are not given adequate consideration in curriculum development or teaching practice. Jing, an instructor of IC, commented:

> When it comes to the interaction between the Han and other ethnic minority students, we teachers, if we can treat their [minority] culture as a kind of resource and link them with the ethnic students I suppose they may show some advantages. However, this is not a standard in our teaching. If we use just one standard to measure all the people it is not fair, of course.
> (Teacher YUN, Jing, Interview, April 26, 2010)

Quan, a senior Naxi scholar of the Yunnan Social Science Academy, suggested that multicultural knowledge could be introduced into the university curriculum. He argued that:

> At the tertiary level, the tertiary institutions should take some measures in transmitting multicultural knowledge given the situation that Yunnan is devoted to becoming a province with strong ethnic minority culture. For example, the students of different disciplines should be given the options to minor in some multicultural courses according to their interest. I think courses like this should be introduced to the universities in Yunnan.
> (Naxi Scholar, Quan, Interview, July 30, 2010)

He commented that YUN is losing its traditional strength in the study of ethnic minority languages. In the past few years, many academic elites have left YUN for perceived better positions. Given this situation he suggested that an ethnic minority university should highlight its unique features. It should be different from other comprehensive universities in terms of research and talent development. Otherwise, the YUN would gradually lose its characteristics and strength.

Jing and Quan's concern, to some extent, suggests the deficiency of current educational policies for ethnic minority learners. Educational policies on ethnic minorities will determine policies of the university and practices such as the medium of instruction, curriculum development, and assessment.

Quan's observation reveals a misguided conception of higher education for China's ethnic minorities: to catch up with mainstream comprehensive universities and become a world-class university. Most ethnic minority universities are more backward than mainstream universities in terms of investment and resources. The different university traditions, histories, policies, and practices must lead to different goals and strategies for university development. As Quan argued, the concept of "talents" should be different between the eastern and the western regions. Ethnic minority universities have a mission to develop special talents for China. The university should provide the knowledge and skills for ethnic students, for quite a number of them will work in ethnic minority areas after graduation. He called for a discussion about using a single curriculum for the ethnic minority universities. He asked "is it necessary for all ethnic students to learn the same foreign language at the tertiary level?" I agree with Quan. In October 2010, I presented at an international conference in Macao on higher education quality assurance. At the speech, a high ranking official from MOE acknowledged that the higher education assessment posed great pressure on ethnic minority universities in China and forced them to develop according to the standards of mainstream universities. MOE has noticed this problem and now supports the development of higher learning institutions with their own characteristics. In this sense, *Duoyuan Yiti* can also serve as the guiding principle for ethnic higher education (Li 2010).

To sum up, the current YUN environment makes it possible to carry out multicultural education. At the individual level, some teachers like Jing, Qiang, and Quan have realized the significance of introducing ethnic culture in to the university curriculum. They have integrated multicultural education and English language education.

However, it seems that the features of the ethnic university are diminishing. This phenomenon, as time goes on, will bring about "cultural discontinuity" (Ogbu and Simons 1998) and "culture exclusion" (Yi 2008) factors that explain the poor performance of EMLs in mainstream education. Lin (2008) presents the similar view by arguing "cultural relevance is essential to retain students in schools and increase their interest and motivation in learning" (p. 76).

Ru, the CPC secretary of the SLF, acknowledges that:

> It is very important to maintain our characteristics as a university of nationalities. We often debated about it in the university internally. Take the enrollment for example, the proportion of Han students is increasing constantly. It seems that we are not a university of nationalities any more but just an ordinary comprehensive university. In the past, we had over seventy percent of ethnic minority students but just some forty percent at the moment.

4.5 Views of Some SFL Administrators and Teachers

It seems to me, we are losing our feature and advantage as a university of nationalities. On the other hand, some excellent children from the countryside cannot afford university education. In fact, many of excellent rural students come from the ethnic minority areas.
(Administrator YUN, Ru, Interview, October 25, 2010)

Xue, a Han teacher who joined the SFL 8 years ago, observed that, "Although this is a university of nationalities, we do not feel this way. Take language for example. What we can see on signs and notice are just Chinese characters. No other languages or scripts are used" (Teacher YUN, Xue, Interview, October 20, 2010).

In a multicultural setting like YUN, students are from diverse multilingual and multicultural backgrounds. They have distinctive cognitive styles, ways of life, values, religious beliefs, and cultural experiences. They have a great interest in discussing their own cultures and learning about other cultures. This finding is in line with Fei's study (2010). Fei investigated eight local universities in Yunnan by surveying 1600 university students. She reported the majority of the informants believed higher learning institutions in Yunnan should attach more importance to the heritage of minority students and introduce ethnic knowledge into the university curriculum. Students claimed they had strong interest in ethnic minority cultures.

From the teachers' perspective, the demographic composition and ethnic studies expertise makes YUN more capable than other comprehensive universities to introduce multicultural education. Besides the large numbers of ethnic minority students, YUN also has many teachers and staff from many different ethnic groups. Most of these individuals hold very strong attachments to their ethnic identity and would like to contribute to multicultural education.

For example, Qiang, a professor from YUN, told me that his multiple cross-cultural experiences armed him with many advantages in linguistic and culture research:

> My nationality? Yi people, of course, because my father is Yi people, I naturally became a Yi, my mom is Han. Forty years ago my parents went to support the border area. So, I grew up in Dai village. Actually I am Yi by blood and nationality. But my hometown is in Dai area. Most parts of me…from my childhood till now deeply influenced by the Dai and Dai cultures, (I have) inherited their culture…I can't speak Yi language, instead (I can) speak Dai language… (I) can listen, speak, read and write, including the written characters, I am more familiar with the (Dai), than the Yi…As an ethnic minority member, in Chinese cultural context, there instead of shame, I feel proud. Why? I feel I can handle things very well while making comparative study of languages and cultures…Take "do" as an example. I can make a long list of "do" in English, Thai Language, Burmese, Jingpo, Dai, and I can make a comparison…But for a Han Chinese, he may have the deficiency in this aspect. If he wants to do it, he has to get to know this area from the start.
> (Teacher YUN, Qiang, Interview, November 30, 2010)

Zhi, an associate professor of YUN, also took great pride in being Bai:

> …My father is Han. My mom is Bai. But I identify myself as a Bai people…I was greatly influenced by especially my mother in terms of personality, so, that is, whenever someone asks me what my nationality is, and I would say these words, "I am very proud of being a Bai" (in English)…It is not a shame, or any other…If you are interested, I hope you can come to visit my hometown. My village is well-known now. It is a thousand-year old ancient village, actually there are around five laurels attached, national ones…In the past,

(people) used to feel this village was the kind of backward, wasn't it? Likely to complain, about poor sanitation, or hard life, but now after the promotion, (you) feel these things, became a kind of feature.

(Teacher YUN, Zhi, Interview, July 13, 2010)

Given the specific nature of ethnic minority universities, it is relatively easy for students to access information on multicultural education. In this sense, ethnic minority universities have dual roles to play: to develop qualified ethnic talents for the twenty-first century and to promote multicultural education. Ouyike (2005, p. 76) once pointed out:

> Ethnic minority universities are important sites to introduce and transmit ethnic minority cultures. One of the functions of this kind of university is to make ethnic minority students transmit and publicize their ethnic culture through school education. Therefore, ethnic students should know their ethnic history and culture. If the graduates of ethnic minority university know well about the history and culture of different ethnic groups it will be easy for them to communicate with the local people and fulfill their duties well by working according to the local reality.

Quan also appealed for a mechanism to develop advanced ethnic minority talents through tertiary education. He believed that ethnic minority universities should take seriously their duties to develop ethnic talents and transmit minority culture.

> In Yunnan, each university, especially YUN, should develop advanced ethnic and folk talents in certain areas. These ethnic talents are different from the Han talents. They are the elites fit for this piece of land. They are suitable to promote the socioeconomic development and transmit the ethnic minority culture in China. I am afraid YUN should take the initiative to do this. As Yunnan is building a "strong province of ethnic culture," the local tertiary institutions should take some measures to achieve the goal.
>
> (Naxi Scholar, Quan, Interview, July 30, 2010)

Quan argued that college students are very busy within the current Chinese education system. They have many subjects to learn and many examinations to pass. Therefore, the courses regarding ethnic minority culture should not be too intense. They could be elective courses. Students could choose among them according to their personal interest. There could be courses on Yunnan culture. Quan (2010) said that the tertiary institutions in Yunnan should offer some courses like this.

Here I would argue that multiethnicity should not be just a label for YUN or be demonstrated by some special activities on the festival days. Instead of being a token ethnicity, it should be displayed in curriculum design, instructional materials, teaching styles, testing procedures, and campus culture. It should be also displayed in the attitudes, perception, and beliefs of teachers, students, administrators, parents, and community members. A counseling program is necessary as is a call for community participation.

However, before any actions are taken, a fundamental question must be answered. What are the driving forces for curriculum reform in a university of nationalities? I see the power of reform in the power of breaking up old mindsets in management and development. The above-mentioned evaluation system for higher education in China is a double-edge sword. It promotes and prevents curriculum reform for ethnic minority universities. On the one hand, the evaluation system encourages local universities such as YUN to reform so as to catch up with the mainstream universities in general. On the other hand, the top-down evaluation system may result in blind copying of mainstream universities due to fear of a negative ranking. Foucault (1977) once argued that normalizing power had spread from the prisons to most other institutions. While looking at the case of YUN I believe Foucault's observation makes a great deal of sense. It seems that the operation of power not only exerts surveillance over EMLs. Various examinations also normalize the judgment of quality higher education. The ambitious strive to build first-class university is a case in point.

As for YUN in particular, the university is able to make policies and politics that are favorable to carrying out multilingual and multicultural education. For example, unity has long been a goal of YUN (Hansen 1999; YUN 2006). As Banks (2010) points out:

> Academic balance of unity and diversity should be a central goal of nations in teaching and learning democratic societies. Unity must be an important aim for nation states to respond to diversity within their populations. They can protect the ethnic minorities and enable them to accept democratic values such as justice and equality (Banks HKU Speech, 2010).

YUN has striven to develop ethnic minority talent for the twenty-first century. To achieve this great mission and to improve the learning outcome of ethnic minority learners should be priorities for the university. These goals are a very good base for carrying out multicultural education. On the one hand, the academic achievement gap between the mainstream majority and ethnic minority calls for curriculum reform to reflect the cultures, identities, hopes, and dreams of EMLs. On the other hand, the ever-increasing racial, ethnic, linguistic, and cultural diversities call for reflective global citizens who can function within the national civic culture. Minorities expect to feel included as a part of society. They should experience equality, tolerance, and recognition. In this sense, an integration of professional skills and multicultural education will help achieve the unity and progress among ethnic multilingual learners.

4.6 The Process of Data Collection

The process of screening informants was very time-consuming and complicated. Prior to beginning my fieldwork, I had intended to choose some informants who were representative in age, gender, ethnicity, and language diversity. To single out the most representative informants I adopted purposeful sampling. I chose the fourth-year English major students of YUN according to two conditions. First, they had to be authentic ethnic minorities. (I defined the "authenticity" in this study in the selective criteria later). Second, they had to be advanced multilingual learners. With the support of the administration, I obtained a list containing personal information on all fourth-year English majors who were enrolled in 2006. The list showed there were 100 English majors and 50 of them were of ethnic minority background. The latter were very complex. Some of them were born in ethnic–ethnic families (both parents are from non-Han ethnic groups) and some were born in ethnic-Han families (one parent is ethnic minority and the other is ethnic Han). According to relevant laws and China's household registration system, children born in ethnic-Han families can be registered as either ethnic minority or ethnic Han as they wish.

The student list contained personal information. Besides details such as student number, name, gender, ethnicity, birthplace, and party membership, the list also contained information such as dormitory address, dormitory type, phone numbers, and students' administrative duties in the university or class. In regard to the student population of English majors, the number of females far outweighed the males for both the majority Han and ethnic minorities (see Table 4.2). Grade 2006 enrolled students came from 14 ethnic minority groups among which the Yi was the largest. And 7 of the 15 minority groups in Yunnan were represented. They are the Yi, the Bai, the Dai, the Lisu, the Naxi, the Hani, and the Lahu.

The composition of Grade 2006 (Table 4.3) suggested that the source of student enrollment was much diversified. It included students belonging to some socioeconomically developed ethnic groups such as the Yi, the Bai, and the Naxi who lived in the flat areas. It also included some socioeconomically less developed ethnic groups such as the Hani, the Lisu, and the Lahu who lived in the remote mountains and border areas. Students from the dominant ethnic groups such as the Yi and the Bai took administrative positions in their classes. The total number of

Table 4.2 Demographic features of the fourth-year English majors at YUN (2006)

Ethnic groups	Ethnic distribution		
	Female	Male	Sum
Yi	15	2	17
Bai	5	2	7
Dai	5	0	5
Lisu	3	1	4
Tibetan	3	1	4
Naxi	3	0	3
Hani	2	0	2
Hui	2	0	2
Lahu	1	0	1
Zhuang	1	0	1
Li	0	1	1
Dong	1	0	1
Mongolian	1	0	1
Man	1	0	1
Han	46	4	50
Total			100

4.6 The Process of Data Collection

Table 4.3 Characteristics of senior ethnic minority students at YUN (2010a, b)

Ethnicity	Sum	Living conditions		Administrative posts in class
		Apartment	Dormitory	
Yi	17	3	14	3
Bai	7	0	7	3
Dai	5	2	3	1
Lisu	4	1	3	1
Tibetan	4	1	3	0
Naxi	3	0	3	0
Hani	2	0	2	1
Lahu	1	0	1	0
Zhuang	1	0	1	1
Li	1	0	1	0
Dong	1	0	1	0
Hui	1	1	1	1
Mongolian	1	0	1	0
Man	1	0	1	0
Note		Students who can afford apartments accommodation are relatively rich and generally from middle class families. Students pay RMB 800 per year for a two-person apartment but just RMB 400 for a 4-person dormitory room.		

ethnic student cadres was 11, which accounted for more than one-third of the total number of student administrators in this grade. Their posts mirrored the "cultural capital" of ethnic minority groups. For example, a Dai girl was elected the class commissioner in charge of recreation because the Dai people were acknowledged as an ethnic group with talent in singing and dancing.

When I tried to narrow down the target students I created some selective criteria. I wished to select the informants in terms of gender, ethnicity, educational background, multilingual proficiency, and their demographic characteristics. Ethnic family background was a very important parameter for a monoethnicity family, bi-ethnicity family, or a mixed parentage family. This background would influence children's language acquisition. Likewise, it might influence children's choice of medium of communication in and out of their communities. Educational background means whether they attend school in the city or countryside. This also might influence attitudes toward language learning. Here I was interested in knowing whether the informants were instructed in monolingual or multilingual programs because earlier language learning experiences might have some impact on the study of new languages in college. Chinese proficiency at university is not a particular consideration because university students have to pass very challenging national entrance examinations in which the medium of testing is Chinese. Chinese is a compulsory subject at university as well. Therefore, all the ethnic minority students are assumed to have a good command of Chinese. English proficiency is also already established, not only because they are trained as English majors but also because they are among the 36 ethnic English majors at YUN who have passed TEM-4. TEM-4 is the national English proficiency test for undergraduate English majors in their second year.

Demographic characteristics were also criteria for sampling. As I mentioned in Chap. 2, due to the geographic, historical, and socioeconomic differences, the development of ethnic minorities in Yunnan varies from one ethnic group to another. This leads to different perceptions of language, education, and ethnic development. The preliminary screening showed, in addition to three students from the Hui, Man, and Mongolian ethnic groups who have adopted Chinese as their first language, the other forty-seven students maintained their cultural heritage. So to a large extent, they can be called authentic ethnic minorities.

As my study focused on how ethnic multilingual learners experience tertiary education, I did not survey the junior English majors (year one to year three). I believed that only senior students could make a comprehensive account of their life history, which would provide rich food for an ethnographic case study focusing on thick description and in-depth analysis.

Table 4.4 suggests the scope of the investigation is very distinctive and diversified. In addition to the two major informants, the study was extended to people on two tracks. One was the academic track, which involved university teachers, students, administrators, and relevant scholars. The other was the ethnic or kinship track including parents, siblings, and peer students.

Table 4.4 Basic facts about the informants (Wang 2012)

Informants Number	Identity	Gender		Ethnological background		Language proficiency		
		M	F	Ethnic minority	Han majority	Multilingual		
						2	3	>3
2	Major informants	0	2	2	0	−	+	−
4	Other students	2	2	0	4	NA		
5	University teachers	4	1	2	3	NA		
1	Senior high school teacher	0	1	1	0	NA		
4	Faculty/administrators	4	0	3	1	NA		
3	Parents and relatives	2	1	3	0	NA		
3	Ethnic scholars	2	1	2	1	NA		
2	School counselor	1	1	0		NA		
24								

4.7 The Choice of the Two Major Informants

4.7.1 The Selection of Mammuts

I came to know Mammuts as a visitor to her IC class in the fall of 2009. Being a friend of her IC teacher, I was introduced as a guest visitor and an "experienced" IC teacher from a neighboring university. During my classroom observation, I was invited to join the student discussion and sometimes asked to give some comments on student presentations. My to-the-point comments often won applause and laughter from the students.

There were two reasons for which I chose Mammuts as one of my major informants. First of all, she was a girl of Naxi ethnicity. The Naxi, as some scholars observe, is a "learned, civilized and advanced minority" with "splendid culture" (Chao 1996, p. 208), good at "absorbing other cultures and enhancing their vitality" (Yang 1998). The Naxi are famous for their ancient script, religious rituals, and distinctive life style. Above all, they are one of the few ethnic minority groups that have integrated with the mainstream Han culture but have never been completely assimilated.

Another reason for selecting Mammuts stemmed from my classroom observation, casual online chatting, and face-to-face communication with her, her teachers, and her classmates. In their eyes, Mammuts was "a representative Naxi girl with female traits" and at the same time, she was "lovely and fashionable." I was struck by those terms: "representative," "female traits," and "fashionable." I wanted to know how Mammuts grew up in the trilingual context, what fashions she had been pursuing and how her experiences had influenced her perceptions about language acquisition.

In order to establish a good rapport with Mammuts, I chatted with her six times on Tencent QQ, the most popular instant messaging service in China before I interviewed her formally. It was after about six weeks of causal online conversation that I learned about her family, her hometown, and her hobbies. I also read her blog in her QQ space, which explained her feelings about university life. In my first online talk with Mammuts, I introduced myself. I also talked about my visit to Lijiang in 2005 and my impressions of the Naxi people. I told Mammuts I had paid a visit to her hometown, Shuhe. She was very happy to hear that and sent me several photos of the Naxi people in her home town. She was very proud to tell me her father was a teacher. He taught mathematics before and was currently teaching oral Naxi language in the local primary school. Her brother was also a college graduate and was recently recruited as a local police officer.

This kind of online conversation continued until she started her teaching practice in the winter. She was very generous in sending me a soft copy of her autobiography, which was an assignment for the course on IC. It was a two thousand word narrative written in Chinese. She started her story like this:

> I was born in a Naxi family in Lijiang. My dad is a teacher, upright and honest. And my mum is a farmer, very hardworking. She is a traditional Naxi woman who is good at running a family such as making a daily schedule and budget, preparing the food and saving money for kids' future education.
> (Mammuts, Autobiography, October 26, 2009)

I was absorbed immediately by the opening. Later, I interviewed Mammuts three times in 9 months using both semi-structured and unstructured questions. These ethnographic interviews were conducted in Chinese. The data was then transcribed in Chinese and translated into English later. She volunteered to make oral narratives of some critical incidents that happened in her process of trilingual education. I also interviewed her friends, teachers, and parents to triangulate the data.

4.7.2 The Selection of Noma

Noma was the first girl with whom I had a conversation during my classroom observation at YUN. As the monitor of her class, she was quite active in raising and answering questions in class. It seemed to me she was a prompt and efficient girl with a quick mind. After learning that I wanted to find some ethnic minority students to interview, she took the initiative to brief me on basic information about the minority students in her class. She also helped me contact some of them in advance. As a repayment, I helped her edit her script for the CCTV Cup English Speech Contest and I shared my personal monograph on English learning. Most teachers told me Noma had always been a warm-hearted and hospitable student. Jing, her teacher of IC, talked about Noma with great enthusiasm:

> Noma is one of the most excellent students I have ever met. She exceeds her peers in academic performance. I am especially impressed by her active participation in the class discussion, her insights into varieties of issues in intercultural communication and her confidence and courage to speak out what she thinks. She has the intellectual curiosity and the eyes to see what others can't see. Her opinions, comments and suggestions benefited a lot of others in her class. She is surely a leader type. For her personality, she is very nice, kind and always ready to help others. She is a person who likes to share her knowledge as well as material things.
> (Teacher YUN, Jing, Interview, December 30, 2010)

To triangulate my impression of Noma I also talked to some of her peers via an instant messenger called QQ. Most of their comments on Noma were very positive. Juan was a Han woman from Zhejiang Province. She was one of Noma's best friends, classmates, and roommates. She highly praised Noma like this:

> In my impression, Noma is a very kind and innocent girl. Like many other ethnic minority students she is warm and generous and at the same time down-to-earth. She is easy to get along with and willing to help others. In daily life, she is very optimistic, and she always brings us a lot of fun.
> (Student YUN, Juan, Online chat, October 12, 2009)

4.7 The Choice of the Two Major Informants

Qing was also a classmate of Noma as well as the Chinese Communist Youth Leagues' secretary of the class. Due to his position, Qing had much communication with Noma. He said that:

> She is a lady full of passion and ability. It seems that she has endless energy. She is warmhearted, friendly, careful and responsible for work. On the other hand, she is sentimental, confident and good at expressing herself. She is quickly adaptive to new environments, hardworking and dedicated to her career. However, she is not so reasonable in logic thinking sometimes and might go astray while doing things.
> (Student YUN, Qing, Interview, December 14, 2009)

During 6 weeks of observation and talking with her teachers and schoolmates, I found that Noma could be an appropriate informant for my study. My first assumption was that Noma was a typical beneficiary of China's preferential policy for ethnic minority students. She was an example of a self-made woman who had made great effort to excel at her university by taking leading roles in academic excellence, political progress, and extracurricular activities. I decided to explore the life story of Noma, for I wanted to understand how a Hani female college student perceived the tertiary education system and how she used it to improve herself. I also hoped to gain knowledge as to how Noma dealt with the academic and identity challenges. I was very mindful that Noma came from a Hani farmer's family, which is different from Mammuts, in terms of cultural heritage. That is to say, I wanted to figure out whether Noma used strategies similar to Mammuts in dealing with these challenges.

As I had done with Mammuts, I interviewed Noma three times from November 2009 to December 2010. I also talked with her six times online between and after these in-depth interviews. Like Mammuts, Noma also shared me with her cultural autobiography. After I read the first draft of her autobiography, I was immediately attracted by the title "Live like Summer Flowers." She started the essay like this:

> When I started to write my life story, a wonderful title occurred to me, to live like flowers in summer. Someone has said that "Let life be beautiful like summer flowers and death like autumn leaves.[5]" I love this saying so much for it contains the philosophy of life. I would like to take this as the title of my life story.
> (Noma, Autobiography, December 22, 2009)

It was the first time I read Noma's essay, written in modern Chinese. I read it as a beautiful prose from which I could feel a young girl telling me her story with her heart and soul. I was moved by the story and surprised with her Chinese proficiency, which was much better than that of the average Han student.

4.7.3 Data Analysis

I finished the first round of data collection at the end of 2009 and went back to the field site twice in July 2010 and January 2011, to revisit my informants and to

---

[5] It is a quotation from the collection *Stray Birds* written by Rabindranath Tagore.

Table 4.5 Types of data (Wang 2012)

Data for description	Data for accounts
National and local policies	Interview scripts
University history	Blogs, pictures
University documents	Cultural autobiographies
Pictures and artifacts	Oral narratives
Student lists	Online dialogue transcription
Field notes	

gather missing data. I then started to code and analyze the data according to the analytic framework I presented in Chap. 3. This framework involved the university curriculum, language policy, ethnic heritage, and the informants' life histories. All the data were coded and processed according to the themes growing from the theoretical model. Storylines emerged during the process of data analysis.

In my study, the data were categorized into two types: the data for the background description and the data for incident accounts (see Table 4.5).

I used content analysis techniques widely accepted for qualitative study in education. I coded the data according to the themes, trends, patterns, and conceptual categories (Strauss and Corbin1990) informed by my literature review and survey questions. My data analysis consists of two parts: macro analyses and micro analyses (Duff 2007).

The macro analysis aimed to study the social, cultural, and historical contexts in which the major informants lay in while the micro analysis pinpointed to study the "multiple, and sometimes contested identities, perspectives, values and practice" (Duff 2007, p. 976).

Pavlenko (2007, p. 167) points out four major weaknesses of content and thematic analyses:

> The lack of theoretical premise...the lack of established procedure for matching of instances to categories...the over-reliance on repeated insistences...exclusive focus on what is in the text... [and] lack of attention to ways in which storytellers use language to interpret experiences and position themselves as particular kinds of people.

According to Pavlenko, "content analysis without a theoretical framework and a clear methodological procedure may end up with a laundry list of observations, factors, or categories" (2007, p. 167). To address the weaknesses of content analyses which are over reliant on text, I analyzed the text message, the context of the text, and the form of narration. I also tried to understand the relationship between ethnic, linguistic, and cultural realities and the autobiographic data. As to what Pavlenko (2007, p. 181) has pointed out:

> Linguistic autobiographies cannot and should not be treated as observation notes, transcriptions, or collections of facts. Rather, they should be treated as discursive constructions, and as such be subject to analysis that considers their linguistic, rhetorical, and interactional properties, as well as the culture, historic, and social contexts in which they were produced and that shape both the telling and the omissions.

Through triangulation of linguistic, observational, and interview data I hoped to draw a true picture of the experiences and mindsets of the sampled ethnic multilingual learners.

In terms of thematic/content analysis, I took into account not only what was said and written but also what was omitted and implied. I read the autobiographic data and tried to detect meaning between the lines. I tried to explain the relationship between the visible data, the literature concerned, and the invisible sociocultural context. I presented the data in a narrative style in chronological order. Prior to presenting each case, I give a brief introduction to the ethnic and family background of each informant. I also reviewed the literature of the Naxi and the Hani to establish a relationship between the target students and their sociocultural backgrounds. The cases of the two major informants will be presented and discussed in separate chapters, according to the themes extracted from the literature review and research design.

4.8 Summary

In this chapter, I gave a detailed introduction to the history of YUN and its SFL. I also elaborated the SFL curriculum and discussed its implications. It was pointed out that YUN has experienced policy changes and an adjustment of students' development plans. It seems that YUN is trying to catch up with mainstream universities at the cost of losing its special features as a multicultural university. It was suggested with its traditional strength in ethnic minority education and research, YUN should reconsider its current policies and goals. Needed is a sensible curriculum for ethnic multilingual learners. Finally, I talked about the field site and discussed the processes of data collection and analysis.

References

Banks, J. A. (2010). *Diversity and citizenship education in multicultural nations*. Presentation at Faculty of Education, The University of Hong Kong.
Berry, J. W. (2003). Conceptual approaches to acculturation. In K. M. Chun, P. B. Organista, & G. Marín (Eds.), *Acculturation: Advances in theory, measurement and applied research* (pp. 17–37). Washington, D.C.: American Psychological Assoc.
Chao, E. (1996). The invention of Dongba culture among the Naxi of southwest China. In M. J. Brown (Ed.), *Negotiating ethnicities in China and Taiwan* (pp. 208–239). Institute of east Asian Studies, University of California Berkeley.
Duff, P. (2007). Qualitative approaches to second language classroom research. In J. Cummins & C. Davison (Eds.), *Handbook of English language teaching, Part 2* (pp. 973–986). Philadelphia: Kluwer.
Fei, M. M. (2010). Higher education demand of cross-border ethnic minorities undergraduates in Yunnan in the multicultural education background. *Academy, 4*, 49–52.
Foucault, M. (1977). *Discipline and punish*. London: Penguin.

Hansen, M. (1999). *Lessons in being Chinese: Minority education and ethnic identity in southwest China*. Seattle, WA: University of Washington Press.

Li, Z. H. (2010). *The trend and practice of evaluation of instruction quality of tertiary institutions in China*. Paper presented at an International Symposium on: Higher Education Quality Assurance. Macao Polytechnic Institute, Macao.

Lin, J. (2008). Education and cultural sustainability for the minority people in China: Challenges in the era of economic reform and globalization. In Z. Beckerman & E. Kopelowitz (Eds.), *Cultural education—cultural sustainability* (pp. 69–84). New York and London: Routledge.

Ma, Y. H. (2010). *Identifying the school of foreign languages and becoming talents: An orientation talk with the freshman students*. Unpublished speech at Yunnan University of Nationalities.

Ogbu, J., & Simons, H. D. (1998). Voluntary and involuntary minorities: A cultural-ecological theory of school performance with some implications for education. *Anthropology and Education Quarterly, 29*(2), 155–188.

Ou, Y. K. (2005). *A general introduction to the higher education of ethnic minorities*. Beijing: Ethnic Nationalities Press.

Parekh, B. (1986). The concept of multicultural education. In S. Modgil, G. K. Verma, K. Mallick, & C. Modgil (Eds.), *Multicultural education: The interminable debate* (pp. 19–31). Philadelphia: Falmer.

Pavlenko, A. (2007). Autobiographic narratives as a data in applied linguistics. *Applied Linguistics, 28*(2), 163–188.

School of Foreign Languages, YUN. (2008). *The enrollment information for the English major undergraduate of Grade 2008*. Retrieved on August 3, 2010 from http://202.203.144.4/english/shownews.asp?id=73

School of Foreign Languages, YUN. (2009a). *English major undergraduate development plan for grade 2009*. Retrieved on April 4, 2011 from http://202.203.144.4/english/shownews.asp?id=364

School of Foreign Languages, YUN. (2009b). *SFL Minute Issue No.7*. Retrieved on March 3, 2010 from http://202.203.144.4/english/shownews.asp?id=273

Strauss, A., & Corbin, J. (1990). *Basics of qualitative research: Grounded theory procedures and techniques*. Newbury Park, CA: Sage.

Wang, K. (2004). *Half century's teaching of foreign languages*. Kunming: Yunnan Press of Nationalities.

Wang, G. (2011). Bilingual education in southwest China: A Yingjiang case. *International Journal of Bilingual Education and Bilingualism, 14*(5), 571–587.

Yang, F. Q. (1998). *Cultural pluralism and Naxi society*. Kunming: Yunnan People's Publishing House.

Yi, L. (2008). *Cultural exclusion in China: State education, social mobility and cultural difference*. London and New York: Routledge.

Yunnan University of Nationalities. (2006). *Fifty-five anniversary of Yunnan University of Nationalities*. Kunming: Yunnan Press of Nationalities.

Yunnan University of Nationalities. (2010a). *A brief introduction to general education courses and foundational courses for science and humanity majors of Yunnan University of Nationalities*, unpublished.

Yunnan University of Nationalities. (2010b). *Guidance of YUN undergraduate program training plan (On trial)* (Unpublished).

Yunnan University of Nationalities. (2011a). *Glory of sixty years: A pictorial for the 60th anniversary of Yunnan University of Nationalities* (Unpublished).

Yunnan University of Nationalities. (2011b). *Sixty anniversary of Yunnan University of Nationalities*. Kunming: Yunnan Press of Nationalities.

Chapter 5
The Case of Mammuts

> *We are the descendants of nine heavens' nine brothers.*
> *We are the descendants of seven layers' seven sisters.*
> *We are the mighty race who has conquered ninety-nine huge mountains.*
> *We are the energetic race who has climbed over ninety-nine huge slopes.*
> *We are the race who cannot be killed by skilled killers.*
> *We are the race who cannot be smashed by the skilled hammerers.*
>
> The Naxi Genesis

In this chapter, I narrate the case of Mammuts, a female Naxi student at YUN, a local university of nationalities in Yunnan. First, I present the sociocultural context of the Naxi people consisting of their demographic features, their language and culture, their educational level and local policies and practice that promote ethnic culture. I review the studies of the Naxi people by Chinese and western scholars and I discuss the implications of these previous studies. In the biography section, I introduce Mammuts' family and educational background, and I report her pains and gains as an ethnic minority student in the local university of nationalities. I mainly discuss the problems that Mammuts encounters at her university. These include language shift between daily and classroom life, tension with the university curriculum, psychological problems, and identity conflict. On the other hand, I also talk about her enjoyable off-campus life as a teaching assistant in a local English school, as a Korean club member, and as a trainee in the Mary Kay program. Finally, I analyze the YUN curriculum and discuss the capital and agency of ethnic multilingual learners in an unbalanced power relationship.

5.1 The Sociocultural Context of the Naxi

5.1.1 Demographic Features of the Naxi

The Naxi are one of the 25 ethnic minority groups that inhabit in Southwest China. The Naxi have a population of 320,000 (Editing Committee 2009). The Naxi people call themselves "Naxi," "Naruo," or "Nahan." Na is an adjective meaning "big" in written form and "black" in oral language.

Most Naxi people live in Northwest Yunnan, and a small population inhabits Southwest Sichuan Province. The largest Naxi group lives in Lijiang city with a population of 240,580 (Statistic Bureau of Lijiang City 2011a, b) and a small number live in the other prefectures of Dali, Diqing, Nujiang, and Kunming.

Literature (Editing Committee 2008a, b, 2009) shows that the ancestors of the Naxi are proto-Qiang, a nomadic tribe from Northwest China. The ancient Naxi had a commercial economy and established many regional towns. The ancient city of Lijiang was called the "Silk Road of the South" (*Nanfang Sichouzhilu* 南方丝绸之路). It linked inland China with Southeast Asia and West Asia through old *Chama Gudao* 茶马古道 (Tea and Horse Trail). Throughout history, the Naxi had frequent communication with the Han, so many Naxi people used the Han language to communicate. During the Ming dynasty (1368–1644), Mu magistrate, the local Naxi administration, kept close ties with the central Chinese government by contributing to it gold, soldiers' salaries, and grains. In addition to the Han, the Naxi also had close relationships with the Tibetans and the Bai. During the Ming dynasty, the Naxi extended their rule to Tibetan-inhabited areas, and Tibetan monks were invited to Lijiang to teach students and build temples.

Since the Yuan dynasty (1271–1386), Lijiang has been under the jurisdiction of the central government. In 1276 AD, Lijiang became a *Lu* 路, an administrative region in Yunnan. The *Tusi*[1] 土司 (native chief) named Mu was appointed as the hereditary magistrate of Lijiang Prefecture in 1386, and in 1770, Lijiang County was established. After the founding of the PRC, the central government set up Lijiang Naxi Autonomous County in 1961, and in 2003, Lijiang County became a part of Lijiang City.

5.1.2 The Naxi Language and Culture

The Naxi speak two dialects—the west dialect and the east dialect. Naxi language is a branch of the Tibetan-Burma language subordinated to the Sino-Tibetan language. The Naxi adopted a minority writing systems, the Dongba and Geba. Dongba is pictography (see Picture 5.1) influenced by Chinese characters. Geba is a phonetic script. Later, a modern written script based on Latin was created, but people seldom use it nowadays.

---

[1]*Tusi* refers to local native chiefs who are designated by the central dynasty to rule the areas in their hometown and neighborhood.

5.1 The Sociocultural Context of the Naxi

Picture 5.1 The Dongba/Chinese calligraphy (He 2016)

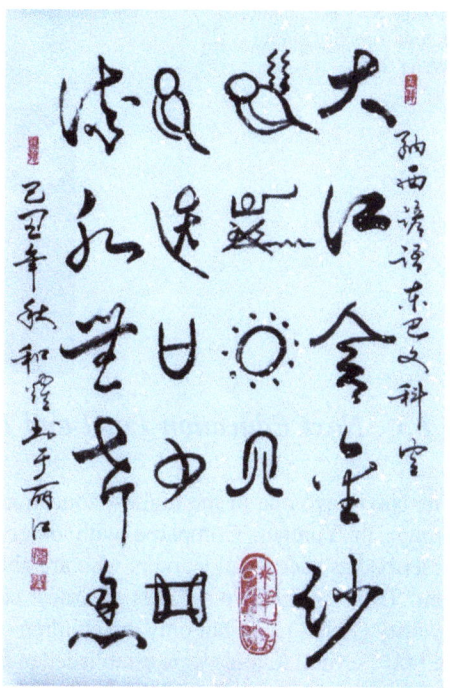

The contemporary Naxi now write Chinese and speak Naxi among themselves. They speak Putonghua to non-Naxi people. Now the Dongba script is only used in tourist products or for decorative purposes. It is difficult to distinguish a Naxi from a Han by physical appearance or written language. Difference can only be seen from the intangible features of the Naxi people, such as their methods of communication and their attitude toward life.

Dongba Jiao 东巴教 is a minority religion, influenced by Tibetan shamanism. Naxi ritual practitioners, who serve as priests, are usually called Dongba (东巴). They are in charge of a variety of rituals such as exorcisms, healings, funerals, and sacrifices. Yang (2006a, b, p. 66) defined Dongba as the "Naxi elite, who are trained and know the Naxi traditional culture." Dongba script was listed as the World Memory Heritage by UNESCO in 2003. Now Lijiang ancient city has received the titles of "National Historical and Cultural City" 国家历史文化名城 (1986), "Key Scenic Area of National Level" 国家级重点风景区 (1988), and the "World Culture Heritage" (1997). However, Dongba practices were viewed as "feudal superstitious activities" (Chao 1996; Hansen 1999) during the Cultural Revolution Campaign[2] 文化大革命运动(1966–1976). Dongba priests were criticized and persecuted (Chao 1996).

---

[2]The Cultural Revolution Campaign (1966–1976) was a violent, disastrous mass movement, which led to social, political, and economic upheaval in the People's Republic of China. It has been blamed for 10 years of nation wide chaos.

Picture 5.2 The memorial arch of *Tianyu Liufang* (Wang 2011)

5.1.3 Naxi Education Level and Features

The Naxi have one of the highest educational levels among the 25 ethnic minority groups in Yunnan. Compared with other ethnic minority groups, the Naxi are described as successful learners who are able to "succeed within the education system" (Hansen 1999, p. 65). The earliest school was established during the Yuan dynasty (1271–1368) but only the children of local *Tusi* (native chiefs) could attend. In 1418, several schools were established in Lijiang, and Han teachers were employed to implement Han style education. The Mu chief built a pavilion called "Wanjuan Tower" (*Wanjuan Lou* 万卷楼) in which thousands of volumes of classic Chinese literature were stored. The horizontal inscribed board of tower *Tianyu Liufang* 天雨流芳 meaning "let's read books" in Naxi is still hanging over the gate (see Picture 5.2).

In order to popularize basic education, the Lijiang administrators in various historical periods made great efforts to establish schools. *Yi-Xue School* 义学 was set up for children from poor families. According to the *Lijiang County Chronicle* in the Qianlong reign (1735–1795), there were five *Yi-Xue* schools in the rural areas of Lijiang such as Fudong, Baisha, Shuhe, Qihe, and Jiuhe (Cai 2001). Throughout the Qing dynasty (1644–1911), two Naxi people were awarded membership in the Hanlin Academy[3] (*Hanlinyuan* 翰林院), seven were awarded the titles of Jinshi[4] 进士, and more than sixty received the title of Ju'ren[5] 举人 (Li 2007a, b, c).

In modern China, the literate population of the Naxi people, compared with other local ethnic minority groups, ranks first in Yunnan (Guo 2001). The fifth national

---

[3]Hanlin Academy was an academic and administrative institution founded in the eighth century during the Tang dynasty by Emperor Xuanzong. Membership in the academy was confined to an elite group of scholars, who performed secretarial, archival, and literary tasks for the court. In general, Hanlin refers to outstanding scholars at the national level.

[4]Jinshi is a type of degree offered to those passing the ancient Chinese imperial examination. The degree helped the recipient to obtain an official post in the court. Now Jinshi refers to elite scholars who have passed imperial examinations.

[5]Ju'ren is the winner of the provincial examination in Ming dynasty China. Here it refers to elite scholars who have passed provincial civil examinations.

census in 2000 suggested there were 3005 undergraduates and 122 postgraduates of Naxi nationality. Yu (2009a) even reports that there are more than 100 PhD students of Naxi ethnicity. The latest population census in Lijiang (Statistical Bureau of Lijiang City 2011a, b) reports there are 6695 Naxi university students among every 100,000 people, which is above the provincial figure (5778 tertiary students among every 100,000). This is a dramatic contrast to 1328 among every 100,000 in 2000. However, some other scholars argue that the high literacy of the Naxi is misleading as few of them can read and write their native language—the Dongba script.

Since ancient times, Naxi people have been good learners and have paid great attention to culture maintenance and literacy development. Parents attach great importance to the family education and social education (He 2006). Senior members of the Naxi family have the responsibility to teach the younger people conventional rules dealing with social communication, ceremonies, and religious activities. In modern Naxi society, parents are trying their best to support their education and are very proud of their children's academic attainment (Zhou 2002).

In 1905, the Senior Primary School of Lijiang was established and very soon the Lijiang Secondary School was set up. Courses offered consisted of Chinese, English, Mathematics, Physics, Chemistry, Geometry, Algebra, Music, Painting, and Politics. The establishment of public basic education was significant (Guo and He 1994), and since then Lijiang has become the cultural center of Northwest Yunnan (Li 1998).

5.2 Studies of the Naxi

As a "learned, civilized and advanced" minority with "splendid culture" (Chao 1996; He 2004), the Naxi people and Dongba culture have gained more and more attention from western explorers, botanists and ethnographers (Rock 1947; Goullart 1955; Jackson 1979; McKhann 1995; Mathieu 1996; Oppitz and Hsu 1998). Field studies of the Naxi have been ongoing for over half a century. For example, Hansen (1999) traced the education of the Naxi people since the 1980s and discussed their identity construction. She pointed out that many Naxi were able to "succeed within the education system" but minority schools did not teach "the culture or history of specific Minzu [ethnic groups (p. 65)]." Sydney (2002) investigated the contemporary Naxi residents of the Lijiang basin. Sydney (2002) argued that the old cultural heritage, the designation of the Naxi as an ethnic group, Chinese minority policies, and economic transformation of the Lijiang basin all helped the Naxi shape their multiple identities. Since the 1980s, more and more Chinese scholars have begun to study the Naxi and Dongba culture.[6]

---

[6]Dongba culture is a new term coined in the 1980s and emphasized by the Naxi intellectuals and local administrators in Lijiang as representing the "core of Naxi heritage" (Chao 1996). However, some western scholars call it an "invention of tradition" (Hobsbawm and Terence 1983) to legitimize the Naxi identity.

A large number of Naxi scholars spend their whole lives studying and publicizing Naxi culture. Some scholars focus on tracing the origin and migration of Naxi people (Fang 1944; He and Yang 1992; Mu 1995; Guo and Yang 1999; Yang 2006a, b), some discuss the features, identities of Naxi people, and achievements of Naxi study (Ge 1999; Mu 1995; Bai 2001; Li 2001, 2007a, b, c; Guo and Huang 2005; Guo 2008; Yu 2007, 2009a); and some talk about the future development of Naxi culture (Liu 2005; Yang 2006a, b; Mu 2006). Among these studies, Yu's work on identity construction of the Naxi people in educational settings is very impressive. She describes her informants as "Chinese with Naxi characteristics" (Yu 2009b). These studies, together with those of western scholars, highlight the Dongba as a splendid culture and the Naxi as an advanced and civilized nation. To support this argument, Guo (2008) summarizes some features of Naxi people: (1) strong self-identification and reflection; (2) internal sense and patriotism; (3) enterprising spirit and learning ability; (4) deep, conscious, and honest personality; (5) open-mindedness and flexible attitude toward religious beliefs; (6) harmonious conception of humans and nature; (7) smart social and political choices; and (8) integrative competence. Zhou (2002) listed more traits such as self-confidence, cohesion, tolerance, humanity and honesty.

5.3 Local Policy and Practice

On February 3, 1996, an earthquake measuring 7.0 on the Richter scale hit Lijiang and brought most of the city into ruin. The quake caused great damage to Lijiang but it also brought about a chance for unprecedented economic development. The Lijiang local government considered the earthquake a turning point of Lijiang's reconstruction. A slogan coined at that time was "the great disaster will bring about great opportunity and great development."

Since Lijiang became a World Cultural Heritage site in 1997, the Yunnan government has taken a series of steps to promote Lijiang under the scheme of "building the great ethnic province." (民族文化大省建设) For instance, the People's Congress of Yunnan Province passed two regulations which were very relevant to the sociocultural development of the Naxi. One is the Protective Regulation of the Ethnic and Folk Culture in Yunnan, and other one is the Preventative Regulation for Dongba Culture in Yunnan. The former is an umbrella policy made to protect the ethnic and folk culture of Yunnan in general, and the latter is a local policy to reinforce the protection, transmission, and promotion of Dongba culture in the Lijiang area.

With 20 years of "leap-forward" development, now Lijiang has become a world famous cultural attraction and domestic travel spot. Since 1997, Lijiang was awarded the titles of "the most popular city in China for European tourists," "the world's most livable city," and "the best city for tourism in China." The "Lijiang Model" (*Lijiang Moshi* 丽江模式) focuses on protecting world cultural heritage and developing it in a sustainable way. The "*Shuhe* Experience" (*Shuhe Jingyan* 束河经验) integrates cultural heritage protection and small town tour development.

In the 12th five-year plan for socioeconomic development for Lijiang (CPC of Lijiang 2011), the municipal government decided to build an international airport, an international classic tourist site, a base for international cultural exhibitions, and a great Shangri-La commercial center. On the whole, the local policies and practices suggest sustainable development of the Naxi culture.

5.4 The Story of Mammuts

5.4.1 *Family and Childhood*

Mammuts was born and raised in an ancient Naxi town named Shuhe 束河. Shuhe is about 7 km north of the Lijiang ancient city. Shuhe was famous in its history for its leather processing industry and bamboo handicraft production. It is the origin of *Chama Gudao*[7] (茶马古道 the Ancient Tea-House Trail) and hometown of the Mu,[8] the most influential native chiefs in Lijiang. It is also the hometown of He Zhiqiang, the first Naxi governor of Yunnan Province in the early 1990s. His household is just 20 minutes' walking distance from Mammuts' house.

Shuhe in history was called *Danfen Hanshu Zhidi* (丹凤含书之地), meaning a place of culture and prosperity. It is a miniature of Lijiang ancient city for it has much well-preserved residential architecture and many beautiful sites such as an old road, an ancient bridge, and a pavilion. Currently, Shuhe is almost a must-see visit for many domestic and international tourists who travel to Lijiang. Twenty years ago the tourist industry in Shuhe did not exist, so Mammuts lived a "quiet life" in a "backward and isolated" village with her family.

Mammuts was born into a Naxi family. Her father was a teacher at a local elementary school, and her mother was a farmer and housewife. Mammuts regarded her mother as a traditional Naxi woman who was able to handle domestic affairs well. For example, she was good at making a daily budget, preparing food, and saving money for her children's education. As a member of a very big family of the Mus, Mammuts had many relatives living in the same village, so visiting the relatives was a frequent occurrence.

---

[7]Chama Gudao (the Tea and Horse Trail) is located in Southwest China and was used by the caravans who transported tea and other commodities to the east. Nowadays, Chama Gudao is used in a metaphoric way, signifying a corridor for ethnic economic exchange in Southwest China.

[8]Mu and He are the two major surnames of the Naxi. Mu is a surname for the ruling local heritage families, and He is an awarded name from the emperor referring to the ruled masses. It is quite interesting that many descendants of the He family were the high ranking officials after 1949, while the offspring of the Mu became senior intellectuals or professionals.

5.4.2 School Journey

Mammuts went to Shuhe Central Elementary School where her father worked then as a mathematics teacher. Both her elder brother and Mammuts received basic education in this village school for two reasons: first, it was close to home, and second, it was easy to be supervised by their father. Mammuts enjoyed elementary school as most of her peers were the Naxi from the same village. Liang, one of her close schoolmates recalled, "At that time, we sang together, played together, went to school together, looked for pig food together and cooked together. It is still a sweet memory even till now" (Student YNU, Liang, Online chat, March 11, 2010).

Most of Mammuts' teachers in her elementary school were her fathers' colleagues, so she was treated like the other teachers' daughter. From the elementary to junior secondary school, Mammuts was a top student in her class. She talked about that period in her autobiography: "I studied well and I was always a good learner so that my mother and my grandparents often praised me" (Mammuts, Autobiography, October 26, 2010). In an interview, she claimed her happiness came from being a "big fish" in a "small pond." She said, "I chose a small secondary school, a local school. I was one of the top students in the school, and my teachers were very kind to me" (Mammuts, Interview, January 22, 2010). However, after she was admitted to No. 1 Senior Secondary School of Lijiang Ancient City District (see Picture 5.3), she experienced great pressure and frustration in the first two years. She recalled this experience in the first interview:

> Everything changed in the senior secondary school. As my class was a top class in the school, my entrance grade was in the middle. But in the high school my score in Mathematics, Physics and Chemistry dropped dramatically as if I was beaten by a bat. My score dropped so quickly that I almost failed in all courses or just remained very low marks. I almost collapsed…I went through three year's high school in struggle without any confidence. It was my grey days.
>
> (Mammuts, Interview, January 22, 2010)

Picture 5.3 No. 1 Senior Secondary School of Lijiang Ancient City District (© Xu 2011)

5.4 The Story of Mammuts

Actually, Mammuts' "good old days" seemed to come to an end after she was enrolled in the key senior secondary school in Lijiang city. The school environment was dramatically different from the village school.

The No. 1 Senior Secondary School of the Ancient City District (SSSACD) is located in the north range of the Dragon Snow Mountain. It is one of the key high schools in Yunnan Province. During the past three years, SSSACD was quite well known in Lijiang as its students attained the top ranking in the national matriculation examination. "It is not only a key school, but also a birthplace of heroes," Mu, the principal of SSSACD, told me, "Five national heroes are the graduates of our school" (Teacher SSSACD, Mu, Interview, January 15, 2011).

The old library was located in an ancient palace of a Tusi chief. A plate inscribed with "there is no end to learning" (*xuewu zhijing* 学无止境) is still hanging over the library entrance (see Picture 5.4).

After Mammuts was admitted to the senior secondary school, she experienced a series of difficulties and challenges like other ethnic minority students who are enrolled in the mainstream Chinese school system. These difficulties could be seen in the shift of language, tension in main stream curriculum, psychological problems, and identity issues.

Picture 5.4 The old library of SSSACD (© Xu 2011)

5.4.3 Language Shift Between Daily Life and Classroom

The after-class language environment in the senior secondary school was very different from before. Mammuts began to speak Naxi as a child and could understand little Putonghua (Mandarin Chinese) before she went to primary school. She told me she had some problems in Chinese. To be specific, as a primary student, she could not understand Putonghua. In fact, she was used to speaking Naxi language with her family and in her communities. This continued till junior secondary school. She recalled that "as long as the class was over (Students were required to speak Putonghua in class), everybody switched to speak the Naxi. And no one spoke Chinese" (Mammuts, Online Chat, September 25, 2009). However, when she was admitted to the senior secondary school she had to communicate with others in Putonghua:

> We had more Han students in the class. And even if we had less Han students we had some highly Han-assimilated students from Yi and Lisu communities. Anyhow, there were more and more people speaking Putonghua then. Even you did not speak Putonghua you had to speak the local Han dialect. I had little chance to speak the Naxi since that time.
> (Mammuts, Online Chat, October 7, 2009)

Written Chinese competence has troubled Mammuts from senior secondary school to university. Mammuts talked about her performance in the national matriculation examination:

> My Chinese score in the national matriculation examination lagged me quite behind and put me in an unfavorable situation. My Chinese was really not good enough. For example, when I was required to write an article in Chinese I did have a good idea but I could not express it well in Chinese. That is to say my expression was constrained by my Chinese proficiency.
> (Mammuts, Interview, January 22, 2010)

Later when she talked about one of her major courses at university—Translation—she told me she had problems in understanding Chinese accurately compared with the Han students. She admitted that:

> My understanding of Chinese was not in the right place. I didn't realize this point until I found my Chinese was so inadequate to express myself. I did want to improve it. When he (the teacher of translation) asked us to translate the classic Chinese poems into English I found I was stuck. To tell the truth, I wished I had better Chinese. That is to say, if I was asked to decode the subtle meanings I would be short of words. It was only at this moment that I thought I should have studied Chinese well.
> (Mammuts, Interview, January 22, 2010)

But soon her worry about her Chinese proficiency faded as the translation course was only offered for one year as she reported:

> There was no translation course after that …so I could no longer feel the importance and urgency of improving my Chinese. I could feel the significance for a while, but I lost that sense when the course terminated.
> (Mammuts, Interview, March 30, 2010)

Ling, who taught the translation course, reflected on the difficulties of ethnic minority students:

> Their Chinese proficiency was very problematic. For example, in a Chinese–English translation assignment, students might meet a sentence with an excerpt from some ancient Chinese poem. It could be one or two lines of a Chinese poem. Students would complain, "It is too difficult. We cannot understand them." But it seemed to me, some of them (the text) were just idiomatic expressions. They were supposed to be mastered, but most students were strange to them. So I warned them, "Your modern Chinese proficiency tends to degenerate". It is very dangerous, for few people write in Chinese now, and they don't like writing in Chinese either. What they prefer is the fast-food culture. In my teaching of translating and writing, I can spot their problems in Chinese proficiency.
>
> (Teacher YUN, Interview, November 16, 2009)

From this episode, it can be seen that language shift brought Mammuts more problems. First, Mammuts had to make a decision to study in the local village school or the key junior secondary school downtown. In the former school, the dominant population was the Naxi, and in the latter, the main school population was the Han and other ethnic groups. For the purpose of getting a better education, Mammuts chose the key middle school at the cost of speaking less Naxi. What was even worse was that the language tested in the national matriculation examination was her second language, Mandarin Chinese, rather than her first language, Naxi. Although Putonghua had been the only medium of instruction since her primary school, Chinese learning was not emphasized, as she had lived in a native language-friendly environment, where Naxi was the medium of communication. At the university, improvement in Chinese was ignored by the university curriculum and by ethnic minority students themselves due to the big pressure to master a third language, English.

The policy of using majority language in the national matriculation examination marginalizes ethnic minority groups, whose Putonghua is not well developed and whose first language is not valued. This policy, to some extent, may either reduce EMLs' access to tertiary institutions or if admitted, put them in an underprivileged position. Informed by this episode, the roles of L1 and L2 in the mainstream curriculum need further review.

5.4.4 Tensions with Curriculum

Mammuts experienced quite a number of problems in adapting to the university curriculum. The YUN curricula for English majors were very demanding for the ethnic minority learners. *The 2009 Undergraduate Development Plan* expected the English major undergraduates (SFL, YUN 2009a, b):

- To have a good command of fundamental Marxist and Leninist theories in language and culture
- To be familiar with China's guidelines, polices, and regulations

- To have a solid English pronunciation foundation and strong skills in listening, speaking, reading, writing, and translating
- To master linguistic, literary, humanist, and scientific knowledge
- To have a good command of the basic theory in English phonology
- To have a broad understanding of the national conditions of China and sociocultural knowledge about English-speaking countries
- To master research methods such as literature review and information technology inquiry
- To understand English-teaching methodologies
- To have a good competence in communicating in Chinese
- To be familiar with one or two additional foreign languages.

The YUN curriculum seems to aim higher than the national curriculum in talent development. During an English faculty meeting, an even more ambitious goal was set, that is, to build "a first-class discipline in Yunnan and well-known major in China" (SFL, YUN, Minutes 090413).

However, Shi, the creator of this curriculum, was very clear about the huge difficulty in achieving such a mission, given the low admission scores of ethnic minority students in the national matriculation examination. He said that:

> Students of ethnic minorities in our university, according to my understanding, have bonus marks in the national matriculation examination. The bonus grades can be as high as 20 to 30 points. Secondly, some of the English major students are upgraded from the "preparatory division" or *Yuke Bu* in Chinese. This kind of student accounts for 75 % of the total students enrolled by our faculty. We are a second-choice university (average university), so the quality of the student source cannot be compared with that of Yunnan University, Yunnan Normal University and Kunming University of Science and Technology.
>
> (Administrator YUN, Shi, Interview, September 6, 2009)

The weakness of ethnic minority students was well acknowledged by many faculty members. It was believed that since the "starting point" of tertiary ethnic minority students was lower than that of their Han peers they were bound to undergo more challenges. Qiang, a young professor of SLF, argued that:

> I think only a small number of ethnic minority students can start their tertiary education at the same level of the Han students. It is true that they can never stand at the same academic starting line of the running race like their Han cohorts. Why do I say so? It is absolutely right that the central government should set the same starting point or stage for all students but due to the limitation of location and instruction conditions, some students from ethnic minority areas have never seen native speakers so the enrolled students are very different in terms of their English foundation.
>
> (Teacher YUN, Qiang, Interview, November 30, 2010)

Professor Yin, a professor who has served on the faculty for more than ten years, echoed the above view by arguing that "the poor foundation is a fact. It will definitely influence the development mission of the English major students." He pointed out that the academic foundation, the range of knowledge, and the limited vision of the world may affect the learning outcomes of ethnic multilingual students.

5.4 The Story of Mammuts

With such higher academic standards and lower academic preparation, Mammuts suffered from the hegemonic curriculum. For example, on various occasions she told me of her loathing for the test-oriented teaching. It seemed that "examination" was such a sensitive word that it had become a burden troubling her studies and life. She criticized most of the classroom instruction at her university as exam-oriented.

> Take English literature for example. This course sounded good, but it was just taught for examination. Although I had never read anything, I had to sit for the test. And I still could get a score of 70 or 80. This is ridiculous, but we have no choice. This is the university system. You have to pass it to get credit. I am still doing this.
> (Mammuts, Interview, January 22, 2010)

As for the effect of testing, she confessed that she could benefit little from these examinations:

> To tell you the truth sir, what I could answer in the exam would go as soon as the test was over. It seemed that I prepared just for the test and I would not use anything (the knowledge and skill) after the test. I think it (examination) was a waste of time.
> (Mammuts, Interview, January 22, 2010)

She told me frankly that she liked teachers who were humorous in class, who could speak English fluently like native speakers, and who taught not for testing. The three courses she loved most were Translation, Listening Comprehension, and Intercultural Communication. She mentioned one of the teachers she met in her second year. She taught Listening Comprehension. She was dedicated to skill training and never took examinations so seriously as other teachers. Mammuts talked about this teacher with great admiration and respect:

> She took examinations lightly. For instance, if we had a mid-term examination today she would not call it a mid-term test. She just called it a small quiz, so we had no feeling of taking an examination. And when the final examination was coming she would say something like "Don't be nervous. We just do as usual, and this test is to figure out whether you can understand". She could describe the exam in a very nice way. I think an examination should be like this.
> (Mammuts, Interview, January 22, 2010)

When I asked Mammuts why she did not like some other teachers she said:

> I don't say other teachers are weak in academic competence. They are pretty strong, but their pronunciations are somewhat Chinglish (Chinese English) and they use Chinese style English sentences. I don't mean their English is poor. I just don't like that feeling.
> (Mammuts, Interview, March 30, 2010)

Another problem which puzzled Mammuts quite often was the purpose of learning English. She said:

> I have my own understanding of English learning. I want to study English well not for gaining certificates as many as possible now. I don't think certificates are too important for me. Certificate is not my ultimate objective of English learning. I just try my best to speak out English. I wish to speak out freely what I mean in English. I want to express myself in English naturally.
> (Mammuts, Interview, January 22, 2010)

As an English major, Mammuts also told me about her dissatisfaction with some of the English courses offered. It seemed that some courses such as English Grammar, General Introduction to Linguistics, and Shakespeare Study were just too abstract and too profound to understand, while some other courses were too short to learn something useful. She talked about Translation, one of her favorite courses as an English major: "If the teacher really wants to teach something useful, the course should be given more time and offered for an additional semester even a year." In my last interview, Mammuts complained about the curriculum designed for her grade:

> In terms of the English major curriculum, I suppose some curricula should be reformed, though I have no idea how to do it. Take me for example. After spending four years as an English major, I had expected I could have harvested a bowl of gold, but I am not sure at the moment.
> (Mammuts, Interview, July 22, 2010)

The biggest frustration Mammuts had at university was her failure in the national test for English majors. In China, all English majors are required to take two very important examinations: TEM-4 in the second year and TEM-8 in the fourth year. In her grade, more than 70 % of students passed the TEM-4, and Mammuts was one of those who failed. She felt very ashamed about the test result. "What a poor mark I got," she reflected later:

> TEM-4 is not a very important examination for me. But as an English major student if you cannot pass it, you will feel a bit strange. After you pass it, you will feel the same as others. You can say I am at least a qualified English major. This (the certificate) is a placebo.
> (Mammuts, Interview, January 22, 2010)

Fortunately, Mammuts learned a lesson from her test failure. She worked very hard and passed the test in her third year.

Mammuts' tension with her university curriculum further addresses the significance of multicultural education. It seems that the SFL curriculum was far beyond Mammuts' linguistic and cultural competence because the entire goal was set in reference to the standards of mainstream comprehensive universities. The lower "threshold" for admission determined by the preferential policies put both the university and EMLs in an awkward position. In this case, Mammuts had to choose either to pass the examination to establish her legitimacy as an English major or be excluded from the mainstream system and labeled as an academic loser. It was not until she passed TEM-4 that she was identified as a qualified English major undergraduate in her community of practice (EFL learners in the English Department). Furthermore, the examination-oriented instruction not only frustrated Mammuts, but also reinforced her disadvantage in the mainstream system. To solve these problems, a curriculum reform from the perspective of multicultural education is required. Such reforms should transform the total school environment (Banks 2009) including perceptions, materials, courses of study, teaching styles, and university policies.

5.4.5 Psychological Problems

A counseling service is a psychological aid provided by most western tertiary institutions for the students who need emotional or mental support. YUN established a counseling office in April 1991. The duty of the counseling office is to provide free consultation service for all YUN staff and students. In 2004 the education center for psychological health was established at YUN. Professional personnel were recruited to carry out psychological health education, counseling, and research. A 24-hour intervention hotline was set up. Now students at YUN can take advantage of the counseling service in four ways: hotline, online, QQ instant message, and walk-in.

The weakness of ethnic minority students came about not only because of their academic problems, but also because of their difficult adaption to the new environment. The online counseling website of YUN said that, by September 24, 2011, there were 156,037 clicks and 688 posts asking for help.

Apart from academic problems, Mammuts also mentioned some psychological problems she suffered at the university. It seemed to her most students at YUN were lacking emotional support. She recalled her worst time at the university:

> The university cared little about the students' psychological health. I didn't realize this point till I took a selective course called Psychology. For example, although something goes normally the students may experience some changes in the mental activity or intentions. But the university shared little with us. Take myself for example. Even if I felt something was almost wrong with me sometimes I didn't know what to do. Sometimes, I was very frightened by great panic. I knew I didn't have to be scared, but I was. Meanwhile, no one guided me. I think a kind of psychological care is very critical for college students. If you have a healthy mind it will be easy to do other things. You will do well in studies or anything else. Some students fail just because they cannot maintain a healthy mind. Personally I pay great attention to keeping my mental health.
>
> (Mammuts, Interview, March 30, 2010)

Dao and He, two of Mammuts' roommates and best female friends, told me their impression about Mammuts after she failed in TEM-4: "She kept silent for quite a while; we could do nothing but encourage her to work hard and take another try. She was in great depression and studied very hard." (Student YNU, Dao and He, Interview, March 15, 2010)

Ru, the CPC secretary of Mammuts' faculty, also talked about the lower self-esteem of some ethnic minority students in the School of Foreign Languages:

> Most of them come from the poor frontier mountain areas. On the one hand, they are open-minded, but on the other hand, they are very conservative. This conservatism doesn't mean they are blocked in mind but they are in very low self-esteem. So I often told them, "Poverty is not your fault. What counts most is how you look at poverty, how you would study hard to change this situation. You shall not just look down upon yourself and feel sorry about yourself. If you are ashamed of eating Chinese cabbage while seeing others having meat, that is not right." What we need to do is to overcome our psychological obstacles. So the strong lower self-esteem is a characteristic of ethnic minority students in our university.
>
> (Administrator YUN, Ru, Interview, October 25, 2010)

In the third interview, Mammuts told me she went to see the university psychological consultants twice during her first year. I asked her whether the consultation was helpful, and she said:

> It was somewhat helpful for that particular case. However, our university has just one or two consultants. That is just a display and does not function well. I think each faculty should be equipped with one psychological consultant, or a teacher of psychological background, who can give a lecture once a week. You know in four years we may come across different troubles at different periods.
>
> (Mammuts, Interview, July 22, 2010)

As I mentioned before, the counseling system is a crucial component of the total school environment (Banks 2009). However, it can be seen from this episode, there are some misunderstandings about counseling services among both teachers and students of YUN. Many students did not know sound mind should be maintained in advance and some preventative intervention would help solve their problems. It is obvious that the counseling system of YUN should be further strengthened. I analyzed the counseling system in the discussion part later.

5.4.6 Conflict with Parents

In general, Mammuts was a good girl at home and generally obedient to her parents. She developed independent perceptions of life and studying after she became a university student. These perceptions might be partly at odds with her family's teaching and university requirements. For example, in terms of her future career, her parents expected her to go back to her hometown and become a civil servant. But she argued:

> I want to go outside to try my luck as I am still young. I know it will take time and skills to convince my mum and obtain her support. Anyhow, I will try my best to make it happen so that I won't regret later.
>
> (Mammuts, Autobiography, October 26, 2009)

Till the final semester, the argument between Mammuts and her parents was not resolved. In the third interview, she confessed:

> This is a critical time of our conflict. It is a time to make a decision. The fourth year will come to an end so my mom said "come back immediately and take the examinations for this or that". And my dad also echoed my mum by asking me to take this or that kind of examination and it seemed to them I would have a peaceful life after that. My mom believed that it would be good for a girl to live like that all her life.
>
> (Mammuts, Interview, July 22, 2010)

I asked Mammuts' father how he looked at Mammuts' determination. He told me he would not push his daughter too much. As for him, there was no big difference for Mammuts to work in Kunming or Lijiang. "I don't see any difference to work in Kunming or Lijiang; it is also the same if she works in Beijing. Now it is easy to travel, she can go home anytime." He commented, "It may be better for her to develop in Kunming. After all, Lijiang is a small place, though you see people come from all over the country." At the same time, he told me Mammuts' mother still hoped very much that her daughter would come back to Lijiang to work. "If she works in Lijiang, then we can look after each other," he added.

Facing much pressure from the society and her family, Mammuts refused to compromise. She told me she would live her life according to her desires. Now Mammuts is teaching some toddlers in an English school in Kunming, but she is still struggling with the decision whether to go back to Lijiang or to stay in Kunming. As she commented, "Life is not easy here in Kunming" (Mammuts, Interview, July 22, 2010). Life is always unexpected. When I almost finished the first draft of this book in July 2011, Mammuts had come back to Lijiang to prepare for the civil service examination. Now she is a clerk in a local bank in Lijiang. She told me in the latest online chat, "I don't like this job at all because it doesn't fit me."

The main conflict between Mammuts and her parent is value orientation. Mammuts' off-campus experiences in traveling widely and working a part-time job made her witness the conspicuous differences in terms of lifestyles. Her stay-in-the-city mentality was particularly enhanced after she became an English major and worked with native English-speaking colleagues at the Shane English School. Her parents wished her to study for the sake of a peaceful life and protection, while Mammuts saw city life both as a challenge and opportunity. With an enterprising spirit nurtured by her Naxi heritage (Guo 2008), Mammuts would rather try her luck despite various difficulties in the urban areas.

5.4.7 Identity Issues

As a student of a university of nationalities, Mammuts assumed that the campus life at YUN would be more lively and diversified. On the contrary, she was not able to feel the multicultural atmosphere on campus. She told me her impressions of YUN:

> I cannot feel any dense atmosphere of ethnic minority groups on the campus. Ms. Cun, a graduate of YUN, told us, when they celebrated National Day or other festivals (of certain ethnic minority groups), the ethnic minority students always sang and danced. Someone would dance the Dai, and someone would do the Naxi dance. I could not feel it was a university of nationalities. YUN is just a name. Life here is no different from that of the Han.
> (Mammuts, Interview, January 22, 2010)

> I hope very much especially on ethnic holidays we can display our culture and convey our feeling. For example, the Naxi should display their culture on Naxi holidays, and the Dai should demonstrate theirs on Dai holidays. I hope the kids of Naxi and Dai can be good at singing and dancing like their ancestors.
> (Mammuts, Interview, March 30, 2010)

Despite various difficulties and hardships, Mammuts gained much as an English major student at YUN. Above all, the new identity of a college student emancipated her from the stressful and suffocating environment of the high school. At the university, she made new friends and started to enjoy life on and off campus.

Owing to studying in a multiethnic university, Mammuts made some good friends of different ethnicities. She told me her best university friends were her roommates. They often studied and enjoyed life together by doing things such as watching movies, eating out or shopping online.

She acknowledged that she had learned much from her friends from different cultures.

> I have many friends now—some Chinese, some foreigners. I have some change in my perceptions and approach to solving problems. It seems to me, some foreigners' solutions are better. If so, I will learn and adopt idea from them. For example, I agree it is important to separate public from private interests. I also prefer going Dutch for dinner with my friends now.
>
> (Mammuts, Autobiography, October 26, 2009).

Studying in a mixed ethnic environment also helped her learn and understand her peers from different ethnic groups. When the investigator asked for her view on the preferential policy (adding 10–20 points to the total score in the national matriculation examination for those students from remote ethnic minority areas), she responded:

> If they are really from the remote areas I think it is reasonable to be awarded some bonus points in the entrance examination. You know, it is really very different for you to study in a developed area or a remote area. You have to make more effort to study well if you are from a remote area. But if you are living in a big place you will benefit from a lot of good policies. They (students from remote places) need chances too, don't they? They should be given more chances. They should not be thrown into a cold palace and deprived of seeing the sunshine all their life.
>
> (Mammuts, Interview, January 22, 2010)

At the same time, when she communicated with the non-Naxi, her Naxi identity was highlighted, consciously or unconsciously. She told me, with more travel experience and cross-ethnic contact, she became more and more proud of being a Naxi. She told me she would speak just Naxi in and out of her community wherever she met her folks. When she met new friends, she would tell them about her Naxi background:

> I didn't say I am a Naxi when I was in Lijiang, but I started to claim my Naxi identity since I came here (Kunming). It could be conscious or unconscious anyhow when I told others I was a Naxi. I told people my ethnicity since my first year at this university. Whenever I met any new friends I would tell them I was a Naxi.
>
> (Mammuts, Interview, January 22, 2010)

Many a time, Mammuts boasted the merits of the Naxi people as "kind," "unsophisticated," and "honest." She said:

> When the natives of Lijiang travel outside they may find the other people may not as be hospitable as the local Naxi people. They cannot do it as well as the Naxi. When I came to Kunming at the very beginning, I felt as if I was coldly treated by others.
>
> (Mammuts, Interview, March 30, 2010)

5.4 The Story of Mammuts

Whenever Mammuts found her Naxi identity was challenged, especially when Lijiang or the Naxi people were criticized without a good reason, she would be quite irritated and would counterattack immediately. She told me this story: A female Han company employee listed a number of bad things she saw in Lijiang such as the cheating of vendors, promiscuous males in the local bars, and the promotion of souvenirs by a tour guide. Mammuts argued with the employee, by pointing out these things could be true, but that Lijiang should not be defined by just one case for "you cannot encounter these things all the time." She thought this woman's comment was too extreme. She explained, "We are trying to safeguard something by instinct. Or perhaps we are reminding ourselves something. This is a right conduct, isn't it?" (Mammuts, Online chat, September 28, 2009).

When she reflected on her life at home she reported feeling quite cozy and happy. She described her home life like the following:

> I had a routine work to do when I was at home on vacations. I would go for a walk with my mother every day after dinner. I would walk with my mom hand in hand. We always would walk around most of the town watching some performances, joining in the Naxi dance, having some barbecue, buying some small ornaments or visiting my grand aunties. When I reflected on these days at Kunming, I felt so warm and happy. So wherever I go in the future, I will miss my parents and will repay them for their kindness.
>
> (Mammuts, Autobiography, October 26, 2009)

Mammuts told me whenever she went home she would be very happy to celebrate her Naxi festivals. The *Sanduo Festival* 三朵节 was a case in point. On this particular day, the female Naxi, young or old, would dress up in their traditional clothing, and sing their folk songs and dance a local dance called *Datiao* 打跳. However, Mammuts told me she did not celebrate the festival by heart at the beginning. "I celebrate them before for I thought it a big fun, but now I celebrate these festivals by heart since I left my hometown," Mammuts reflected in the second interview.

As an English major with Naxi background, Mammuts took a new look at Lijiang from her distinctive position. She criticized that general English proficiency of Lijiang. She complained that:

> Some English spelling in the signs of parks and bus stops are wrong. (I consider) these signs the face of a city. It should be constructed in a better way. If we can achieve this people will show more respect for Lijiang. Lijiang is so valuable that I think we should let people respect Lijiang (by correcting these mistakes).
>
> (Mammuts, Interview, January 22, 2010)

She believed that her mastery of three languages and her Naxi background would help her make some contribution to her nationality someday:

> In the long run, I often think about it when I am going to sleep or when it is quite late at night. I want to be an "ambassador" for Lijiang culture. I want to do this work though I cannot tell you what kind of job it is. I want to do something relevant, introduce the Lijiang (Naxi) culture to the outside world or import other cultures to Lijiang. I am very happy when I talk about Lijiang to the strangers. This is a heart-to-content feeling…I am a native of Lijiang so I am very confident to talk about my local culture.
>
> (Mammuts, Interview, January 22, 2010)

Like her ancestors, Mammuts also held a strong identification with China. Actually she was very proud of being a Chinese, too. She thought of the Naxi as one of 56 ethnic groups in China. She told me she often showed her patriotism in her own way. For example, most of her electronic gadgets were made in China, though she knew the quality of some were not as good as foreign products of the same type. I asked her in the second interview if the quality of Chinese products would be improved if many people insisted on using them. She responded, "I am not quite sure. Actually I have questioned this myself, too. But I think since there are people I know doing like this, I would rather believe it and bet by trying to use Chinese products." (Mammuts, Interview, July 22, 2010)

Mammuts claimed frankly that she was very patriotic. She told me her patriotism came from her school and family education. When she was a senior secondary school student she participated for three years in a routine ceremony every Monday morning—"Speaking under the national flag." (see Picture 5.3) In her senior secondary school, a thematic class meeting was held every week. Most of the themes involved moral education and psychological health. Mr. Mu, the principal of No. 1 Secondary School of Ancient City District, told me that his school had attached great importance to moral education and positive psychology. In 2005, the Political Education Department was renamed as Moral Education Department. The students' moral performance became the criteria for selecting Three-merit Students[9] (*Sanhao Xuesheng* 三好学生). The first condition in moral evaluation was stated as "Love our country; respect the national symbol; maintain the national dignity, reputation and ethnic unity; have ethnic self-esteem and social responsibility" (Editing Committee of History of No. 1 Lijiang Ancient City Secondary School 2009, p. 295). The No. 1 Ancient City Secondary School has published five books on thematic class meetings and one journal on school counseling. Five national heroes were the graduates of this school.

Mammuts acknowledged that television programs also played important roles in building up her patriotism.

> In fact, this sense of patriotism came from the movies of patriotic theme I saw when I was young. My father loved to see this kind of movie, and I was influenced, too. When I grew up, I had more contacts with foreigners, and I often watched TV news. After experiencing more and more of this kind of thing, my sense of patriotism was developed step by step.
> (Mammuts, Interview, March 30, 2010)

After she had visited the Huawei Technology Corporation, Ltd., a leading international telecom solutions provider in Shenzhen, she remarked "Woo, I don't expect that we have such an excellent national industry in China. Although I am not an employee of it, I am very proud that our China has this kind of enterprise" (Mammuts, Online Chat, October 7, 2009). The visit to Huawei not only helped

---

[9]Three-merit Students refer to students of excellent morality, intelligence, and fitness. They are similar to Straight A students in the West but, in addition to academic performance, their moral and sport merits are also considered.

Mammuts strengthen her national identity but also helped her set her life goal. She observed:

> The Huawei employees are so young and full of vigor and vitality. They seem overwhelming, and I feel certain pressure from them. In my eyes, they are well-educated people with strong ability. When I saw they filed out the gate of Huawei, I was shocked by the power they displayed. I have an idea right away. I want to have a good command of knowledge, but refuse to become a bookworm. I want to be a person with knowledge and ability at the same time.
>
> (Mammuts, Interview, January 22, 2010)

This section mainly documents Mammuts' comments on the university culture, her perception of the Naxi, and her performance as an ethnic minority. It seems to Mammuts that multicultural phenomenon is invisible at YUN. She expected that YUN would be a multicultural university in a real sense. As an ethnic minority herself, she shows great empathy for other ethnic minority students and supports the national preferential policy for ethnic minority people.

At the same time, Mammuts displays strong Naxi identity by highlighting her ethnicity in public, fighting against the stigmatization of her people by outsiders and reflecting on ways of further improving her group's image. Her actions fit the typical attributes of the Naxi—strong self-identification and reflection (Guo 2008). Her changed attitude toward festival celebrations from halfhearted to wholehearted shows her "cultural self-consciousness" (Fei 1999). Her attitude indicates the success of patriotic education throughout the Chinese education system from primary to tertiary education, as well as parental influence. Furthermore, the Naxi inherit patriotism due to Confucian education and their experience fighting against the Japanese during World War II. The economic emergence of China since the late 1990s also intensifies the 1980s generation's nationalism. Her praise of the Huawei people is a case in point.

5.4.8 The Enjoyable Off-Campus Life

Mammuts had never been out of Lijiang before she went to a university in Kunming. The life in Kunming, the provincial capital of Yunnan, created many "firsts" for Mammuts. She told me

> It was my first time to take a train to Kunming, the first time to see so many high rise buildings, the first time to spend spring festival away from home, the first time to travel by plane and the first time to see real sea in Shenzhen.
>
> (Mammuts, Online chat, September 25, 2009)

Actually, it is through so many the "first times" that Mammuts found "Life can be lived in another way. You can play different roles in life and can step back sometimes to look at life" (Mammuts, Interview, March 30, 2010).

5.4.9 Happy Vacations

Since her first university summer vacation, Mammuts had visited many places in different parts of China to meet new people and experience different cultures.

> I want to know what kind of places they are living in and what their lifestyles are. Each of these experiences can be very small and concrete. In addition, I want to train my survival and adaptive skills such as finding a place to live, finding the road, talking to strangers, etc. I hope to learn the skills to survive in a strange environment.
> (Mammuts, Online Chat, October 22, 2009)

Now Mammuts has traveled to some big cities such as Shenzhen, Shanghai, Hangzhou, and Changsha. She traveled mostly by herself with the money she saved from her living allowance made from part-time jobs. Before she departed each time, her mother would show her disapproval by worrying about traffic accidents, cheating by evil people, and even murder on the train. But every time she returned home safe and sound. Mammuts summarized her travel experiences in the following way:

> As far as people were concerned, they were not that bad as my mum said. (She worried just) because she had no personal travel experience. Therefore, her guess was arbitrary. What I mean is that you will never understand many things till you experience them. Most people in the society are good people in general.
> (Mammuts, Online Chat, October 22, 2009)

Holiday traveling was a very valuable experience for Mammuts. This experience not only enriched her knowledge of the outside world, but it also taught her survival skills. Shuhe historically was a part of *Chama Gudao,* along which many Naxi people conducted business. In the process, they encountered various cultures and had their minds broadened. Like her ancestors, Mammuts loved traveling and developed her "enterprising spirit and learning ability" (Guo 2008).

5.4.10 Being a TA in Shane

To improve her oral English, Mammuts often went to English corners in the first two years of her university study. Since July 2009 she worked as a part-time teaching assistant in Shane, a local English school run by native English speakers. At Shane, her job was to communicate with students, head teachers, and parents. She did telephone coaching three times per week. She told me that she joined Shane to talk with native English speakers and make friends. "I appreciate Shane's motto 'English is for life,'" she reflected.

The Shane experience not only helped Mammuts improve her English, but it also built her self-confidence and strengthened her will to pursue her desired career. In my latest interview, Mammuts specially mentioned Carl, a colleague at Shane from the United Kingdom. One day, Mammuts did not look well at school so Carl asked her what was wrong. She told Carl her conflict with her parent over her future job. Carl said, "You should make a decision out of your heart. If your choice is not against your heart you should tell your parents clearly their choice is not your choice. You should have your own life."

Carl's encouragement helped Mammuts make up her mind to pursue her own career. She told her parents her decision during the winter holiday of 2010, but they could not accept her idea.

What benefited Mammuts most from Shane was not the improvement in her English proficiency and her teaching. It was her perception of language learning for life. With this perception, she adopted a positive attitude toward school examinations and certificates. At the same time, by working with foreign colleagues she learned "another way of life" marked by self-reliance, independence, and critical thinking.

5.4.11 Dae Jang Geum Club

With the aim of learning Korean and experiencing a new culture, Mammuts joined a club named Dae Jang Geum (Jewel in the Palace) with one of her roommates in 2006. The Dae Jang Geum 大长今 was a very popular Korean TV drama broadcast in the mid-2000s in China. Dae Jang Geum Club (DJGC) was a salon established by some Korean teachers in the business school of a local Kunming university. Most club members were Korean Christians and included college teachers, college students, high school students, housewives, and businessmen. Besides Korean lessons, BBQ, and sport, DJGC also organized some charitable activities such as developing children's literacy in remote schools. Mammuts remembered a tough journey to Cha'ke Town, a remote mountainous village in southeast Yunnan.

> We went to a very backward remote school with very poor sanitary conditions. But no Korean complained during the hard journey including the young kids who were just five-or-six years old. I was quite moved by this scenario. To be frank, I was tired out in exhaust and starvation. I started to complain but they (the Korean) didn't.
> (Mammuts, Interview, March 30, 2010)

The trip turned out to be tough. Fan, a roommate of Mammuts as well as a member of the Cha'ke team, described the journey:

> The road was flooded away, and it was raining hard. We went there by wearing rain boots...The school was composed of two rows of flat houses. One row was used as classroom, and the other the dormitory for both teacher and students. The floor was mud-made, and a blackboard was set in a rack. We taught them some simple characters or alphabets in the morning and played games with them in the afternoon.
> (Student YUN, Fan, Interview, November 25, 2010)

Mammuts reflected on the lessons of this trip:

> (If I have this ability), I will help those poor but enterprising girls. How to say, I think girls are more sensible. She will be more sensitive for your help and may try to help others later.

> I learned this point by watching TV. It seems that it is very different for you to help a boy or a girl. If you help a girl, it makes a big difference in terms of psychology and other perspectives. I believe it is true. If I have an option to help a boy or a girl I am very likely to help a girl.
>
> (Mammuts, Interview, March 30, 2010)

As for Mammuts, the DJGC was not only a social gathering but also a stage to learn new cultures. What struck me most was her visit to the rural school. This experience is very crucial for college students in contemporary China. Banks (2009) once talked about talents for the twenty-first century. He believes knowledge, skill, attitude, and commitment are critical qualities for the current century generation. In Chinese tertiary curricula, knowledge and skill often outweigh commitment and service. If YUN strives to become a world class university for minority nationalities, it should first develop the students with talents that enable them to serve the local community and the nation. I am very happy to see Mammuts had the intent to help people in need with her knowledge and skills.

5.4.12 Mary Kay Implication

Mary Kay Inc. (MKI) is an international marketing company that sells skin care and cosmetic products. The vision of MKI is to "provide women with an unparalleled opportunity for financial independence, career and personal fulfillment and to achieve total customer satisfaction by delivering the products and services that enhance a woman's self-image and confidence" (Mary Kay Inc. 2010).

What attracted Mammuts to MKI was not only its cosmetic products, but also its philosophy of female life. After taking some courses such as "how to start a businesses as a woman" at the Mary Kay, Kunming Branch, Mammuts learned about makeup and skincare. After she had attended some lectures delivered by the beauty consultants she exclaimed:

> A female can be very graceful and beautiful. It is their (beauty consultants) self-confidence and beauty from the inner most that deeply attracted me. Women from Mary Kay are really beautiful and attractive. I learned that a female has to be economically independent first and then spirit and personality independent. Anyhow women must have their career at first.
>
> (Mammuts, Interview, July 22, 2010)

In her latest blog, Mammuts talked about her philosophy of life: "Lovely people, lovely story, and lovely life." She told me she had been tracing beauty since her childhood:

> When I was still a young girl I wanted to become a beautiful woman in the future. The same is still true now. When I see the young ladies wearing lipstick I will get excited. I love it (lipstick) so much as it is very attractive to me…After I came to YUN, I changed a lot. I am good at making up now. I can do quite well in making up. I can do it anytime.
>
> (Mammuts, Autobiography, October 26, 2009)

5.4 The Story of Mammuts

As far as Mammuts was concerned, Mary Kay was not only selling cosmetic products but also promoting the philosophy of beauty, love, and feminism from the western perspective. With aims of beauty-seeking and self-reliance, Mammuts accepted the philosophy naturally. As for her future family life, Mammuts prioritized faith first, family second, and career third. When I asked her how to keep a balance of family and career she told me frankly:

> I think I won't quit my job soon after I get married. I have to work. In my family, I will try my best to fulfill the duty of a wife. I will try my best to make my family life perfect in spite of any difficulties. I will never be tired of playing well my role as a wife. I won't give up my job for employment is important for a family. As for me, family and career are both important. They should be balanced well with great effort.
>
> (Mammuts, Interview, March 30, 2010)

It can be seen here, with the traditional Naxi attributes of an open-mind and flexible attitude (Guo 2008), Mammuts integrates the western philosophy with her Naxi heritage aiming for a balance between family and career.

5.5 Discussion and Implications

In the previous section, I traced the life history of Mammuts as an ethnic multilingual student from elementary school to university. Her personal story reflected some pains and gains that ethnic minority students experience while they strive to excel in the mainstreams education system in contemporary China. In addition to academic challenges, Mammuts also faced a dilemma of maintaining her ethnic identity or being assimilated into the mainstream for better life chances. In the following section, I will discuss Mammuts' case from two perspectives: mainstream university curriculum and power relationships.

5.5.1 *Curriculum and Disempowerment*

Apple (2004) argued that "Education… is… a site of conflict about the kind of knowledge that is and should be taught, about whose knowledge is 'official' and about who has the right to decide both what is to be taught and how teaching and learning are to be evaluated" (p.vii). This argument reveals a power relationship in education: to achieve the will of the dominant social group and to provide education for the good of the majority. In this hegemonic discourse, ethnic minority learners are in most cases at a disadvantage. They have no voice in the content and form of curriculum. They are passive test-takers, although some may benefit from preferential policies for school admission. Once admitted, they have to follow what is stipulated for them in terms of what kind of knowledge is to be learned. Furthermore, the preferential policies are limited by many extra conditions. For example, the beneficiaries are only selected from certain ethnic groups in terms of population size, geographic locations and socioeconomic development. Mammuts told me that before the national matriculation examination, she got a form explaining preferential conditions for ethnic minority students. After studying the conditions very carefully she found the Naxi were excluded from the shortlist of policy beneficiaries.

As I have described in Chap. 2, the drastic socioeconomic development in contemporary China provides opportunities as well as challenges for those EMLs who are lucky to be admitted to higher education. The expansion of higher education in China is pushing tertiary institutions to compete for academic status. This has intensified the pressure on all students, not just ethnic multilingual learners who come from less advantageous backgrounds. For Mammuts, the change of language environment, lack of Chinese proficiency, and the demands of curriculum and assessment pushed her into a very difficult position when competing with the majority students. As a result, she had to either adapt to the mainstream curriculum by passing TEM-4 to prove that she was a qualified English major student (legitimate participant) of the English Department (community of practice) or suffer from the depression and marginalization due to repeated failure.

The ethnicity-detached university environment brought some frustration into her life and studies. There seemed to be a kind of resistance within Mammuts, which could be seen from her criticisms of the university curriculum, the teaching content, the instruction style, and the examination policies. We know life chances can be very different from person to person due to the complex sociopolitical/economic structures in contemporary China. On the one hand, the national trilingual policies do provide possible opportunities for ethnic minority learners to pursue their dreams and to fight for an equal chance for upward mobility. On the other hand, good-will polices do not always bring about good results. Educational structures such as university curriculum, study environment, university policy, teacher perceptions, and university administrators have a critical impact on EMLs' learning outcomes. The coercive power relationship (Cummins 2009) implied from Mammuts' case proved to be detrimental to her healthy development as an ethnic multilingual learner. It is quite clear that there are still large gaps between university policies and practice and the needs of ethnic minority students.

At present, YUN calls itself "a cradle for high-level and top-quality talents" for the ethnic regions, "an important base for ethnic studies" and a "window of Yunnan open to the outside world" (Yunnan University of Nationalities 2006, p. 25). Around 50 % of registered student at YUN come from the ethnic minority areas in Yunnan and some other Chinese provinces. However, neither the academic strengths nor the demographic features of these students are taken into account while designing the curriculum or creating a campus culture. Therefore, many ethnic minority students like Mammuts are struggling with two challenges: academic attainment and identity negotiation.

5.5.2 Capital, Agency, and Empowerment

In the previous section, I discussed the coercive power relationship between Mammuts and her university curriculum. I argued that Mammuts was disempowered to some extent and disadvantaged in the mainstream system. However, I also noticed that the disempowering situation could be changed through the constant interaction between EMLs and their environment.

Take language for example. I was very surprised throughout my interviews with Mammuts. Her oral Chinese is much better than some of their Han cohorts. Her Putonghua pronunciation is crystal clear like fountain gushing and her oral English was fluent and accurate. I asked Mammuts, her father, and her primary schoolmates how Mammuts could speak such a standard version of Putonghua and English. They attributed her Putonghua pronunciation to the instruction of her Chinese teacher in the primary school. Her commitment to mastering authentic English paid off. Mammuts' devotion to building up linguistic capital suggests that both she and her family attached great importance to multilingual acquisition. These findings resonate with Chao and Yu's observation that the Naxi people are good at learning and open to new knowledge and skills (Chao 1996; Yu 2008; 2009a).

Despite some unfavorable conditions for ethnic multilingual learners, the university environment did provide Mammuts chances to seek new knowledge and develop different perceptions. For example, she took every means possible to empower herself by engaging in diversified academic and social activities. In her first three and a half years, she took courses like Psychology, Tourist Culture and Beauty Appreciation, and Classic Chinese Poem Appreciation, to name just a few. These courses, to some extent, helped Mammuts have a better understanding of the natural beauty, female fulfillment, and women's responsibilities in the family and in society. With an ever-increasing amount of linguistic and cultural capital, she was able to reflect on the university curriculum, her hometown, and her career development.

Off campus, Mammuts assumed many academic-related posts such as that of a TA in a local English school and a private English tutor. She also worked at forming social networks. For example, during her vacations she worked in Shuhe first as a bar tender and then as a waitress in a local restaurant. By communicating with people from different cultures and walks of life, she developed her survival skills and made pocket money. Her experiences in the Korean-sponsored club and her frequent domestic traveling allowed her to learn about cultural differences and developed her critical thinking, open-mindedness, and international vision.

D'Angelo (1971) saw "critical thinking" as a process of "evaluating statements, arguments and experiences" and "a positive attitude toward novelty and seeking answers to various questions and problems" (p. 7). Mammuts developed her "critical thinking" step by step in the process of trilingual education. For instance, as I mentioned before, she found she could learn something from westerners in terms of career decisions and interpersonal skills. However, Mammuts did not accept western ideology blindly. For example, she criticized the feminine lead in an American TV series called "Gossip Girl":

> It seems that they (the girls in the movie) could not make a rational judgment about right and wrong. They didn't have firm faith. The way they acted was misty and short of serious consideration. As for this point it is not as good as Chinese. I suppose they are too frivolous.
>
> (Mammuts, Interview, January 22, 2010)

In her second year at university, she even criticized an expatriate teacher. She thought that teacher was of "poor quality" and short of teaching experience. For example, he never talked about anything in the textbook but just organized some drills. "He was just a native speaker," she commented. "It is not enough to employ a native speaker without considering their educational background and teaching experience."

Mammuts' questions about the qualifications of the expatriate teacher show not only critical thinking, but also empowerment, an ability to negotiate her identity through multilingual education.

Open-mindedness could be seen from her willingness to learn new things. She reflected on her change as a college student in her autobiography:

> After I came to Kunming as a college student, dramatic change happened to me. Now I am skillful in making up. I can handle each step of makeup. I made a lot of friends both at home and abroad. My perception and way of dealing with problems changed, too. I found some westerners could handle some problems well, so I learned from them. I also learned something from the Han schoolmates. They were meticulous in doing things and good at rational analysis. I would often handle things emotionally before.
>
> (Mammuts, Autobiography, October 26, 2009)

The above-mentioned changes in Mammuts also show that she achieved integration through longer term adaptation and cultural contact. As Berry argues, longer term adaptation may lead to longer term accommodation among groups in contact with each other. Included are "learning each other's languages, sharing each other's food preferences, and adopting forms of dress and social interactions that are characteristic of each group" (Berry 2005, p. 700).

Mammuts' view of friendship also showed that she was open-minded like her Naxi ancestors. I once asked what her standards were for making friends. I asked her whether she had more Naxi friends or Han friends. She responded:

> I have no fixed standard to make friends. If he or she is different from me I will have the intention to make friends with them. I won't think too much at the beginning. I just communicate with them. I don't care whether he/she is ugly or beautiful, big or small. If I find this person has some merit in this or that aspect, I will communicate with him/her more frequently.
>
> (Mammuts, Interview, January 22, 2010)

Her open attitude toward friendship, new experiences, and different cultures show an acceptance of "ethnic diversity within national unity" (Fei 1989, 1999). Fei (2003) argues that "diversity within unity" is a combination of *gemei qimei* 各美其美 (to understand yourself and discover your own form of beauty) and *meiren*

5.5 Discussion and Implications

zhimei 美人之美 (to befriend others and appreciate radiance of different people). Using Fei's point of view, I interpret Mammuts' concept of life and friendship as being a flow of inner recognition and outside admiration. The driving force behind this recognition and admiration is not short-term goals but instead is a simple and pure Naxi spirit. This spirit serves as a cornerstone for ethnic development and personal advancement.

Here I argue that it is the combination of tertiary education, off-campus experiences, Naxi cultural heritage, and personal agency that empowered Mammuts. I assume that her empowerment comes from the integration of capital and agency provided by educational institutions and Naxi heritage. Her valuing of cultural integration over cultural assimilation has helped Mammuts overcome all the difficulties she has met with as an ethnic minority student.

The school curriculum helped Mammuts build up new linguistic capital as well as an ability to question the existing educational practices.

Tertiary education in a multilingual context broadened Mammuts' visions of language and culture. Her education allowed her to reflect on her multiple identities from time to time. It is through this kind of "tertiary socialization" (Byram 1989, 1997; Doye 2003) that Mammuts underwent cognitive, affective, and behavioral transformation. This allowed her to better understand and deal with intercultural issues (Feng 2007a). As Feng (2007a, p. 275) pointed out:

> It is important to note that an individual who becomes intercultural does not abandon his/her own social group or reject his/her social identities. He/She is willing to step outside the closed boundaries, engage with otherness, bring the two or more than two cultures into relationship and take up different perspectives to view the world.

Trilingual education can provide a platform from which learners experience new pedagogies and form appropriate strategies to handle their problems in their life and studies. We must bear in mind that Mammuts does not represent the majority of EMLs in China, who are still struggling with school attainment and social inclusion. Therefore, a well-tailored curriculum should be developed to meet the diversified needs of EMLs.

As a descendant of the Naxi, a highly developed ethnic group in Yunnan and China as well, Mammuts displayed many distinctive characteristics. For example, she was good at absorbing other cultures and enhancing their vitality (Yang 1998). Being taught three languages and being exposed to many cultures empowered Mammuts to reflect on her own values, beliefs, and behaviors from time to time. As a result, she became "willing to extend her social identities" (Feng 2007a, p. 275). For example, she refused to copy others blindly and developed her critical thinking skills. Her criticism of the performance of the expatriate English teachers is a case in point.

She also used an adaptive strategy when she was confronted with a cultural dilemma. She built up her international vision for trilingual education in China, which is to develop a "global citizenship with local and global roots" (Delors et al. 1996, 17). In this sense, like her ancestors, Mammuts dealt with westernization and sinicization successfully (Bai 2001; He 2004; Yu 2009a, b) by displaying the "spirit of persistence and creativity found in the Naxi epic Genesis" (Yu 2009a, p. 24).

Mammuts' life story shows that individuals are not passive receivers within coercive power relationship. Actually, individuals can negotiate their identities by activating their dormant linguistic and cultural capital and can create social and symbolic capital through active engagement in and off tertiary institutions in pursuing cooperative power relationship. Armed with this knowledge, one can challenge the legitimacy of common practices in higher education.

It can be seen that Mammuts held multiple identities in and out of school. Some of these identities were assigned to her as a result of the language she used and her "core cultural heritage" (Chao 1996) as a Naxi. She cherished her Naxi identity so much that she was reluctant to sacrifice her "core cultural heritage" to the forces of urbanization, modernization, and globalization. She acknowledged that her outlook might have changed after she became a college student, but the "core" of her Naxi heritage remained as strong as before.

5.6 Summary

In this chapter, I documented the life history of Mammuts and reported her pains and gains as an English major at YUN. I also discussed the power relationships and their impact on Mammuts. However, I would like to point out that Mammuts' story is not necessary the case of other EMLs in China as the Naxi have a high degree of identification with Confucian education and regard Chinese education as a pathway to ethnic revitalization and development. Therefore, the Naxi people may respond positively toward "cultural homogenization" and successfully establish themselves as an advanced group with their prominent performance in mainstream education. The unique case of the Naxi is very different from many other ethnic groups in terms of their Chinese language proficiency, historical relationship with the central Chinese empire, high position in state education, personalities of individuals, acquaintance with the Chinese educational system, and acknowledgment of the Chinese political system. Mammuts' case suggests that an ethnic minority group with a high integration with the dominant culture rather than a resistant attitude is more likely negotiate identity successfully within the accepted political framework and super identity of the *Zhuanghuaminzu* 中华民族 (Chinese nation). However, as Wray (2004) pointed out, "multitudinous power relationships operating within particular ethnic and cultural localities may create different ways of thinking about agency and empowerment" (p. 24). As a result, people may see a very different picture of other ethnic multilingual learners in contrast to Mammuts. In the next chapter, I will introduce the case of Noma, a female Hani English major at YUN.

References

Apple, M. (2004). *Ideology and the curriculum*. New York: Routledge.
Bai, G. S. (2001). *Colors and the folk customs of the Naxi*. Beijing: Social Sciences Publishing House.
Banks, J. A. (2009). Multicultural education: Dimensions and paradigms. In J. A. Banks (Ed.), *The Routledge international companion to multicultural education* (pp. 9–32). New York: Routledge.
Berry, J. W. (2005). Acculturation: Living successfully in two cultures. *International Journal of Intercultural Relations, 25*, 697–712.
Byram, M. (1989). *Cultural studies in foreign language education*. Clevedon: Multilingual Matters.
Byram, M. (1997). *Teaching and assessing intercultural communicative competence*. Clevedon: Multilingual Matters.
Cai, S. F. (2001). *An educational history of Yunnan province*. Kunming: Yunnan Educational Press.
Chao, E. (1996). The invention of Dongba culture among the Naxi of southwest China. In M. J. Brown (Eds.), *Negotiating ethnicities in China and Taiwan* (pp. 208–239). Berkeley: Institute of East Asian Studies, University of California Berkeley.
CPC of Lijiang. (2011). The draft of the 12th five-year plan of socioeconomic development in Lijiang. Retrieved on May 1, 2011 from http://www.lijiangtv.com/viewnews-8868-1.html
Cummins, J. (2009). Pedagogies of choice: Challenging coercive relations of power in classrooms and communities. *International Journal of Bilingual Education and Bilingualism, 12*, 261–272.
D'Angelo, E. (Ed.). (1971). *The teaching of critical thinking*. Amsterdam: B. R. Grüner N.V.
Delors, J., Al Mufti, I., Amagi, A., et al. (1996). *Learning: The treasure within—report to UNESCO of the international commission on education for the twenty-first century*. Paris: UNESCO.
Doye, P. (2003). *Foreign language education as a contribution to tertiary socialization*. Paper presented at the Durham symposium on intercultural competence and citizenship, Durham University.
Editing Committee. (2008a). *A general introduction to Mojiang Hani Autonomous County of Yunnan Province*. Beijing: Nationality Press.
Editing Committee. (2008b). *A brief history of the Naxi nationality*. Beijing: Nationality Press.
Editing Committee. (2009). *Yunnan provincial facts*. Kunming: Yunnan People's Publishing House.
Editing Committee of History of No. 1 Lijiang Ancient City Secondary School. (2009). *The History of No. 1 Lijiang Ancient City Secondary School*. Kunming: Yunnan Press of Nationalities.
Fang, G. Y. (1944). A critical study of the Moxie people. *A Collective Journal of Ethnology, 4*.
Fei, X. T. (1989). Plurality within the organic unity of the Chinese nation. *Journal of Beijing University, 4*, 1–19.
Fei, X. T. (Ed.). (1999). *Plurality and unity in the configuration of the Chinese people*. Beijing: Publishing House of Minzu University of China.
Fei, X. T. (2003). Some monologues on culture self-consciousness. *Academic Study, 7*, 5–9.
Feng, A. W. (2007). Intercultural space for bilingual education. In A. W. Feng (Ed.), *Bilingual education in China: Practices, policies, and concepts* (pp. 259–279). Clevedon, Buffalo: Multilingual Matters.
Ge, A. (1999). *Dongba bone prognostication culture*. Kunming: Yunnan People's Publishing House.
Goullart, P. (1955). *Forgotten kingdom*. London: John Murray.
Guo, D. L. (2001). The Naxi traditional culture and its protection. *Yunnan Social Sciences, 6*, 52–55.

Guo, D. L. (2008). *Selected works on Naxiology*. Beijing: Nationality Press.
Guo, D. L., & He, Z. W. (1994). *A history of the Naxi*. Chengdu: Sichuan Nationality Press.
Guo, D. L., & Huang, L. N. (2005). Practice and exploration of inheriting Dongba culture in schools. In Z. X. He., D. L. Guo & G. S. Bai (Eds.), *The Proceeding of the 2nd International Academic Conference of Lijiang Dongba Culture and Art Festival* (pp. 227–233). Kunming: Yunnan Press of Nationalities.
Guo, D. L., & Yang, S. G. (1999). *A history of the Naxi*. Chengdu: Sichuan Press of Nationalities.
Hansen, M. (1999). *Lessons in being Chinese: Minority education and ethnic identity in southwest China*. Seattle, WA: University of Washington Press.
He, L. M. (2004, March 6). Inheriting and studying Dongba culture by theory of creativity. *Lijiang Daily*, 4.
He, Y. (2006). Study on the relationship of Lijiang ethnic culture and education. In S. H. Mu (Ed.), *A living key town along the tea and horse road: Dayan ancient city in Lijiang* (pp. 295–301). Beijing: China Nationalities Press.
He, Z. H., & Yang, S. G. (1992). *A history of Naxi literature*. Chengdu: Sichuan Nationality Press.
Hobsbawm, E., & Terence, R. (Eds.), (1983). *The invention of tradition*. Cambridge: Cambridge University Press.
Jackson, A. (1979). *Na-khi religion: An analytical appraisal of the Na-khi ritual texts*. The Hague: Mouton.
Li, J. (1998). Cultivation and education: On education in the Naxi history. *Journal of Nationalities Education, 4*, 39–44.
Li, X. (2001). *A road close to the gods: Dongba painting*. Kunming: Yunnan Art Publishing House.
Li, J. (2007a). *A developmental transition of Naxi culture in Lijiang*. Beijing: Publishing House of Minzu University of China.
Li, Y. H. (2007b). An analysis of the psychological health and its effect of 4782 freshmen in ethnic minority universities. *Journal of the 4th Military Medical University, 28*(8), 58–760.
Li, X. M. (2007c). Identity puzzles: Am I a Chinese instructor or a nonnative speaker? In M. Mantero (Ed.), *Identity and second language learning: Culture, inquiry, and dialogic activity in educational contexts* (pp. 23–44). Charlotte, NC: Information Age Publishing.
Liu, C. (2005). Impact and integration between tourism development and Naxi culture protection. In Z. X. He, D. L. Guo, & G. S. Bai (Eds.), *The Proceeding of the 2nd International Academic Conference of Lijiang Dongba Culture and Art Festival* (pp. 551–562). Kunming: Yunnan Nationalities Press.
Mary Kay, Inc. (2010). Company perspectives. Retrieved on April 20, 2010 fromhttp://www.fundinguniverse.com/company-histories/Mary-Kay-Inc-Company-History.html.
Mathieu, C. (1996). *Lost kingdoms and forgotten tribes: Myths, mysteries and mother-right in the history of the Naxi nationality and the Mosuo people of southwest China*. Paper presented for the degree of Doctor of Philosophy of Murdoch University.
McKhann, C. F. (1995). The Naxi and the nationalities question. In S. Harrell (Ed.), *Cultural encounters on China's ethnic frontiers* (pp. 39–62). Seattle: University of Washington Press.
Mu, L. C. (1995). *Revealing the secrets of Dongba culture*. Kunming, China: Yunnan People's Publishing House.
Mu, S. H. (2006). *Lijiang Dayan: An important city on the Ancient Tea-Horse Trail*. Beijing: Nationality Press.
Oppitz, M., & Hsu, E. (Eds.). (1998). *Naxi and Moso ethnography: Kin, rites, pictographs*. Zürich: Völkerkund Museum Zürich.
Rock, J. F. (1947). *The ancient Na-khi kingdom of southwest China*. Cambridge: Harvard University Press.
School of Foreign Languages, YUN. (2009a). English major undergraduate development plan for grade 2009. Retrieved on April 4, 2011 from http://202.203.144.4/english/shownews.asp?id=364
School of Foreign Languages, YUN. (2009b). SFL minute issue no.7. Retrieved on March 3, 2010 from http://202.203.144.4/english/shownews.asp?id=273

References

Statistical Bureau of Lijiang City. (2011a). A survey report of the census in Lijiang. Retrieved on September 8, 2011 from http://xxgk.yn.gov.cn/canton_model56/newsview.aspx?id=1724919

Statistical Bureau of Lijiang City. (2011b). *An analysis of 2010 national economy of Lijiang.* Retrieved on June 7, 2011 from http://xxgk.yn.gov.cn/canton_model58/newsview.aspx?id=1625436

Sydney, W. (2002). Town and village Naxi identities in southwest China's Lijiang basin. In S. D. Blum & L. M. Jensen (Eds.), *China off center: Mapping the margins of the middle kingdom* (pp. 131–147). Hawaii: University of Hawaii Press.

Wang, G. (2011). Bilingual education in southwest China: A Yingjiang case. *International Journal of Bilingual Education and Bilingualism, 14*(5), 571–587.

Wray, S. (2004). What constitutes agency and empowerment for women in later life? *Sociological Review, 52*(1), 22–38.

Yang, F. Q. (1998). *Cultural pluralism and Naxi society.* Kunming: Yunnan People's Publishing House.

Yang, F. Q. (2006a). *The Naxi cultural history.* Kunming: Yunnan University Press.

Yang, J. (2006b). Learners and users of English in China: Just how many millions are there? *English Today, 22*(2), 3–10.

Yu, H. B. (2007). Identity and schooling among the Naxi. *Asian Ethnicity, 8*(3), 235–244.

Yu, H. B. (2009a). Naxi intellectuals and ethnic identity. *Diaspora, Indigenous, and Minority Education, 3*(1), 21–31.

Yu, H. B. (2009b). Naxi students' national identity construction and schooling: A case study of Lijiang No. 1 Senior Secondary School. *China: An International Journal, 7*(1), 167–175.

Yunnan University of Nationalities. (2006). *Fifty-five anniversary of Yunnan University of Nationalities.* Kunming: Yunnan Press of Nationalities.

Zhou, J. H. (2002). *Naxi culture impression.* Beijing: Nationality Press.

Chapter 6
The Case of Noma

> *I heard there was a place called Noma-Amy with delicious food and beautiful landscape. Where is it? It is at the divide of the sky and the earth, at the divide of human and divine.*
>
> Haba-The Ancient Hani Epic

6.1 Sociocultural Context of the Hani

6.1.1 Demographic Features

The Hani are one of the oldest, and the second largest, ethnic minority groups in Yunnan. The Hani are mainly distributed in the lower range of the Yellow River and in mountain areas near the Mekong River. The population of the Hani in Yunnan is 1.63 million (Yunnan Bureau of Statistics 2012). As for the origin of the Hani, there are four assumptions in academic circles. The first one says that the Hani come from the north of China and are descendants of the ancient Di and Qiang tribe. The second one assumes that the Hani originated in East, Southeast and Northeast China. The third one supposes that the Hani are mainly an indigenous people from the Honghe area. The last one believes the Hani are a hybrid offspring resulting from the marriage of northern nomads and southern rice paddy tribes (Editing committee 2008b, p. 19).

Throughout the past 2000 years, the Hani were called "He Ren" in general. "He" means mountain, and "Ren" refers to people. He Ren means "hill people living on mountain slopes." Another interpretation is that Hani refers to a female-dominant community (Editing committee 2008b, p. 4). The Hani also call themselves Kado, Yani, Haoni, Biyue and Baihong (Heni), according to their different residential areas. The overseas Hani are called Akah and can be found in Myanmar, Thailand and Vietnam.

Hani people speak mainly three local dialects: Haya, Bika and Haobai, which are composed of 10 sub-dialects. Hani language is believed to be a branch of Yi language within the Sino-Tibetan language family. The written phonetic script of Hani was created in 1957 by the national linguists, but it is not widely used today.

Tsang's study (2005) suggested that 408,782 Hani people were bilingual language speakers by 2004.

Before *Tusi*, the native chiefs, were appointed as the local administrators of the central government, Confucian ideology had very little impact on the Hani's social and political life. The establishment of a compulsory *Tusi* system promoted the integration of the Hani and the Han. For example, in the Qing dynasty (1644–1911), if the offspring of *Tusi* wished to assume power from their fathers they had to go to school to receive a Confucian education. The Section on Schooling in the *Yunnan General History* said that (cited from Li 2005, p. 14):

> It was proposed that the heirs of *Tusi* in Yunnan could take over the power of their fathers on the condition that their heirs had to learn the Confucian teaching at school and develop good manners. When their father or elder brothers passed away they could go back to their hometown to take the post of native chief. The local officials could select some literate children to go to school and then sit for the examination of civil servants.

According to the book, *Brief History of the Hani*, during 1573–1620, a local *Tusi* called Long Shangdeng went to Beijing to receive the title of native chief. During his stay in Beijing, he visited many celebrities there. Following his return to Dali, he was very active in learning classic Chinese, building Confucian schools and writing papers to publicize Confucian and Mencius teaching. Due to his effort, Confucian culture was transmitted into the mountain areas of Liuzhao[1] 六昭, and the local Hani had early access to classical Chinese. The Hani in Mojiang and Pu'er had very early access to Confucian teaching. By 1904 there were 23 Hani who had education of more than 10 years, and four of them were awarded the title of *Xiucai*[2] (秀才).

Hani culture is transmitted in four ways (Zhao 2007): family genealogy, history education, social behavior and labor skills. Li and Che (2007) summarize five types of Hani traditional education: transmitting and developing agricultural skills, handicraft making, herb seeking, traditional religion and ethnic cultivation. Alternatively, He (2005) categorizes three main aspects of Hani education: production and labor work, ethics and Mopi culture. Hani culture involves material products (farming, hunting, handcrafting) and spiritual wealth (ethics and Mopi culture).

Elders and "Mopi", Hani witches, are in charge of Hani education. Family education is usually carried out at the dinner table, during labor, at festival celebrations and during worship. Oral narrative, singing, demonstrations and participant observation are the basic means of cultural transmission. Long and He (2005) see Hani education as a network woven together by home and family. Labor skills, moral education and Mopi culture are highlighted. Elders in each family teach children about work and life. Clans also play critical roles in Hani education. Family

---

[1] At the beginning of the seventh century, there were six big ethnic tribes inhabiting the Er'hai area in Yunnan. The six large ethnic tribes were called Liuzhao.

[2] *Xiucai* refers to one who passed the imperial examination for talent selection at the county level during the Ming and Qing dynasties.

gatherings, worship ceremonies, weddings and funerals are important occasions to reflect upon clan regulations. Vocational and traditional education are embedded in family and community activities. Li and Che (2007) highlight the characteristics of traditional Hani education as follows:

> In terms of the content, it is practical as the knowledge serves the needs of life and production. In terms of the approach, knowledge is delivered by imitating and doing things on site. In regard to the knowledge instructors, the knowledge is primitive and experimental. In regard to the knowledge receivers, the knowledge is multiple and overlapped (p. 86–88).

6.1.2 Characteristics of the Hani People

Hardships in farming and migration shape the Hani world view. *Congpopo* is a Hani epic that documents the hard journey of migration from the remote North to the Southwest China. The epic is composed of seven chapters. The first one documents the birth of the Hani people as hunters and gatherers. The second and third chapters describe the formation of matriarchal and patriarchal societies. The fourth chapter outlines the formation of tribes and communes. The fifth chapter narrates the stagnation of social development. The sixth chapter records wars in Hani history. The last chapter documents the restoration of social development (Wang 2003).

The Hani see the world as composed of God, ghost, nature, and people. Each group lives in its own place with its own family tree. Family trees are very important for the Hani. Each Hani has to memorize the family tree. Hani people believe human beings have a natural life and also a soul. When the soul leaves, people become sick or even die. Death is a natural phenomenon. When people die, their souls will rejoin their ancestors. Hani people have established their own understandings about the relationship of humans and nature. On the one hand, they think people should follow God's will in handling human–nature relationships. On the other hand, in terms of interpersonal relationships, they favor "tolerance and peace" (Long 2008).

The following is some literature documenting impressions of the Hani (Lei 2002). In *Chronicle of Pu'er Prefecture,* the black Woni were described as "mild and gentle people who preferred black clothes." The *History of the Dai* says "Woni are industrious throughout their life. They are frugal in spending money but good at accumulating wealth." And the *History of Yuanjiang Prefecture* said "Woni are simple and honest, good at cultivating." The *History of Mengzi County* claimed that "the Woni, self-called Hani, are gentle and timid. They dare not do anything like burglary. They are kind and able to get along well with others." *The History of Kaihua Prefecture* depicted the Ai'ni as "a simple and honest nationality that dare not do anything illegal and will never take possession of anything picked up on the road." The Hani lived in isolation for a long time, even during the Republic of China (1911–1949). *The Draft of Yuanjiang History* documented: "They are very proud and stubborn, few can understand Chinese. They live in remote mountain areas and seldom go to downtown" (Lei 2002, p. 258). The above presents us with contradictory profiles of the Hani. On the one hand, they are kind and gentle so they are easy to get along with and to be governed. On the other hand, they are proud and stubborn thus they are isolated from the mainstream.

After studying the Hani living on the southern bank and along the Red River, Zhang (1996) summarizes seven features of the Hani: hardworking, intelligent, strong, simple, friendly, upright, and honest with high self-esteem. To Zhang, if the Hani were not diligent and intelligent, they could not have survived in such a terrible natural environment and could not have created the world-famous "terraced paddy field."[3] Long (2008) studied some Hani expressions like "Angjiaojiao" (meaning labor exchange), "Bajiaojiao" (meaning money loan), "Angbamu" (referring to compulsory work to help build houses), and "Pudaza" (signifying mutual economic assistance). He argues that "this nationality's unity and mutual assistance, as well as the peaceful coexistence are critical factors to ensure the social stability of the Hani community" (p. 32). He points out further that "the traditional morality of the Hani can be seen from their tradition of assisting the people in poverty and need, treating others with benevolence" (2008, p. 32). Wang (2003) argues that the Hani have three main features. First, they are mild and gentle, which can be seen from their endurance of pain, no competition, and unity first. Second, they are warm and generous, so they appreciate sincerity and honesty. Third, they are persistent and strong-willed. This may be generally true about the interaction among members of the same ethnic group. There is variation among members and toward other people. Bai and Wang's study (1998) discloses some weaknesses of the Hani such as being sensitive, upset, blue and irritated, suspicious and cowardly, introverted and resistant.

6.1.3 Socioeconomic Development

In spite of a large population, the Hani are a "needy and poverty-stricken" people who hold the lowest rank (38.3 %) in the "quality of life index" (People-in-Country Profile 2011). The national average index is 62.7 %. Mojiang, Noma's hometown, had been a "poverty-stricken county" throughout its history. It was listed in 1986 as one of the 41 poorest counties supported by the central and provincial governments. Further, in 1994, Mojiang was listed again by the Yunnan Provincial government as one of the 73 most poverty-stricken counties supported by the *Seven Yunnan Poverty Elimination Projects* (Zhao 2002). Infant mortality is 107 out of 1000, and the average life span reaches only 58 years. Pu (2005, p. 295) points out that "the backward economy of the Hani area is resulted from the backward education, which is checking the prosperity and welfare of the Hani people."

---

[3]The terraced paddy field was awarded the World Culture Heritage designation by UNESCO in 2013.

As the largest population in Mojiang, the Hani people receive very poor education. By 1948, there were 2261 school-aged students in Mojiang and only 68 were Hani. The secondary education in Mojiang was very backward in 1949. Literature (Chinahani online 2008) suggested that there was only one secondary school with just 72 Hani children (0.02 % of the Hani population). By 1950, there was only one secondary school with 190 students in four classes.

In the past, most Hani families only sent their boys to school. Even now, the dropout rate of the female students in the secondary school is quite high compared with other ethnic groups in Yunnan (Pu 2005). Modern schooling in Mojiang started in the early 1900s. Lianzhu Academy (联珠书院) was the first public school, established in 1907. It was composed of 87 students and two teachers. In 1912, a new school was set up in Mojiang County, enrolling 50 students. By 1949, there were 48 public schools with 2033 students. This accounted for only 10.8 % of the school-aged children.

Table 6.1 documents some facts about education in Mojiang since 1907. Since 1949, basic education developed dramatically in Mojiang. By 1999, Mojiang had achieved 6-year compulsory education, and by 2000 Mojiang had wiped out adult illiteracy. By 2004, Mojiang had 191 primary schools consisting of 1016 classes. The school population was 27,335, and teachers and staff amounted to 1661. It was reported that 99.6 % of school-aged children were admitted to primary schools.

At present, all school-aged Hani children can receive nine-year compulsory education. Preschool education has also been introduced to the Hani communities at the township level. By 2004, there were four kindergartens with 2092 students. In the Republic of China (ROC) period (1911–1949), there were only two preschool classes in the Lianzhu Primary School with 160 young children. The "Two Basic Project"[4] 双基工程 passed the annual national appraisement in 2006.

Table 6.1 Education in Mojiang (data from a general introduction to Mojiang Hani Autonomous County of Yunnan Province; A brief history of the Hani people; Chinahani online 2008; Chinese ethnicity and religion online 2010; Pu'er education and information online)

	Preschool/students	Primary school/students	Secondary school/students		Vocational school/students	College students
1907	NA	87	junior	senior	NA	NA
1912	NA	50	NA	NA	NA	NA
1949	2/160	NA	1/43	NA	NA	NA
2004	4/2092	191/27,335	14/16,593	2/2393	1/2832	NA
2008	8/NA	79/NA	15/NA	2/NA	1/NA	3000*

Note: NA means not available, and 3000 is the total number of college students from 1994 to 2008

---

[4]The "Two Basic Project" aims to popularize nine-year compulsory education and eliminate illiterate adults. The ex-premier Peng Li promised at a UNESCO conference that China would eliminate illiteracy by 2000 and would achieve the 9-year compulsory education by 2010.

Like primary education, secondary education developed rapidly during the past 30 years. By 2004, Mojiang had 14 junior secondary schools and one ethnic secondary school with a student population of 16,593. Senior secondary education was divided into two tracks: general high school and vocational secondary school. Before 1949, there was only one senior secondary school with 43 students. Only 14 of the 43 finished their schooling. By the middle 1980s, five senior high schools were established in Mojiang. By 2004, Mojiang had two high schools and one vocational school with a student population of 2393 and 2832, respectively. In 2008, 97.70 % of school-aged children were admitted to primary school (Editing committee of Pu'er Local History 2009). The average years of school attainment amounted to 6.41 years. The expenditure on education was 125 million Yuan which was 8.6 % above the level of the previous year (Wang 2009). Now, an educational network ranging from preschool to senior secondary school is well established.

Other measures include the joint special programs for ethnic minority students (Pu'er local history editing committee 2009). For example, bilingual education (teaching Han script with Hani interpretation) was introduced in Shuikui Junior Primary School. In the first year, the Hani was the medium of instruction and starting from the second year, more Chinese was introduced. At that time, teachers often did home visits to inspect their students' study conditions. The Hani students in the village showed great respect for their teachers and studied very hard in a positive atmosphere.

In terms of higher education, there was not a single Hani college student before the 1950s. Now, there are about 3000 Hani university students among whom 10 have obtained PhD degrees and four are university teachers (Li 2008). However, the literacy level of Hani people is still very low in comparison to most ethnic groups in Yunnan. The high dropout rate of female students is a case in point. It is a pity that no dropout rates are reported by the official documents.

6.1.4 Hani People's Perception of Education

He (2005) argues that the traditional education of the Hani has both a positive and negative influence on modern education. These impacts are ideological and behavioral. The ideological impacts can be detected from the Hani's mindset of pragmatics, perception of studying just for becoming cadres[5], the emphasis on liberal arts and the ignorance of science and technology. For example, some Hani parents believe that if their children cannot become cadres after going to school, then what they need to learn is some practical knowledge such as understanding Putonghua or the way of doing business. For most Hani people, education is a

---

[5]Cadres are people who take leading political or administrative roles in factories, communes, governments, schools, the military and similar organizations. This is the number one choice for ethnic minority graduates after they "get rid of the destiny of being farmers.".

stepping stone for upward social mobility. They wish to become cadres and leave the status as farmers (*Tiaochu Nongmen* 跳出农门).

Wanting to be cadres is understandable as many Hani live in very isolated areas. Because of the limited socioeconomic development, some knowledge or skills taught at school may not be useful in their hometowns. Thus, to become cadres is the only motivation for school-aged children. With drastic higher education reform, graduates from tertiary or secondary technical schools are not assigned jobs anymore. As a result, the mindset of "it is no use to study" is being revitalized among some ethnic groups. Another mindset of the Hani, as He (2005) observed, is the desire to study liberal arts instead of science or engineering. She argues that, in terms of the content of Hani education, most knowledge is about social science. For instance, most Hani people admire heroes or the intelligent such as local chiefs, headmen, Mopi, blacksmiths and carpenters, who are engaged in labor.

The Hani also advocate learning by doing. For example, they acquire most knowledge or skills in the workshop or family. This mindset echoes with the modern educational concept of integrating theory with practice. However, the Hani ignore the knowledge that cannot be put into practice immediately. With this perception, some Hani people are only interested in simple mathematics and literacy. They assume that fundamental knowledge in math, physics, and biology has nothing to do with rural life and production. Except those who wish to become cadres after graduation, many Hani children are called back home by their parents after they finish primary or secondary school. He (2005, p. 377) criticizes this mindset because it results in "high enrollment, high dropout and low attainment."

6.1.5 *Local Policies to Promote the Education of the Hani*

The Yunnan provincial government has initiated special preferential policies since the 1950s to promote education for the Hani from elementary to tertiary levels. In 1952, the first ethnic minority primary school was established in Mojiang, and students were provided with accommodation and stationery for free. In 1988, the first ethnic class of the Mojiang No. 1 Middle School started to enroll ethnic students. In 2006, the first junior ethnic experimental school was established in Mojiang. This signified a complete education system for ethnic students, from preschool to high school. The school mainly enrolls students of ethnic minority background from the remote and mountainous areas.

One of the important measures in promoting education for the Hani is the preferential admission policies for the ethnic minority learners. These policies are made by both central and local level governments to ensure easy access to educational institutions at various levels. For example, in 1952, the Yunnan Institute of Nationalities made a special policy on enrollment. The university applicants of the Han, the Hui, the Bai, and the Naxi groups must be between 18 and 30 years old with a junior secondary school diploma or above. As for the applicants from other ethnic groups like the Hani, the minimum requirement was a primary school education.

Since 1979, the enrollment policy for the national matriculation examination was adjusted to select the best applicants. However, overall consideration was given to ethnic minority applicants. For example, since 1984, the ethnic applicants could be enrolled with 10–30 bonus points in the national matriculation examination. Moreover, some local governments such as the Honghe Hani and Yi Autonomous County made special quotas for the ethnic groups from the frontier or poor mountain areas. Eight ethnic groups (the Hani, the Yi, the Miao, the Yao, the Dai, the Zhuang, the Buyi, and the Lahu), receive 10–30 bonus points in the secondary technical school and normal school enrollment examinations.

The preferential policy also applies to ethnic applicants to tertiary institutions. For instance, due to backward local socioeconomic development, the entrance score of ethnic students is about 10–30 points lower than that for nonethnic students. The Yunnan University of Nationalities set up a "Preparation Program" (*Yuke Kecheng* 预科课程) to offer preliminary foundational courses for ethnic students. The "Preparatory Division" (*Yukebu* 预科部) of the university offers special remedial courses to help minority students bridge the gap between secondary and higher education.

6.2 The Story of Noma

6.2.1 *Family Background*

Noma was born into a Hani family in Mojiang County in the late 1980s. Mojiang is the only Hani Autonomous County in China with over 80 % of its population being Hani. By 2008, the population of Mojiang was 368,582. The Hani are the largest ethnic group in Mojiang with a population of 227,879 (Editing committee of Pu'er local history 2009).

Mojiang is located in the south of Yunnan Province, covering an area of 5312 m^2. As a mountainous county astride the Tropic of Cancer, Mojiang has three nicknames: "Hometown of the Hani," "Hometown of the Tropic of Cancer" and "Hometown of the Twin."

Noma's home town is Sangtian 桑田, a village attached to Lianzhu Town 联珠镇, the capital of Mojiang County. Mojiang is 152 km from Pu'er, the capital city of the Simao Prefecture. Since the Qing dynasty (1644–1911), Lianzhu had been the socio-political center of Mojiang and its administrative center since 1732. Lianzhu Confucian Academy 联珠书院 was the first school offering modern education in Mojiang.

Noma was born into a traditional Hani family. The whole family migrated from Dali to Mojiang as descendants of the Duan family. Her father was a very "advanced" farmer who served in the post of head of commune for decades. He always

6.2 The Case of Noma

took a leading role in community activities such as building roads and worshiping the gods of the mountains. He was an example to his children for sacrificing personal to collective interests. Noma's mother was a traditional Hani woman who was quite well-known for her diligence and capability. She not only raised four children of her own. She also raised her two younger brothers and supported them through higher education in the 1980s.

Noma was the youngest child in her family. I was surprised when I learned that she was the fourth child in the family with two elder brothers and one elder sister. It was not strange for ethnic minority families in Yunnan to have more than two children[6], I was still quite curious how Noma's father could challenge the national policy of family planning and be recognized as "model citizen." I supposed that Noma came into the world by accident. The birth of Noma brought the family not only more pleasure but also more economic pressure. No one expected this Hani girl to become the first female university student in her village and the first Hani girl to visit the United States of America several years later.

6.2.2 Financial Problems

Noma's memories of her childhood are full of poverty and hard labor. She told me she spent her childhood doing housework as many children from poor families did.

> I had endless chores to do at home. It was the nature of children to have fun but I had to do the farm work reluctantly with my parents every day. Thus, my childhood memory was full of resentment and complaint.
>
> (Noma, Autobiography, December 22, 2009)

The cost of education for four children was prohibitive. Although Noma's parents worked desperately hard in the fields, the income from farming was limited, Noma reflected:

> It was not a small sum for a farmer family to pay over 6000 Yuan tuition for four children each year. My parents went all out in the field, but the barren field yielded very little. In drought season, despite our utmost expectation, the crops remained still and fruitless. In cold winter nights, I often picked up the vein of the potato with my mom in the dim light till midnight. My hands and feet were frozen numb and red. I had to struggle to keep awake while picking up the potato each time.
>
> (Noma, Interview, September 25, 2009)

Apart from farm work, Noma would prepare dinner with her mother and finish her homework on time every day. The reward of her hard work would be a chance

---

[6]China has executed a very strict policy since the late 1970s. The couple living in the city or township can have only one child, but a couple in the countryside can have no more than two children. For ethnic minority couples in the remote rural areas, the two-child policy is not strictly implemented.

to go to the local fair on market day in a pretty "old but clean dress," to watch TV in her friends' house, or to eat an apple in the mid-autumn festival.

Many a time, Noma told me that living in poverty during her childhood brought about "an implicit lower self-esteem and frustration." When I questioned Noma about why she felt like this she said:

> (I felt like this) just because we were poor. Once my mother and I tried to sell our self-planted vegetable to others but they (the potential customers) refused to buy our vegetables. They were rich, we were poor, and so I had very low self-esteem.
> (Noma, Autobiography, December 22, 2009)

When I asked Noma how she felt about this more than ten years later, she replied:

> I feel the same, as I still hold the feeling like that. If you are a vegetable vendor you must be poor to some extent. If you are capable of doing other things you don't have to make money by selling vegetables. Because we were poor we had no choice but to sell vegetables. After I became a college student, I made up my mind that I would not sell vegetables anymore. Since then, I was even unwilling to go to the trade fair with my mother anymore.
> (Noma, Interview, January 15, 2010)

Noma had been a happy top student in her primary school. She had been awarded the title of *"Three-merit Student"* (*sanhao xuesheng* 三好学生) from year one to year six. However, due to her examination nerves, she failed in the entrance examination to the key secondary school in Mojiang. She was just one point short of being enrolled at the No.1 middle school, the best secondary school in Mojiang. At that time, she had two choices, to pay an extra RMB1600 per academic year to go to the key school or to attend a vocational school. After serious consideration, she chose the key middle school with the sponsorship of her two uncles:

> My parents had to pay RMB1600 a year for my high school education. That was very expensive at that time. My accommodation at school would cost another RMB800 so it would cost my parents over RMB2000 per year. If my parent did not make a decision to send me to that key school with my uncles' financial assistance I would not become a university student now. I might have gone to vocational school and become a migrant worker later. I might have gotten married now.
> (Noma, Interview, January 15, 2010)

Fortunately, with Noma's efforts, she became a public-sponsored student in her second year due to her learning attainment. Her family did not have to pay the extra tuition fee any more. Noma was very diligent in junior secondary school. However, her elder sister Nomy told me that Noma's personality changed. She was no longer a cheerful girl as she was in the primary school.

Noma's fear of poverty led to her decision to stay in Kunming, the capital city of Yunnan Province, rather than going back to her hometown of Mojiang. She told me clearly in our first face-to-face talk: "Since I have spent so many years studying at university I will no longer go back to the countryside. I have to try my best to study in the city or I will disappoint my parents" (Noma, Interview, September 25, 2009).

Regardless of her hard childhood, Noma also enjoyed some happy memories of her hometown. She told me she was born in a "remote small village with dark green forests, golden paddy fields and lovely playmates" (Noma, Autobiography, December 22, 2009). She did enjoy her family as "my parent never gave special treatment to any single child. They treated us equally as my mother said, 'I treated the four children with equal love'" (Noma, Autobiography, December 22, 2009). Noma's elder sister, Nomy, confirmed this by saying:

> Although we lived in the countryside, we had a very good family atmosphere. We began to know what education would bring us because our two uncles set very good examples for us. As they were good at learning, they received special treatment (they were supported to finish their tertiary education). And they also cared about our study.
> (Nomy, Online chat, September 16, 2009)

Noma was born in the early 1980s. At that time, China had just embarked on economic reforms and opened its doors to the world. The socioeconomic development in Yunnan was very slow, however, particularly in the remote mountain area where Noma lived. The financial situation of a seven-member family like Noma's was even worse. At that time, compulsory education had not been implemented, so school fees were a big burden for an extended family like Noma's. Poverty can lower self-esteem and exclude poor people from education. Fortunately, Noma's parents believed that education could change their life so they supported their children's schooling at whatever cost. With the Hani heritage of persistence and hard work (Wang 2003), they changed their family's destiny.

The memory of a poor childhood and the resulting humiliation has followed Noma. This memory is very common among many ethnic minority students in Yunnan. This memory may either stimulate them to work hard to get rid of poverty, as in Noma's case, or weaken their confidence.

6.2.3 Family Influence

Being the youngest daughter in her family brought Noma no privilege but rather more responsibilities and challenges. However, Noma gave credit to her parents and siblings for helping shape her perceptions of love, life, and friendship.

In Noma's eyes, her father was a quiet, advanced, unselfish, model CPC[7] village cadre. He always took leading roles in village activities such as building roads and participating in religious services. Noma resembled her father in terms of personality and morality. In her eyes, "he is a guy who would rather suffer self-loss but be considerate for others." Noma followed her father's example. She was very unselfish and always ready to help others.

Her mother was a smart and capable woman. She was good at farm work and saving money for her children's education. She also enjoyed singing ethnic folk songs and was curious about new things. For example, in the off-season, she learned to surf the Internet. Noma's parents were quite proud to have a daughter who was

---

[7]CPC refers to the Communist Party of China, the ruling party of the People's Republic of China.

not only a good student but also considerate to others. When I questioned Noma's parent on their daughter being a college student, her mother said, "I am very happy she made progress in her study and became mature. She can get along well with others and is concerned about her parents. She is not only frugal in life, but also willing to do part-time jobs to reduce our economic burden." Noma's father was also satisfied with his daughter commenting, "She has grown up now. I am a CPC member and she joined the CPC at university. I am very happy she has pursued political advancement."

Noma's second elder brother was handicapped. He suffered from a terrible wound to his waist. However, he never complained of his fate. Instead, he lived with a heart of thanksgiving and finally married a local Hani woman. Noma acknowledged that her second elder brother was a good model of self-reliance and optimism. Noma admired her brother, commenting:

> He respected my parents very much and never let them worry about him. When I was very fragile and weak, I would think of my second senior brother. He was so strong and optimistic that I could not find any excuse to give up or complain.
>
> (Noma, Autobiography, December 22, 2009)

Noma's two maternal uncles played critical roles in her education and personal development. As Noma's grandmother died young, it was Noma's mother who brought up her two younger brothers and supported them in finishing their college education. The two brothers treated their elder sister as a mother. Later, the two uncles helped their sister's children finish their education. As Nomy pointed out, "The two uncles treated us with great concern like our parents. They were the policymakers concerning our education in our family."

Noma confessed that she sometimes fell into deep depression due to financial and academic problems. However, she was very brave in facing these issues and solving problems by herself. She reported:

> I told myself that I had to be strong and optimistic. Whenever I called home, I would just report the good news rather than bad news. I would not let my parent worry about me, but let them have pride in me.
>
> (Noma, Interview, September 25, 2009)

From the episodes presented above, I was deeply impressed by the power of the role models provided by family members. I was also impressed by the Hani traditions of family unity and mutual assistance (Wang 2003; Long 2008). Noma inherited the merits of diligence and frugality from her mother, of endurance and appreciation from her brother, of generosity and leadership from her father, and of determination to pursue knowledge from her uncles. It can be seen that her attachment to her family and her ethnic community played a critical role inempowering her to become a successful ethnic minority learner. Without her uncles' financial and intellectual support Noma would never have become a college student later.

6.2.4 Language Shift Between Daily Life and Classroom

Like Mammuts' case presented in the previous chapter, Noma also experienced the challenge of a language shift in her journey through schooling. Noma grew up in a pure Hani community, and Hani was her first language. When she went to primary school she spoke Hani only, but she also picked up a few words in Putonghua from her parents. "I could say a few words in Putonghua at that time," she told me, "but I could not speak it fluently. I learned Putonghua at school." The medium of instruction in her primary school was Putonghua, but the teacher would explain some difficult points in Hani. After school, Noma spoke Hani to her Hani peers and Putonghua to other non-Hani. At home, Noma spoke Hani to her siblings. She acknowledged that her brothers and sister could speak much better Hani than she:

> I only learned to speak Hani when I was young. I lived in a Hani community, and people spoke more authentic Hani. I learned how to count in Hani, but nowadays children can only count in local Han dialect (*Dangdi Fangyan* 当地方言). My mother can count in Hani by saying "tima, nima, shuma, lima" (1, 2, 3, 4), but I can only count in fangyan. With authentic Hani, I can only count from one to ten. Children born in the later 1980s like me knew little how to count in Hani, and my elder brother and sisters know more than I did.
> (Noma, Interview, September 25, 2009)

When I asked Noma whether she wished to learn how to count in Hani, she replied without any hesitation: "I am learning. I want to learn so I often learn from my mother." After Noma went to university, she only spoke Hani when she met Hani friends or called home. In general, she spoke more *fangyan* 方言 (local Chinese) to her schoolmates. "When I spoke Hani, my non-Hani friends assumed that I was speaking Japanese," she said.

Noma's journey to learn Chinese was not so smooth. At primary school, she found it quite difficult to speak and write Chinese. She learned to read word for word and wrote each stroke with her teacher holding her hand. Fortunately Noma was motivated to learn Chinese, and she learned it quickly during primary school.

At middle school, all subjects were taught in Putonghua, and the chances of speaking Hani were less. Noma's Chinese proficiency developed so well that she could write beautiful essays in Chinese when she graduated from her primary school. However, Noma still believed that her Hani proficiency was much better than her Chinese. It seemed to her that Chinese was just a communicative language for life but that Hani was a more animated language for describing things. She said, "Chinese is only a public language. That is to say, every person uses those words and expressions. A public language cannot be delicate, while the Hani is more accurate and animated."

Noma attributed her advanced Hani proficiency to her early childhood acquisition. She said, "Perhaps I had learned more Hani than Chinese when I was very young. Therefore, you can find more traces of the Hani language in me." (Noma, Interview, January 15, 2010).

At university, Noma spent most of her time and energy learning English, although she enrolled in the course College Chinese in her first year. Noma felt perplexed about the two languages. She understood it was very important for ethnic minority students to master the common language—Chinese. She argued that:

> In the Chinese family composed of 56 nationalities, each ethnic group has its own language, but if we want to communicate with one another we have to use Chinese. To master Chinese is an overwhelming trend and fundamental requirement. When you master a new language, you will have more options. Our native language and culture are our property, while Chinese and English are keys to success.
> (Noma, Interview, January 15, 2010)

At the same time, Noma acknowledged that her Chinese proficiency was problematic. She told me some about her classmates could not write a note of absence in standard Chinese. After she studied College Chinese, she shifted her attention to English and Japanese.

> As for Chinese, I read Chinese books often before I went to college but very few now. Now I just read books on building up English vocabulary. I set a goal and then start to do it. It is a pity I seldom read Chinese now. It is the case of China. It seems that I have forgotten many things in Chinese. Now my main contact with Chinese is to read *Information Daily*[8] and surf the Internet. Now many college students surf the Internet just to enjoy recreation messages. They pay little attention to the stuff with culture background. We go to the library just to look for references. We don't go there to read something with any purpose.
> (Noma, Interview, January 15, 2010)

Much like Mammuts, Noma mentioned her translation course at university. She found her translation from Chinese to English was too plain, while her teacher's model version was full of the flavor of Chinese culture. She thought her "sole of Chinese" (Chinese language foundation) was very thin. Though Chinese was a major subject in the national matriculation examination, most students learned Chinese just to excel in the test. In her reflection, this is a narrow-minded perception. She suggested that Chinese classes at university should be offered as elective courses, so that non-Chinese majors could choose those of interest to them. She even suggested transforming the Chinese major classes into elective courses and encouraging non-Chinese majors to sit in. Noma attributed the decline of Chinese proficiency partially to university curriculum and partially to students' reading habits:

> Now many students surf the Internet just for fun. They pay little attention to the stuff which entailed rich language and culture messages. We look for reference for the sake of references and seldom take the initiative to read books in the library. When I was working in an English summer camp I was often troubled by my diction in my speech. I did wish my Chinese was better. It is only when it was the time to apply knowledge that you would regret not acquiring enough of it.
> (Noma, Interview, September 25, 2009)

Like Mammuts, Noma also experienced language shift between daily life and classroom learning, but her story has some very different implications. First, Noma found she could not speak authentic Hani anymore. Her gradual loss of her cultural

---

[8]*Information Daily* is a local newspaper in Kunming, Yunnan, China.

heritage was an important issue for her. To compensate, she sought to learn authentic Hani from her siblings and elders in her village. This sorry-for-loss mentality shows that Noma would rather not lose the attachment to her ethnic community. Kramsch (1998, p. 77) had argued that native language has become the "most sensitive indicator of the relationship between an individual and a given social groups."

Noma had no extra energy to improve her native language skills because she had to spend more time enhancing her second language, Chinese, and mastering her third language, English. Furthermore, she was to learn Japanese as her second foreign language. This is required of foreign language major students in China. As a result, Noma was desperate in coping with four languages. Ignorance of one's native language and limited time to study other languages resulted in less learning attainment. Noma finally failed in TEM-8, the most demanding English proficiency test, the national examination for English majors.

The dilemma of Noma calls for an urgent review of the current policies on language revitalization and planning. For example, what should the priorities be in multilingual acquisition—the heritage language or the nonnative language with market value? What kind of curriculum should be developed to maintain the native language and enhance the new languages?

6.2.5 Learning English as the Third Language

As it is for many other ethnic minority learners, English was the third language for Noma. Noma chose English as her major at YUN for three reasons. First, she loved learning English. She believed English was an international language. If she could master it, she would have more job opportunities in the future.

Second, her uncles and aunts were English teachers in her high school and her uncle was even her own English teacher. Her elder sister also preferred English. Now Noma still remembered how her uncle taught her elder sister English with a little blackboard at home. She recalled, "When he was coaching my sister in English, I just stood beside them and listened. I was very young at that time. Maybe this experience had some impact on me, and since then I dreamed of being an English teacher" (Noma, Interview, September 25, 2009).

At university, Noma was a very diligent student. To improve her English pronunciation, she started her day at 7 a.m. to do morning readings. She believed that morning readings improved her pronunciation and increased her language awareness. She also became a frequent visitor to three English corners on and off her university campus. She told me:

> Other students did morning readings, too, but I forced myself to do more. For example, I would memorize an additional five new words. When they were still enjoying their sleeping, I would get up and memorize two model essays.
>
> (Noma, Interview, September 25, 2009)

Noma did experience great difficulties in acquiring English as a foreign language. She told me her major problems in learning English were pronunciation and grammar:

> As I got used to speaking my native language (Hani), I felt a bit awkward in learning English. I had some problems in English pronunciation. In terms of grammar, English grammar is of SVO[9] structure, while our Hani grammar is SOV[10]. For example, we say "I have my breakfast had" rather than "I have had my breakfast". If I had not learned Chinese and accepted Chinese grammar, I would not have mastered English grammar.
>
> (Noma, Interview, September 25, 2009)

It seemed to Noma that learning Chinese had changed her mindset. She told me if she only spoke Hani she would never have understood what her English teacher was discussing. With her unremitting effort, Noma improved her English proficiency dramatically and achieved prominent academic success. In her resume, I read her brilliant awards: runner-up of the CCTV[11] English speech contest at YUN (2009), Scholarship of Long Shengwen and Certificate of TEM-4[12] (2008).

Noma was strongly motivated to learn English. The motivation came from her expectation of social mobility as the result of mastering an international language. Her motivation also came from her uncle who taught English at her senior secondary school. Noma's case matches Gu's (2008) observation that English learning involves complex issues like motivation, identity, and culture. For Noma, learning English was very difficult as it is different from Hani in phonetic and grammatical structure. Thanks to Chinese, which is similar in grammatical structure to English, Noma found a path to English learning. In this sense, Noma benefited from a positive language transfer. However, whether L1 or L2 learning will facilitate L3 acquisition is still being debated, given the linguistic distance and context (Stern 1983; Ytsma 2001).

6.2.6 Tensions Within the Curriculum

Like Mammuts, Noma also experienced some tensions within the university curriculum. First, she complained about the frequent changes of teachers in the Course of Advanced English. In the past three academic years, her class has had 6–7 teachers for this course. Students had just got used to one teacher's instruction style

---

[9]SVO is the short form of subject, verb and object

[10]SOV is the short form of subject, object and verb.

[11]English speech contest is sponsored by China Central Television, a major state broadcaster in mainland China.

[12]TEM refers to the Test for English majors. It is a national test developed by the National Foreign Language Teaching and Learning Advisory Board to evaluate the English proficiency of English major undergraduate students at colleges and universities. TEM-4 refers to the test for English major band 4. It is a national test of English proficiency for English majors at the end of their second year.

and then they had to adjust to another. She told me she disliked the course Advanced English very much. On the one hand, some teachers' lecturing was boring. On the other hand, some texts were old and tedious. Actually, I knew her textbook very well for I used the same one 20 years earlier as an English major. Since the late 1990s, non-English majors have over a dozen choices of college English textbooks, but the choice for English major textbooks is very limited. Given the large number of non-English majors, publishers compete with one another in order to make a profit.

Noma told me that her three favorite courses were Listening Comprehension, English Writing, and Translation. As for other courses like Audiovisual English, she thought they were boring. I asked her why she did not like Audiovisual English, a course often delivered by native English speakers; she told me that:

> The courses of Oral English and Audio-visual English were usually given by the expatriate teachers. We didn't like their style of instruction very much. At their classes, they played games all day long. You see, when Chinese teachers gave lectures, they wrote a lot of notes on the blackboard, but the expatriate teachers wrote nothing there. They just played games or let us talk, so on and so forth. Their lecturing was very boring and tedious. If they taught like this in the first two years we could accept them, but we could not put up with them in the third and/or fourth year if they still instructed like that. It seems that every expatriate teacher would teach in this way. Our mindsets just could not accept it. I personally prefer the instruction style of Chinese teachers.
>
> (Noma, Interview, September 25, 2009)

In general, Noma took a pragmatic attitude toward the university curriculum and various examinations:

> One of my classmates complained that she had learned little at university, but I think university is a place to build up competence and vision. In addition, universities can be different from one to another. Take our university for example, It cannot provide us many chances and hardware, so we have to strive for more. No one will give you resources if you don't take the initiative to seek them out.
>
> (Noma, Autobiography, December 22, 2009)

Aware of her weak English foundation, Noma took every chance to improve her English and prove her legitimacy as an excellent ethnic minority learner in the mainstream system. To her, examination is a means but not a goal for her academic success. Therefore, she sat for many examinations like TEM-4 and TEM-8, as well as tests for English Tour Guide Certificate, Junior English-Chinese Translation Certificate, Putonghua Certificate, Teacher Qualification Certificate, and Computer Proficiency Certificate. She passed five of these tests and failed two of them.

Although Noma passed TEM-4 smoothly in her second year, she failed TEM-8 in her fourth year. It was the second blow for Noma in her schooling history.[13] Noma devoted much energy to preparing for the test. She quit all her part-time jobs and withdrew from the Student Union. She spent the 2009 Chinese New Year at her elder sister's home so that she could concentrate on preparing for the test. Her sister

---

[13]The first blow was her failure in the secondary school entrance examination. She failed when applying to the key county middle school.

told me during an online talk, "She is at my home now. As the test will start in March, she is very nervous." Unfortunately, Noma failed in this crucial test despite her great effort. She was very frustrated and sad. She wrote a blog to document her feelings after the test:

> Life is filled with changes, most of which may result in our failure or unexpected blow. These days are my gray days; I really can't accept the result or even I hope it were wrong. But I can't cheat myself, in fact, I failed. "It's ok!" I told myself more than a hundred times, but it is useless. It is very important for everyone and so do I, but I lost it. I have gained something and also have paid everything. To be honest, these days are very hard for me. I even dare not look at others into their eyes, and I lost my confidence and smiles. I know I can try again like they said to me, but it is very difficult for me, maybe for everyone.
> (Noma, Blog, May 28, 2011)

In this section, I narrated Noma's tensions within the YUN curriculum: the administration (the frequent change of teachers), courses of study; instructional materials (textbooks), teaching style of expatriate teachers, and her failure in TEM-8. The narration suggests that the total university environment (Banks 2009) put Noma at a disadvantage. One of the major disadvantages is the demanding national English proficiency test (TEM-8) for English majors. To prove her legitimacy as an English major, Noma had to compete with her Han peers. A failure in the exam not only reduces the opportunity for good employment. It also leads to psychological problems such as loss of confidence and low self-esteem.

The tension with the expatriate teachers reflected a conflict in the culture of learning between East and West. The instruction style that fits for the dominant Han or western students may not function well at the YUN because of the diversified linguistic and cultural backgrounds of the students.

6.2.7 Psychological Problems

Like Mammuts, Noma went through some lingering psychological problems, a reflection of her frustration due to the examination failure. In her autobiography she reflected, "I had my blue days because of interpersonal relationships among teacher and student and students themselves. Those were thorny issues at that time" (Noma, Autobiography, December 22, 2009).

What struck her most was the sudden passing away of her most beloved teacher, Yong. This incident not only made her very sad, but it also changed her perception of life and death.

Yong was a woman who taught Noma Intensive English reading during her second year at YUN. In Noma's eyes, Yong was a teacher of grace and knowledge. Many a time, Noma talked about Yong with great gratitude and respect:

> She knew many things, but she was never arrogant, so I admired her very much. She was very kind to me and introduced to me the first tutoring opportunity. I kept this job till now. Although she has passed away, I will keep this job as long as possible. She was a very

serious teacher in teaching. She was very modest and honest. From her, I learned that I had to be honest and humble.

(Noma, Interview, January 15, 2010)

Noma was very sad for months when her beloved teacher died of cancer. She could not understand how such a nice teacher could have left her so suddenly. She said of her teacher, "She worked very hard for years, but she could not afford to buy a new apartment and had no chance to drive a car. I suppose it was due to fate. But I had never thought that she would leave us." Noma was in deep sorrow for a long time. It took her one month to resume her normal life. The loss of Yong made her realize the shortness of life and the significance of being healthy:

I never expected that. I never expected that Yong would leave us. Now I guess it is her fate. That is the fate. I suppose that she was very painful with tumor. Her passing away might help to reduce her pain. I know it would happen to her sooner or later, but was unfair to her daughter.

(Noma, Interview, September 25, 2009).

Many other students could not understand Noma's lingering sadness over Yong. Some students said: "Yong has left us for years. Why do you still mention her?" But for Noma, Yong was a role model of scholarship and morality. Noma expressed her deep respect for Yong. She wrote in a blog two years later:

Since November 2009, I began to miss her. I don't know how many people will think of her at this moment but at least "Monster" (a nickname of a female student) and I miss her. We wish her a good journey in another world. Don't worry about us.

(Noma, Blog, May 1, 2011)

As I have mentioned, the Hani are a sensitive and introspective ethnic group with a very high self-esteem (Zhang 1996; Bai and Wang 1998). They have a natural view of life and death. They do not believe in reincarnation (Long 2008). Hence, many internal and external factors will influence their psychological health. Noma's lower self-esteem arising from her poverty-stricken childhood was reinforced by her failure in the national English test. The death of her beloved teacher was a big blow and a lingering sorrow that haunted her for years. This episode indicates the urgent need to provide quality counseling for ethnic minority students.

6.2.8 Culture Shock and Reentry Shock

When Noma was admitted to YUN, she had no idea how to adapt herself to the new environment or to communicate with other newcomers. She recalled:

As a matter of fact, I felt very uneasy and uncomfortable when we came to YUN in the first year. People did not know what they should say and how to talk to each other, for most of us came from different parts of China. You would feel better if you were classmates or from the same secondary school. If you came from the same place, you would treat each other like brothers and sisters.

(Noma, Interview, January 15, 2010)

Under the influence of some senior students, Noma joined the Student Union (SU). Since she had more free time at university, she thought it was good to gain some social experiences and fulfill her dreams. She told me she benefited greatly from joining the Student Union:

> By working in the Student Union, I developed my social skills and experiences. As I worked for the Public Liaison Division, I had to do many things. When other students were napping or doing shopping, I had to go to the SU office to work…I contacted a lot of things at SU. SU was very complicated as the society. I found some students there were very sophisticated. She could please both the upper leader and the subordinate. I consider this sophistication a kind of ability. Maybe she would play some tricks sometimes, but she was really capable.
> (Noma, Interview, September 25, 2009).

After staying in Kunming, the capital city of Yunnan Province for more than three years, Noma found she could not adapt to the life in her hometown anymore. She found the provincial capital city was more attractive. When she was young, she often went to the trade fair in the county capital with her parents. She admired the modernity of the county city life, but today she has changed her mind:

> At that time, I assumed that the county city was so good, but now I found it very dirty and people's *Suzhi* (quality) was not so good and needed further improvement. After you have traveled a lot, you will have a different feeling. Now Kunming is competing for the selection of civil city. I had no sense like this when I was young. If you compare the two cities, you will know which one is better.
> (Noma, Interview, January 15, 2010)

Historically, the Hani have been called "mountain people." They lived in the remote and geographically isolated areas and seldom went to town (Lei 2002). In modern China, due to the underdeveloped social economy in their area, few Hani have experienced traveling outside their community. Noma's feelings of isolation and loneliness are understandable. Therefore, I borrowed the concept of "cultural shock" from the study of intercultural communication to refer to the dislocation of EMLs who have moved out of their original communities for better education or work opportunities. It is usually believed that, "cultural shock" or "reentry shock" may bring about some "acculturative stress" (Berry 2003), due to dislocation from a familiar environment.

Under these circumstances, orientation in university life becomes most important. University clubs should play more active roles, and "intercultural communication" should be offered as a course of general education so that all students, regardless of major, will know how to talk with people of different backgrounds. Only in this way will the ethnic minority culture, as Postiglione (2009) has expected, be brought into the spotlight without dislocating ethnic communities.

Noma's admiration of city life and her estrangement from village life is very normal. To prevent the brain drain in ethnic minority education at all levels, it is critical to break down the vicious circle of poverty and illiteracy (Wan and Yang 2008).

6.2.9 Challenge of Being Class Monitor

Noma had been the monitor of her class from 2006 to 2010. She was also the director of the Public Liaison Division of the faculty Student Union. Her regular duty was to carry out class activities and recommend stipend and scholarship candidates. Because of her management abilities, she was very popular among her fellow students and teachers.

Qing, a Tibetan male student told me during an online talk his impression of Noma. In his eyes, Noma was a warm-hearted, generous, responsible monitor, always ready to help others. He told me Noma was very considerate of others and always treated people with sincerity. She lived a simple life. I asked Qing for a concrete example:

> When you need her help she would never escape with any excuse. For example, if you are sick she will inquire about your illness and give you some medicine. If there is any message of recruitment she will inform the whole class at the first notice.
> (Student YUN, Qing, Online chat, December 14, 2009)

Noma described herself in her resume as an open-minded, honest, active, independent girl with very good communication skills and team spirit. Under her leadership, her class was awarded the title of Excellent Class of YUN and "May Fourth Movement League[14]" at provincial level. When I asked her whether she had leadership abilities, she replied:

> When I was working in the Student Union, some classmates mentioned about it and later in the summer school and the secondary school where I worked as a student teacher, some teachers also talked about it. So I guess I may have leadership, but I am not sure.
> (Noma, Interview, May 30, 2010)

Noma told me of an episode involving her class. A middle-aged male teacher took the place of a female teacher of intensive English after the she went abroad to pursue her PhD. The ex-teacher was a very active and open-minded woman. She encouraged students' participation in her class. The new teacher preferred the teacher-centered approach, so his class was very boring and dull. The sudden change in teaching style incurred resistance. Noma reflected:

> In those days, most students were very frustrated; they just sat still in the classroom. The resistant and refusal atmosphere prevailed in the class. So I talked to them when the class was over, "How could you do like this (refuse to listen)? If you have anything to say, write me a note and I will negotiate with the teacher. However, you should know it was not easy for a teacher to stand in front of us giving lectures for hours. If you do want to learn, you can learn from each teacher despite his instruction style. Each teacher has his/her scholarship for you to learn. In addition, the faculty would not change the teacher at random for the sake of your like or dislike. This is the reality."
> (Noma, Interview, September 25, 2009)

---

[14]The May Fourth Movements was an intellectual revolution that happened between 1917 and 1921. The movement aimed to achieve national independence, emancipation of the individual and reconstruction of society and culture. May Fourth Movement League is an honorable title for the outstanding student community at tertiary institutions in Yunnan Province.

With Noma's mediation, the teacher accepted students' criticism and improved his style of instruction. When he left YUN to pursue his PhD overseas years later, his students found it hard to say good bye to him. The experience convinced Noma to know that interpersonal communication rather than confrontation is crucial. If she could convey students' opinions to teachers in private and positive ways, teachers might accept students' advice and students might accept the teacher gradually:

> You know if some students are critical of teachers they may hold a rebellious attitude. I am different from them for I not only have to study but also communicate with teachers as monitor. I cannot contact teachers with this rebellious attitude. I have to consider the effect and consequence.
> (Noma, Interview, January 15, 2010)

Another issue that troubled Noma considerably was the recommendation of scholarship/stipend candidates. On the one hand, she did wish that all her fellow students could obtain the scholarships/stipends. On the other hand, the quota of scholarships was very limited. Noma told me:

> Other classes might fight for the chance of scholarships/stipends and even play tricks. I hope to consider all the students' interests, but it is very hard when it comes time to recommend scholarship/stipend candidates. Both our teachers and we student cadres feel quite embarrassed at this moment. As you can see, we have more female students in our faculty, and the females are abominable. They are not like males who were straight forward. Female students will not say a lot in front of you but gossip a lot behind so I felt great pressure sometimes. I would try my best to be fair and I would handle the case based on fact.
> (Noma, Interview, September 25, 2009)

Honesty and frankness were also Noma's standards for friendship. She liked to make friends with those who were kind and honest. Therefore, after Noma found some of her roommates cheating in applying for stipends, she was very irritated.

> One female student filled out false information in the investigation form of household economic condition. Even if you want to change something, how can you change your parents' information by claiming they are losing labor power, handicapped? That is impossible; I know her parents work for the township government and middle school. I cannot accept the cheating of students especially who I know quite well. If I know the truth, I cannot accept it.
> (Noma, Interview, January 15, 2010)

However, Noma refused to report the cheater after she found out the truth. Later, the cheating was reported by another student, and the cheater was forced to return the money (about RMB750). Noma told me, "If I were the reporter I would not have done that for I didn't have the heart to do that. Since she had changed the message and submitted the form, I would not complain anymore." It is quite clear that Noma faces the dilemma of maintaining fairness and justice as a class monitor or following the Hani tradition of tolerance, harmony, and peaceful coexistence. In this incident, it seemed that fairness yielded to the powerful Hani habitus of interpersonal relationships.

Honesty and kindness were important teachings in Noma's family. Since childhood, Noma, her brothers and sister were taught to be honest. Her elder brother had been scolded by her mother for telling lies, and she herself was given a beating by her mother. She recalled:

> When my mother came to me with a thin stick I was very sad of being wronged. She had used the stick to threaten me but this time she hit me by a slap in my face. I hated her very much for I had been a docile girl and done a lot of housework. However, it was that slap that let me know I had to be honest, and I learned that no lie or cheating could be tolerated.
> (Noma, Interview, January 15, 2010)

It can be seen from this section that Noma was a student with strong leadership and potential. She was very popular among her fellow students. She was a role model in study, in her management capacity, in her attitude toward mutual assistance, in integrity, and in wisdom in handling difficult issues. Nurtured by her Hani heritage, she was generous, active, and always ready to help others. It was out of a natural view of human–nature relationships that Noma succeeded in easing the tensions between rebellious students and their teacher. Her appeasement strategy in dealing with the cheating student also mirrored her Hani values, which emphasized "unity," "tolerance," and "no competition" (Wang 2003).

6.2.10 Thanksgiving Attitude

In my talk with Noma, a phrase I heard repeatedly was "thanksgiving." Noma credited her success as a college student to her parents, her two uncles, her teachers, her schoolmates, and the state's preferential policy for ethnic minority groups. She wrote in her autobiography:

> I want to thank my parents first. They didn't have enough to eat at difficult times but tried their best to educate us. Many girls of my age now have become mothers and are living hard life. I thank my parent for they not only brought me up but also taught me life was hard and not easy. My parents are just ordinary and kind farmers. They wish to give more to their children but they cannot. What they can give us is nothing but all their love. Family is not sunshine but more valuable like the sunshine. Even if I travel to the end of the earth I can still feel the sunshine of my family.
> (Noma, Autobiography, December 22, 2009)

During her holiday visits, Noma would help her parents do farm work. She called her parents on both Mother's Day and Father's Day though she knew they had no idea of these two western festivals. Her mother was very moved by her daughter's greeting each time. She even gave half of her scholarship to her mother once and promised to buy her parents something with her first month's salary. "I want to thank my teachers," Noma said, "They lit up my road ahead and signposted my development. Teachers are candles. They burn themselves silently and present us with their love and concern in spark."(Noma, Autobiography, December 22, 2009).

Even now, Noma visits her former teachers when she goes home. She writes them one or two letters per semester to send season's greetings or report on her life and study at YUN. I asked Noma how she could maintain such a frequent contact with her ex-teachers. She said:

> When I was a middle school student, Yan, a beautiful and sentimental teacher read us a letter from her ex-student. She was moved to tears when she was reading it to us. I supposed that was the happiness of being a teacher. So I told myself later if I could go to university I would write to my teachers. And then I made it.
> (Noma, Interview, May 30, 2010)

Due to her leadership and hospitality, Noma won the support of her schoolmates. They often studied together, gossiped together, ate out together, and shopped together. When Noma was sick, her roommates often came to see her and helped her with her lessons:

> I want to thank my friends. It was them who accompanied me and shared with me the good and bad times in life. When I was in need, they would give me a hand without any hesitation and help me go through those hard times. We don't have to say too much with one another for we are the youth on the way of growing.
> (Noma, Autobiography, December 22, 2009)

In the spring of 2009, Noma worked in her local senior middle school as a student teacher for a senior-level class. After she finished her last class, her students surprised her by presenting her with a stuffed toy frog and by singing her a touching song. Noma could not remain composed and broke into tears. She responded with a choking: "Thank you all the students in Class 202. I can return nothing more but full-hearted gratitude and blessings. Thank you for the best memory you brought me, and I wish you academic progress and an enjoyable school life" (BLON-3).

Noma also mentioned that she was a beneficiary of the national preferential policy for ethnic university applicants. She was awarded 20 bonus points added on to the total marks of the national matriculation examination. "Without 20 points for ethnic minority students, I could not have come to YUN," she told me. Sometimes, she would discuss the significance of thanksgiving with her classmates:

> Owing to good state policy, we were so lucky to study at this university for ethnic groups. If we studied at other (non-ethnic) universities we might not have so much money (scholarships and stipends) and the ratio of scholarships would be not so adequate.
> (Noma, Interview, January 15, 2010)

Due to the nature of YUN, students usually have more opportunities than those of mainstream universities to be supported by various scholarships and stipends. However, not all ethnic students were grateful for the patronage they received. When disaster struck, such as the earthquake in Sichuan, students were asked to donate money. However, some ethnic minority students in Noma's class refused to donate. She felt irritated. She complained:

> Sometimes I tried to mobilize my classmates to donate money for other students in need or pay fees for class activities, but they told me they had no interest and commitment. So I

said, since you have got scholarships/stipends, you should know how to return and repay the society.

(Noma, Interview, January 15, 2010)

I asked Noma whether she would repay the society if she was very successful in the future. She said, "Yes, of course." I asked her how. She said, "I will patronize one or two students. I suppose I can make it. It is not the Project Hope,[15] which is too much for me. If I have the ability I would donate some money and support some students" (Noma, Interview, June 15, 2010).

She told me she intended to sponsor primary students and support them for as long as possible. "I like to support basic education for I know how a kid would feel if he/she cannot go to school. I prefer to support the younger students" (Noma, Interview, June 15, 2010).

Noma's thanksgiving attitude supports Lee's (2001) observation that parents of ethnic multilingual learners make great sacrifices to obtain a good education for their children. And the children reciprocate with gratitude and dedication throughout their schooling.

Noma's appreciative attitude resulted from both her Hani heritage and family's teaching. Hardship typified the Hani migration; so when they settled down and developed terraced paddy fields, they were grateful for the blessing of their mountain God. In the Hani community, mutual assistance is a very common practice, so Noma was used to "giving" rather than "taking." It was this simple philosophy that won Noma more friends from both the Hani and non-Hani communities. Her parents, siblings, and university teachers all provided role models for her. Noma practiced this attitude toward other individuals and the state. I appreciate Noma's aspiration to help young girls. At this point, she has much in common with Mammuts.

6.2.11 Being Chinese with Hani Characteristics

Before I Interviewed Noma, she did not think too much about her ethnic identity or her Hani culture. In her autobiography, she reflected on our communication:

I talked with you, I knew almost nothing about the value of being a member of an ethnic minority group. I only knew I could speak my native language, but never realized my language was a kind of "capital." After I had written something for you each time, I gained a lot, which was hard to describe. By reflecting on my personal story, I went over my life journey and found some driving force. It was you who let me know and find my ethnic value. (Noma, Autobiography, December 22, 2009).

---

[15]Project Hope is a Chinese public service project initiated by the China Youth Development Foundation (CYDF) and the Communist Youth League (CYL) Central Committee. Started on October 30, 1989, the project aims to improve schools in poverty-stricken rural areas with an aim of helping children complete elementary school.

According to my observations, Noma increased her "culture self-consciousness" (Fei 2003) through being an informant in my study. Frere (1994) sees this kind of conscientization as the first step on the road to empowerment. "Conscientization is the process through which oppressed people realize their cultural values are legitimate and worth maintaining" (Lee 2001, p. 60).

Postiglione (2009) argued that "ethnic minority students see school as an embodiment of future prosperity but distant from their values and the traditions of their communities" (p. 504). This observation is very true in the case of Noma. Noma's understanding of Hani culture was fragmented. Her knowledge about the Hani mainly came from simple readings and family memories. She said: "The Hani are an industrious and kind ethnic group. It is composed of 11 different branches speaking 11 dialects. Hani people prefer unity and mutual assistance. Inter-branch marriage is quite common for Hani people" (Noma, Interview, May 30, 2010).

Noma, as a Hani, held mixed feelings. On the one hand, she was very proud of being a Hani. When she was at home, she visited her county library and read some books on Mojiang's history. She also participated in the national examination for English tourist guides. One part of the test was devoted to the general knowledge of Yunnan and its ethnic minority groups. She mentioned the epics of Hani although she could not understand them quite well. She celebrated the Hani torch festival 火把节 in October and Hani New Year with her parents. She also hoped to learn embroidery from her mother and counting in the Hani from her grandfather. Like many Hani women, Noma's mother liked singing and even composed songs. She often sang these to Noma, but Noma seemed not very interested.

Jilong Festival (Dragon Worship Festival 祭龙节) is a native ceremony to worship the God of the mountain. In lunar May, Hani people kill pigs and carry out the ceremony in front of a big tree in the village. Noma's father was always an active organizer and participant. "It is the male's duty. The female has no qualification to do that," Noma told me. I asked why her father was so active. Noma told me her father was not only the ex-head of the commune but also a model CPC member. Noma told me her father was a mixture. On the one hand, he kept strong a faith in communism. On the other hand, he always took a leading role in village worship activities. In terms of religion, Noma had a half-hearted belief:

> Something in the village is superstitious, I suppose. They (villagers) may not realize it is a kind of superstition, but they believe if they do so their families will be safe and healthy. I can't help believing that if we don't follow the rule, something bad may happen. Is that a kind of conventional belief or mindset, I don't know. Anyhow my mother does believe that, and she required we children follow her. In order to make her feel well, we always follow her mind… I will do what she asked me to do as she always did for her mother. If something bad happens, I will feel guilty if I do not listen to her.
>
> (Noma, Interview, January 15, 2010)

So I asked Noma, as a CPC member how she perceived the relationship of political and religious beliefs as I knew CPC members claim to be atheists. She responded, "Communism is a belief or value orientation while worship is a native heritage. As a Hani, we worship the mountain since we were quite young so I don't think it is a contradiction" (Noma, Interview, May 30, 2010).

When Noma met new friends, she would not tell them her ethnicity, but if she was questioned about her hometown she would tell people she was a Hani. Despite exposure to three languages and cultures, Noma still displayed very strong Hani characteristics. For example, she criticized some Han students because of their "bad manners" in interpersonal communication. She praised Hani etiquette:

> Some of my ethnic features can be only seen at home. Etiquette is a case in point. I felt some Han students were casual sometimes, and I would rather accept some ethnic manners. For instance, some Han students just throw something to others or receive offers, without speaking "thank you," but we Hani have to reach out two hands to receive something or hand something. At home, I was taught how to serve guests tea. You can fill a cup of water, but not too full.
>
> (Noma, Interview, May 30, 2010)

Unconsciously, Noma had been maintaining her Hani identity and fighting against anything detrimental to Hani culture. For example, she had a childhood Hani playmate who worked in Guangzhou as a migrant worker. When a group of high school classmates met in Kunming she was very shocked to find the man could not speak authentic Hani but only spoke Hani with a Cantonese accent. "I could not accept that and felt very embarrassed, so did my ex-classmates. We began to scold him. We told him he had to switch to speaking authentic Hani, or we would not talk to him any more" (Noma, Interview, January 15, 2010). It can be seen from this incident, that the knowledge of ethnic minority language is an important indicator of one's identity and creates a strong sense of affiliation to one's nationality group.

On the other hand, Noma was perplexed about her increasing acculturation with the Han. She said:

> Now I am here (in Kunming) to study so I am getting away from my native culture and hometown. What I had was what I acquired when I was very young. However, as time goes I find I am losing my originality as a Hani. Now I am somewhat different from the native people.
>
> (Noma, Interview, September 25, 2009)

I once asked Noma, as she was a well-educated Hani, how she perceived her identity as Hani Chinese. She told me she was very proud of being both Hani and Chinese. She believed that Hani was a component of the Chinese nation. Due to patriotic education, she loved China very much. She told me her patriotic awareness increased with the rapid rise of China. She argued:

> If you look at the outside world, you will see much turmoil and disturbance.[16] You will feel so good to be Chinese. We have so many ethnic groups, but we can still develop so smoothly. I think it is not very easy for any country so I hold confidence in this country.
>
> (Noma, Interview, January 15, 2010)

Like the Naxi, the Hani self-identify with their ethnic group. What ties the Hani people together is common hardship, migration experience, concentrated residence, common language, shared religion, and, above all, tight family and community

---

[16]When I interviewed her in late 2009 the West was suffering from a financial crisis.

bonds. In contrast to the Naxi, with a large population, the Hani keep a low profile due to their mild, gentle, and introverted personalities (Bai and Wang 1998; Lei 2002). As for Noma in particular, she received both traditional and modern education. For example, she abided by the Hani traditions in religious worship and holiday celebration. What impressed me most was how she tried to integrate her cultural heritage with the communist doctrine. Like her father, Noma had a strong attachment to China and saw the Hani as a component of the Chinese ethnic family. Perhaps this strong national attachment resulted partially from Noma's patriotic education and partially from China's prosperity during the global recession. Therefore, I would like to call Noma a Chinese with Hani characteristics. I will discuss identity issues at the macro level later.

6.2.12 Dream of Being Noma-Amy

In 2007, a contest called Noma-Amay[17] was conducted in Mojiang to select the most beautiful Hani woman. The winners of the contest were awarded RMB80,000 and the title of Mojiang Tourist Image Ambassador. The selection process included a talent display, questions, and answers. The winners were twin sisters who studied at the Yunnan Arts University. Noma saw this beauty contest as a commercial activity as well as a promotion of Hani culture. She was very regretful that she knew nothing about the contest in advance:

> When the contest called for applications, I was at the university. I didn't know this till it was finished. They should have sent notice to each university in Kunming and invited those Hani students to participate. It was a great pity they did not send a message. We missed it for we knew nothing about it.
>
> (Noma, Interview, January 15, 2010)

Besides the contest, Mojiang County held other activities to introduce Mojiang and Hani culture to outsiders. For example, the Sun Festival 太阳节 and International Twins' Day 国际双胞胎节 are celebrated every year. Noma said, "I think Hani festivals should be publicized but not over commercialized. If is over commercialized, it will lose its original taste." To Noma, Noma-Amy is a Hani icon more than a beauty contest. She believed the contest would help to promote Hani culture and create business opportunities.

During the past two decades, cultural festivals have become very fashionable events favored by both local governments and ordinary people in ethnic minority areas labeled as *wenhua datai jingji changxi* 文化搭台 经济唱戏 (using culture to set the stage for business to put on a show). It has been believed that this mode would attract more domestic and foreign investment. However, Noma thought the beauty contest was not well organized because many Hani college students like her

---

[17]Noma-Amay was the birth place of the Hani in their legend, meaning a beautiful plateau in the north of Ai'lao Mountain, which was regarded as a land of promise.

were not informed in advance and because the tone of commerce outweighed that of Hani culture.

6.2.13 Dream, Reality, and Conflict

Noma was a girl full of dreams. In our conversations, she told me, she wished to be a teacher, a tour guide, a radio station anchor, or even a volunteer. She said, "In fact, I have no fixed intention on what to do or what to gain. For the long run, I wish I can put what I have learned into practice. I hope I won't let down my parents' wish and become a useful woman." Noma told me she once read a story of a university graduate, Xu Benyu, who worked as a volunteer teacher in a remote village in Guizhou province. His story moved the whole country. Noma said:

> For a long time, I wished to be a volunteer teacher, but I was afraid my parents would not agree. Especially my mother….my mother would be heartbroken if I insisted on doing that. So I thought sometimes, I had to follow her mind to please her. But I will feel regret if I don't do that (teaching in a village). Now I still want to be a volunteer teacher.
>
> (Noma, Interview, May 30, 2010)

As for future employment, Noma and her mother held conflicting ideas. Noma wished to stay in Kunming, the capital city of Yunnan Province:

> After I came out I found a small town was much more backward than a big city. I also hope to find a job in the city. I know it is very competitive and stressful to live in a city, but I may have more chances to realize my personal value. It may be quiet to live in a small town, but the chances of development are slim. For the long run, the backward education will affect the education of the next generation. The educational condition in my hometown is relatively backward.
>
> (Noma, Interview, September 25, 2009)

Noma's elder sister and two uncles understood Noma's decision, and they showed strong support. Her sister argued:

> It would be better to develop outside. After all Mojiang is too small. I know it is very competitive to live outside but as far as Noma's personality and ability are concerned, I suppose it is the best choice to develop outside.
>
> (Nomy, Online chat, February 5, 2010).

However, Noma's mother was strongly against it. She said, "Don't listen to your sister. They are afraid you will come back and live on them. It is your mom (not others) who will raise you."

As for her mother's idea, Noma showed full comprehension. "Why did my mom say that? She often thought that way. It is understandable, for the old people, they wish to be close to her children" (Noma, Interview, May 30, 2010).

Another issue that concerned Noma's mother was Noma finding a boyfriend at the university. She said:

> As parents, we believe she should concentrate on study. Having a boyfriend may affect her study. She had some junior schoolmates who failed in their study just because they had boyfriends as students. Boyfriends even destroyed their prospects.
> (Noma's mother, Interview, October 6, 2009)

On the contrary, Noma's father was not as worried as her mother. He held strong faith in his daughter and believed she could deal with this issue appropriately. He commented, "I have no worry so far. I suppose her mother worried too much about this issue. It seems to me if she can handle it well, I will have nothing to worry about. I trust her."

Fortunately, Noma balanced finding a boyfriend and learning quite well. After some observation, Noma's mother found that having a boyfriend did not affect her daughter's studies. She finally accepted the boyfriend and even asked him to persuade Noma to go back to Mojiang after graduation.

In spite of her dreams, Noma found it was very difficult to find a job in Kunming. After she tried a few interviews, she told me:

> It is so difficult to find a job here (in Kunming). I am losing my confidence. Maybe I have expected too much, but the reality is cruel and serious. What's more, I found I am quite weak in many ways, so I am not confident enough to go into the society now. If I cannot find a job here anymore, I may go back to the village to become a teacher.
> (Noma, Interview, May 30, 2010)

Noma graduated from YUN in June 2010, and finally found a job in a branch of a prestigious national English training school in Kunming. It is the same school where Noma worked as a summer camp intern teacher. Noma worked very hard in this school and won the trust and recognition of both her students and colleagues. In the summer of 2011, she went to the United States as the leading teacher of a study tour group.

To sum up, Noma had low expectations for the future. She was not particular about post-graduation employment. She did not care what kind of job she took as long as it could support her living in the city. Her major motivation for becoming a college student was to "jump out of the farmer status" (He 2005) and repay her parents' sacrifices. Her wish to become a village teacher like Xu also reflected her mentality of thanksgiving. The process of job seeking was very frustrating. She had many interviews and after graduation. Employers seemed to have no interest in the graduates of YUN, due to doubts about the quality of education offered at a university of nationalities.

6.3 Discussion and Implications

In Sect. 6.1 I traced the life history of Noma from primary school to tertiary education as an ethnic multilingual student. Here, I highlighted her story as an English major at a university for ethnic groups. Like many EMLs in China, she experienced difficulties from time to time in acquiring new languages and adapting to a new environment. However, Noma was positive from the very beginning and took every chance to empower herself with all the resources available. In the following section, I will explain how her attitude and heritage, combined with tertiary education, empowered her as a minority student. I will also discuss power relationships and their impact on the identity development of ethnic minority learners.

6.3.1 Perception, Policy, and Practice

Noma is from the Hani, a less-developed ethnic group who have lived in poor mountain areas for generations. The greatest desire for most Hani students is to "jump out of the farmer status" through education and "become cadres" in the future. That was why Noma's parents, at any cost, tried to make sure their children received the best education affordable. Without a good education, Noma would very likely have married as a teenager or ended up as a migrant worker like some of her schoolmates. Because of the obligation to help her household and escape poverty, Noma overcame many difficulties. She mastered new languages and acquired the social skills to survive in a new learning environment. One of the reasons for Noma to apply to YUN was because the university could provide a wide range of scholarships. Noma's case supports Cao and Feng's augment (2010) that "poverty acts as both a barrier to education and an outcome of lack of education" (p. 100).

Noma's success can be attributed to her parents' perception of education, to her two uncles' academic guidance and financial support, and to her own personal effort. As the descendant of a faded landlord family, Noma's parents understood the significance of education. Her mother helped her younger brothers finish higher education. Noma's mother often mentioned that she lost the chance to go to university because of the "Cultural Revolution." Her two younger brothers were admitted to local universities after the "Cultural Revolution" and were later assigned to stable and well-paid jobs as cadres and teachers. Noma's parents' decision to provide the best education for their children resulted from the life story of the two younger brothers. They had proved that education could change people's destiny. When I interviewed Noma's parents about their contribution to Noma's education, her father said, "As ordinary farmers, we have little power to help her. We just hope for her to work hard and make her dream come true." Many a time, Noma and her elder sister talked about their parents' efforts to help their children develop as far as possible. Noma's sister said:

> My parents paid the price that no family in my village could ever afford. It is due to my parents' priceless effort that we can live our life today. They borrowed money to support us to finish our schooling. Without their support we maybe still work in the fields with our face to the earth and back to the sky.
>
> (Nomy, Online chat, November 29, 2009)

Noma's two uncles also contributed significantly to Noma's success. One of her uncles was her high school English teacher. Her other uncle, a civil servant, had been a "think-tank" for resolving critical issues in Noma's family. The two uncles' advice was like an imperial edict 圣旨. They not only provided financial support but also crucial guidance. From Noma's uncles' actions, I saw the power of the Hani heritage that derived from mutual assistance and family bonds. Actually, Noma had internalized and extended the spirit of mutual assistance to other students in her university by always being ready to offer help to others.

My investigation reveals that Noma's parents and her two uncles not only attached great importance to education, but were also highly sensitive to the national policies for ethnic minority people. When I asked Noma's father why he asked Noma to apply to an ethnic minority university rather than an ordinary comprehensive university, her father responded:

> The decision was made only based on Noma's marks in the national matriculation examination. We had the intention to send her to a teacher's college. But we chose a university of ethnic groups to make sure she could be admitted by a university with the support of the national preferential policy.
>
> (Noma's father, Interview, October 6, 2009)

Noma told me that one of her cousins applied to a law program designed for ethnic minority students at a key university in Yunnan. Noma's life story shows that preferential policies can serve as stepping stones for minority students to gain access to better education. Professor Li Qing'an, the first Hani PhD in Psychology at Beijing Normal University (BNU), once studied in the "Preparatory Program" 预科课程 of YUN. He said "I hope my personal story will shed some light on the development of advanced ethnic talents in China" (Li 2008). He believed that without the "preparatory program," he would never have become a university student.

The preferential policies for ethnic minority groups, despite some disagreement (Ma 2007, 2009; Zhang 2011), provide ethnic minority learners access to higher education. This is very important for those ethnic groups like the Hani who have low socioeconomic development.

6.3.2 Investment, Legitimacy, and Changing Identity

In 2000, Norton discussed the "investment" and "good return" of second language acquisition. She argued that "if learners invest in a second language, they do so with the understanding that they will acquire a wider range of symbolic and material resources, which in turn increase the value of their cultural capital" (p. 10). Noma's life history reveals that a "good return for investment" can be achieved. Noma invested much beyond academic study. She joined the Student Union and worked as a liaison officer. Work experiences brought her more social experiences and management skills. The successful resolution of teacher–student conflicts displayed Noma's capability in dealing with sophisticated interpersonal relationships. She built up the trust of peers and faculty by being a good friend, monitor, and student teacher. Her hard work helped her earn the certificates of TEM-4, computer literacy, and tourist guide.

Due to the pressure of the university curriculum, Noma's efforts to maintain her native language seemed very difficult to achieve. On the one hand, she had to spend more time learning English and Japanese. She was trying her best to master two languages as "the key to success." On the other hand, the motivation to learn her native language was diminishing owing to her pragmatic mindset. Now, Noma can only count in the local Han dialect rather than in authentic Hani. She even told me that when she could not make herself understood in Chinese, she preferred to use English. "I can use a simple English word to express what I mean now. But if you ask me to say it in Hani, I have to say Hani with the loan words in Chinese," Noma said (Noma, Interview, September 25, 2009).

As the senior citizens who have a good command of Hani are passing away, Noma's chances of picking up Hani as a linguistic capital are becoming slim. Code switching between Hani, Putonghua, and Hani with Chinese loan words and expressions supports Huang's observation (2003) that minority languages are losing their authenticity and being replaced by Chinese vocabulary, phonology, and grammatical systems.

Noma's case also presents a picture of how an EML by exerting her agency, is able to achieve role transformation. Noma moves from a marginalized, vulnerable student to a peripheral participant, and then to a capable, legitimate participant of YUN. A "community of practice" (COP) is a notion proposed by Wenger (1998). COP sees learning as a process of situated practice. In order to become a legitimate participant of a certain community, one must learn first from a mentor to accumulate adequate knowledge and skills. In primary school and junior secondary school, Noma was assumed to be a legitimate participant for she was a top student and most of her cohorts were from the Hani community. Lives at home and at school were very similar. The same language, the similar way of life, and the similar conceptualization of the world made her life and study at school very comfortable. Thus, she was regarded as a "core member" in a Hani dominated school.

However, her legitimacy was questioned when she failed in the secondary school entrance examination. She was perceived as a less qualified student and was expected to pay an extra fee. This marginalized Noma until she became a public-sponsored student due to her school attainment. Her legitimacy was again challenged when she failed the TEM-8 at university. The failure in TEM-8 was daunting, but her frustration was not prolonged. Noma remained devoted to her teaching practice. With her positive attitude, she won the respect of her peers. She also gained new recognition in different communities. Much like multiple identities, communities of practice are also dynamic and negotiable. When Noma's legitimate membership was questioned and denied in one community of practice (YUN), she could still be accepted and recognized in another community of practice (the school she worked as a preservice teacher).

I would like to argue that Noma's failure in various examinations was not her fault. What needs to be criticized is the current hegemonic curriculum and criteria for talent selection. These put EMLs in an unfavorable position, given their weak foundations of Chinese literacy. The strength of EMLs, such as multilingual proficiency and intercultural awareness, has never been recognized in the assessment system or in employment policies.

If the national policy is to promote the "development of all ethnic groups" (State Council 2009), then a multicultural educational policy should be instituted to allow for the sustainable development of minority learners. The white paper for ethnic minority groups argues (State Council 2009, p. 144):

> Education among national minorities is an important part of the education of China. The development of education among national minorities is of paramount importance to the improvement of the quality of the minority population and the promotion of economic and cultural development in ethnic minority areas.

From the white paper, it can be seen that education for ethnic minority people has become an indispensable part of the overall Chinese education system. As a result, a series of measures have been taken to enhance education in ethnic minority areas. As Wang et al. (2007) have observed, these policies, despite good intentions, fail to help ethnic minorities develop their cultures.

Noma's life history made me think about the fundamental goals of higher education for ethnic minority learners. As for Noma's university of nationalities, I would like to ask the following questions: Do minority students study to earn the certificate for graduation or for social mobility? Can the so-called professional knowledge and skills they have learned at university help them make a living? Should the university make greater efforts to produce minority elite professionals, such as engineers, doctors and linguists? Or should the university develop ethnic talents for social transformation and nation–state building, with the knowledge, skill, and attitude required for the twenty-first century?

6.3.3 Cultural Heritage, Attitude, and Actions

The omnipresent Hani heritage infuses Noma's perception of the world and determines her actions in handling problems she meets in and out of the university. Noma's case implies that parental teaching and role models are dispensable pillars that support school education. They may influence Noma's identity construction in view of the amount of hardship she experienced. Her early childhood memories together with the role models displayed by her parents and siblings become a kind of "habitus" and "cultural capital," mediated from one generation to the next. This kind of "habitus," as a way of life or a fixed conduct of behavior, is very powerful in shaping people's perceptions and guiding their actions. As Zhao (2007b) observed, "Convention is a kind of reminder of one's ethnic role. It helps to consolidate one's culture and tradition, check one's speech and act by governing everything from one's thought to behavior" (p. 140).

According to Wang (2003), Hani people believe that life is painful, promising, and governed by gods. It is believed that Hani people are born to experience pains,

6.3 Discussion and Implications

so they should work hard. Otherwise, they will not be able to enjoy life in another world. As Wang (2003, p. 137) argued:

> The Hani spent their life by doing hard labor work. As a result, the hard work and perception of enduring hardship were accumulated and passed down from one generation to another. This is the common experience of both the young and old. This common sense was identified and strengthened through the life experience of the Hani people and makes them believe people were born to suffer.

Painful childhood experience resulted in both a positive and a negative mindset for Noma. She treasured the chance to study at the university. She argued:

> I never complained about the hardship and poverty in my life. On the contrary, I was grateful for poverty. It let me know life was not easy and made me strong through hardship. I had an internal driving force that knowledge would change my destiny. So I would take any opportunity to change my destiny. I have never complained that I was born into a poor family. My parents were really so great that I owed them so much...After experiencing so much poverty, I realized that this chance of being a university student was very rare, so I told myself I had to grip the chance.
>
> (Noma, Autobiography, December 22, 2009)

Noma was determined not to go back to her hometown to work because it was still "backward in many aspects in comparison to big cities like Kunming." At the same time, Noma promised to help young children by supporting their basic education. With this "thanksgiving" attitude, she made great efforts to excel in her class. Her performance is in line with Trueba and Zou's (1994) observation that "the process of empowerment...seems to be rooted in their (students') commitment to help their villages... (meaning) to acquire knowledge, and through knowledge, prestige, status, honor and power to make changes" (p. 147).

To overcome difficulties in life, the Hani developed a culture of friendliness and mutual assistance. As a monitor, Noma took a leading role in studying and caring for all students in her class.

The Hani see the world as a complex environment composed of God, ghost, nature, and people. Due to their respect for nature, Hani people never deforest or destroy the natural environment. On the contrary, they try to protect nature and have developed a world-famous, ecologically friendly, terraced paddy rice field.[18] For example, "Ototo" was a conventional provision to guide people to use water reasonably (Long 2008). Hani people established their own understanding about man and nature's relationship. On the one hand, they believe people should follow God's will in handling people–nature relationships. On the other hand, in terms of interpersonal relationships, they favor "tolerance and peaceful coexistence" (Long 2008). The ancient song of Hani told the story of how the God Apymain solved the disputes of seven other gods. Therefore, harmony and coexistence are the guiding principles in handling relations between gods and gods, people and devils, and

---

[18]The terraced paddy field is a distinctive landscape in Yuanyang, Yunnan, China, mirroring the harmonious relationship between people and nature. Honghe Hani Terraced Fields were awarded the title of world heritage site in 2013.

people and wild animals. The creation of the terrace paddy rice field is a case in point, which reflects belief in the harmony of man and nature.

Hani people appreciate harmony and tolerance. This can be seen in relationship between man and nature. Wang (2003, p. 139) argued, "in Hani society, tolerance is a kind of life attitude. It is also a doctrine for the Hani to follow." Noma tried to adopt a "collaborative strategy" (Cummins 2009) to create a balance between honesty and harmony. For example, she resolved the confrontation between her fellow students and one of her teachers through mediation. She also forgave the students who refused to donate money and who cheated in applying for stipends. For Noma, negotiation rather than confrontation helped reduce contradiction and achieve harmony. Although she totally disagreed with students' cheating in applying for stipends, she would not report the cheating, as her intention was to save face for her peers and maintain harmony.

Noma was far away from home, but whenever possible, she tried her best to maintain her Hani identity by talking to her family members in their native language, celebrating Hani festivals, observing nature worship and criticizing her ex-schoolmate who could not speak authentic Hani. She also complained that some of her Han peers could not pass things in an appropriate ways. She wished to promote Hani culture in her own way by attending the Hani beauty contest. From Noma's story, we can see that she took a very positive attitude toward difficulties such as poverty, failure in examinations, interpersonal relationships, and employment.

6.4 Summary

As with Mammuts' case in the previous chapter, Noma's life history displayed the pains and gains of a minority female college student who made great efforts to survive as a qualified English major at YUN. Rather than being resistant to the dominating curriculum, Noma took a collaborative and positive attitude toward the system. Noma overcame difficulties, one after another, and successfully negotiated her multiple identities in a sophisticated and interwoven sociocultural context. Unlike her ex-schoolmate who adopted an assimilationist strategy to remove his Hani accent as a barber in Guangzhou, Noma used an integrative strategy. She achieved acculturation in the dominant society while maintaining her native language and cultural heritage. In the next chapter, I will discuss these two cases further and forecast the prospects of ethnic multilingual education at the tertiary level.

References

Bai, B. Y., & Wang, X. H. (1998). *The Hani's natural life and origin of culture*. Kunming: Yunnan Nationalities Press.

Banks, J. A. (2009). Multicultural education: Dimensions and paradigms. In J. A. Banks (Ed.), *The Routledge international companion to multicultural education* (pp. 9–32). New York: Routledge.

Berry, J. W. (2003). Conceptual approaches to acculturation. In K. M. Chun, P. B. Organista, & G. Marín (Eds.), *Acculturation: Advances in theory, measurement and applied research* (pp. 17–37). Washington, D.C.: American Psychological Assoc.

Cao, H. H., & Feng, J. (2010). Access to education for girls in minority regions of Gansu: A geographic perspective. In H. H. Cao & E. Morrell (Eds.), Regional minorities and development in Asia. Abingdon: Routledge.

Chinahani online. (2008). The development of Hani education. Retrieved on July 1, 2011 from http://www.chinahani.com/newshow.asp?id=78&key=.

Chinese ethnicity and religion online. (2010). Education of the Hani people. Retrieved on May 20, 2011 from http://www.mzb.com.cn/html/report/145506-2.htm.

Cummins, J. (2009). Pedagogies of choice: Challenging coercive relations of power in classrooms and communities. *International Journal of Bilingual Education and Bilingualism, 12*, 261–272.

Editing Committee. (2008a). *A general introduction to Mojiang Hani Autonomous County of Yunnan Province*. Beijing: Nationality Press.

Editing committee. (2008b). *A brief history of the Hani nationality*. Beijing: Nationality Press.

Editing Committee of Pu'er Local History. (2009). Pu'er Yearbook 2009. Kunming: Yunnan People's Publishing House.

Fei, X. T. (2003). Some monologues on culture self-consciousness. *Academic study, 7*, 5–9.

Freire, P. (1994). *Pedagogy of hope: Reliving pedagogy of the oppressed*. New York, NY: Continuum.

Gu, M. Y. (2008). Identity construction and investment transformation. *Journal of Asian Pacific Journal, 18*(1), 49–70.

He, Q. Y. (2005). The impact of Hani traditional education form, content and characteristic on modern education. In Hani Study Association (Eds.), *Selected papers on the Hani culture study series 3* (pp. 367–380). Kunming: Yunnan Press of Nationalities.

Kramsch, C. (1998). *Language and culture*. Oxford United Kingdom: OPU.

Lee, M. B. (2001). *Ethnicity, education and empowerment: How minority students in Southwest China construct identities*. Aldershot, UK: Ashgate Press.

Lei, B. (2002). *A cultural history of the Hani people*. Kunming: Yunnan Press of Nationalities.

Li, Z. R. (2005). The influences of the Han culture on the Hani culture. *Journal of Yunnan Normal University, 37*(4): 14-17.

Li, Q. A. (2008). Guangming Daily. *From a Hani cowboy to a professor of psychology: My personal story*. Guangming Daily, retrieved on June 4, 2011 from http://www.gmw.cn/content/2008-11/06/content_856675.htm.

Long, Q. H. (2008). The traditional morality of the Hani and its contemporary significance. In Y. C. Fang & Z. Q. He (Eds.), *The study of Honghe Hani culture* (pp. 30–38). Kunming: Yunnan University Press.

Li, Z. R., & Che, J. M. (2007). The content, form and characteristics of the Hani/ Akah traditional education. In S. C. Liu., & D. M. Zhao (Eds.), The proceeding of the 5th international conference of Hani-Akah culture proceeding (pp. 77-88). Kunming: Yunnan Nationality Press.

Long. L. G., & He, Q. Y. (2005). Traditional Hani education and its impact on modern education, in HIS (Eds.), China's Hani study. Beijing: Nationality Press.

Ma, R. (2007). Bilingual education for China's ethnic minorities. *Chinese Education & Society, 40*(2), 9–25.

People-in-country profile. (2011). Hani of China. Retrieved on June 4, 2011 from http://www.joshuaproject.net/people-profile.php?peo3=12062&rog3=CH.

Postiglione, G. (2009). The education of ethnic and cultural minority groups in Asia and Latin America. In J. A. Banks (Ed.), *The Routledge international companion to multicultural education* (pp. 501–511). New York: Routledge.

Pu, Y. H. (2005). *Observing the Hani education through the lens of four counties in Honghe prefecture*. In Hani Study Institute of Central Minzu University (Eds.), *China's Hani study Volume 3*. Beijing: Nationality Press.

Pu'er local history editing committee. (2009). *Pu'er year book 2009*. Kunming: Yunnan People's Publishing House.

State Council of the PRC. (2009). China's ethnic policy, common prosperity and development of all ethnic groups. In State Council (Eds.), *White papers of information office of the state council of the People's Republic of China* (pp. 1–153). Beijing: Foreign Languages Press.

Stern, H. H. (1983). *Fundamental concepts of language teaching*. Oxford: OUP.

Trueba, H. T., & Zou, Y. L. (1994). *Power in education: The case of Miao university students and its significance for American culture*. Washington, DC: Falmer.

Tsang M. C. et al. (2005). *Minorities' education in Yunnan: Developments, challenges and policies*. Retrieved on June 5, 2010 from http://www.tc.edu/centers/coce/pdf_files/a11.pdf

Wan, G. F., & Yang, J. (2008). How China best educates its minority children: Strategies, experience and challenges. In G. F. Wan (Ed.), *The education of diverse student populations: A global perspective* (pp. 139–157). London: Springer Science and Businesses Medium.

Wang, Q. H. (2003). *On the culture of the terraced field*. Kunming: Yunnan University Press.

Wang, H. X. (2009). The golden recession: 30 years' glory of Mojiang. *Ethnic Today, 11*, 10–14.

Wang, J., Qin, L. F., Luan, X. F., & Guan, Y. (2007). Interpreting multicultural education in China. *Guizhou Ethnic Studies, 21*(1), 145–150.

Wenger, E. (1998). *Communities of practice: Learning, meaning, and identity*. Cambridge: Cambridge University Press.

Ytsma, J. (2001). Towards a typology of trilingual primary education. *International Journal of Bilingual Education and Bilingualism, 4*, 11–22.

Yunnan Bureau of Statistics. (2012). The main data of the 6th national census in Yunnan. Retrieved on May 1st, 2013 from http://www.stats.gov.cn/tjsj/tjgb/rkpcgb/dfrkpcgb/201202/t20120228_30408.html.

Zhang, X. W. (1996). The Psychological characteristics of the Hani people. In Z. X. Li & Q. B. Li (Eds.), *The proceeding of the 1st International Conference on Hani culture* (pp. 26–35). Kunming: Yunnan Press of Nationalities.

Zhang, J. H. (2011). *University of nationalities through the lens of multiculturalism*. Beijing: Nationality Press.

Zhao, L. (2002). The relationship between Hani culture and other cultures in the process of globalization. *Yunnan Social Science, 4*, 72–75.

Zhao, D. W. (2007). Hani language and Hani culture. *Journal of Simao Teacher's College, 23*(1), 57-60.

Chapter 7
Discussion and Conclusion

> *Every form of beauty has its uniqueness,*
> *Precious is to appreciate other forms of beauty with openness.*
> *If beauty represents itself with diversity and integrity,*
> *The world will be blessed with harmony and unity.*
>
> By Fei Xiaotong

In the previous two chapters, I examined the cases of two ethnic minority students at YUN. I also discussed the impact of YUN curricula on two minority students. It can be seen that as EMLs, Mammuts and Noma experienced both empowerment and disempowerment during their tertiary education. They negotiated multiple identities successfully by active engagement inside and outside the university. Both encountered great challenges in accommodating to the new learning environment and university curriculum. Fortunately, they both made use of their linguistic and cultural capital, negotiating their identities and finally became legitimate peripheral participants in various communities of practice. In this chapter, I will discuss the two cases in depth and reflect on YUN curriculum with an overall remark and will examine the integration of multicultural education with multilingual education.

7.1 Mammuts and Noma: A Discussion of Contrast

7.1.1 Sociocultural Background, Perception, and School Performance

To a large extent, Mammuts and Noma have much in common for both of them come from ethnic minority families and learned English as a third language at university. They both believe learning an additional language like English will better their life opportunities. Both of them are top students among their ethnic peers from their hometowns and both have left for the city to pursue tertiary education. However, their ethnic backgrounds are very different. Mammuts is a Naxi, an ethnic group with a small population, but advanced sociocultural legacy. The Naxi have attached great importance to education throughout history. Noma is a Hani, a large ethnic group who are considered as a "backward mountain people." They attach less attention to education, especially the education of females. Huang's (2009) study of the educational status of ethnic minority groups in western China suggests that by 2000, the average years of education for the Naxi were 6.96 (7.64 years for the male and 6.29 years for the female) while the average years of education for the Hani were just 4.64 (5.58 years for male and 3.62 years for female).

The big divergence in socioeconomic development results in different perceptions by EMLs of education and employment. Yang's investigation (2009) of the divergence of socioeconomic development in the southwest frontier areas shows that it is related to the different educational levels for different ethnic groups. For instance, Noma was the only female college student in her family and village, while Mammuts was one of five Naxi girls in her village receiving a college education. Her elder brother also received a university education. The two informants' cases support Yang (2009) and Xu's (2009) findings of female education for ethnic groups in western China. The cases of the two informants also resonate with Li's observations on the relationship of minority socioeconomic status and the social constructions of ethnicity (2008). For example, Noma like many of her Hani relatives perceived tertiary education to be a stepping stone away from a farmer identity. Her expectations for future employment were not very high. She was willing to take up different kinds of jobs. She looked forward to becoming a teacher in the city, a tour guide or even a volunteer teacher in the countryside. In contrast, Mammuts set herself a higher career goal. She saw higher education as a vehicle to make her into a "graceful and beautiful" lady, a lady with "knowledge and ability." She wished to integrate her professional knowledge with her Naxi heritage with the ultimate goal of becoming a "cultural ambassador." With different memberships in their "imagined communities," Noma and Mammuts took advantage of the resources and opportunities available to them to fulfill their dreams.

Another conspicuous feature of the two major informants is the power they gained from multilingual education, even though both had faced conflicts and challenges in the process of acquiring this education. In facing adversities, they not only built up their professional knowledge and skills, but they also developed their critical thinking skills. They questioned the legitimacy of the imposed curriculum (compulsory examinations, courses offered and qualifications of expatriate teachers) and of the ineffective student counseling system. Their resistance to the dominant curriculum and complaints about the university environment support my hypothesis that "individuals are not passive receivers of knowledge/power relationships."

In spite of this commonality, Mammuts and Noma used distinctively different strategies in dealing with tensions and conflicts. Their differences can be traced to their perceptions, attitudes, and resources. For example, when Mammuts found some of her lessons were too difficult or the teachers' lecturing was too boring, she would choose to skip class as a kind of resistance. Mammuts' action confirms some multilingual educators' observation that resistance may take place during English acquisition (Canagarajah 1999; Norton 2004). Mammuts insisted on attending her favorite three courses: Audio–visual English, Translation, and Intercultural Communication. Instead of relying on the system, she developed her own ways of learning beyond what was provided by the institution.

Noma also encountered some problems, such as the frequent change of teachers, peers' complaints about dull teaching styles and her own failure in the TEM-8. However, Noma chose the strategy of communication rather than confrontation. She used cooperation and collaboration to work toward improvements. She chose negotiation for she believed that "you can learn from each teacher" and "being a teacher is not easy." As for Noma, the "harmony first" mindset is not only a Hani tradition (Lei 2002; Long 2008) but also her family's teaching. Noma's response is also in line with Wang's description (2003) of the Hani as "humble, and cowardly and compromising." It turned out that Noma's collaborative strategy achieved positive results in the end. She succeeded in not only persuading her teacher to improve but also maintaining a good relationship. In this sense, Noma can be labeled as an "active coper" (Berry 2003). Through this negotiation, I see the effect of what Cummins (2009) calls the "collaborative creation of power."

Another distinctive difference between Mammuts and Noma is found in their completely different attitudes toward university practices and extracurricular activities. Noma, as a model student cadre and CPC member, always took a leading role in university activities such as the CCTV Cup English Speaking Contest, sports meets and activities organized by the Student Union. To prove her legitimacy in the mainstream education system, she obtained the certificate of TEM-4, the Certificate for English Tour Guides and the Certificate of Computer Literacy. She joined the liaison division of the Student Union. As the director of the liaison department she organized and implemented many cultural activities. "I have learned a lot from the senior students in the liaison department. Now I know how to communicate with others and gained some social experience," she told me. During my four months of observation, Noma never missed a class unless she was terribly ill. Noma attributed her enthusiasm to her Hani heritage, her family's teaching and her father being a role model. Noma took part in few activities off campus. She only attended the English corners in the neighboring universities and tutored a primary student on the weekend. All her off-campus activities either related to her university major or helped to reduce her family's economic burden.

In contrast, Mammuts was not very active in participating in university activities. She was not a member of any university social clubs. However, her off-campus activities were more diversified. Mammuts' extracurricular activities served three purposes: (1) enhancing her English proficiency, (2) making friends, and (3) gaining social experience. As can be seen from Chapter Five, Mammuts claimed that she studied not to pass examinations or earn certificates but rather to enhance her English proficiency. As a result, she went to English corners and worked as a TA in the Shane English School to learn survival English. Her work in a local bar and restaurant in Shuhe was done to observe people and develop social skills. She traveled frequently in order to experience new cultures and make new friends. She joined the DCJ club and the training course at Mary Kay to satisfy her pursuit of beauty and experience.

When I observed their strategies of negotiating their multiple identities, I found Noma was a "policy-maker" for she believed that she could "make the best from the worst." Mammuts was a "policy challenger" who would rather seek external resources when she could not solve a problem within the university system. Noma took some practical measures in dealing with the present opportunities as they arose. Mammuts looked ahead and made plans for the future. The different strategies of the two EMLs in addressing the challenges of the mainstream education system reflect the "community forces"[1] (Ogbu 1983, 1987) and "socioeconomic status and cultural factors" (Yi 2008), which help explain the different performances of ethnic minority groups.

7.1.2 Cultural Awareness

What struck me most about Noma was her "cultural self-consciousness" (Fei, 2003). Fei (2003) puts forward the notion of w*enhua zijue* 文化自觉 (cultural self-consciousness) and defines the term as "a kind of self-knowledge of one's culture. If someone has *wenhua zijue*, he will know his cultural origin, development, characteristics, the process of formation and future direction" (2003, p. 7). Fei (2003) argues that self-knowledge is necessary for adapting to new environments and cultures. Fei's notion of *wenhua zijue* is in line with what Berry (2003, p. 26) has called "cultural awareness." Berry (2003) defines cultural awareness as "the knowledge about one's heritage culture and the dominant culture (e.g. values, language, way of living)" (p. 26). Barry points out that the degree of identification with one's culture determines a minority's acculturation strategies.

As I mentioned before, Noma's knowledge about Hani culture was vague and fragmented. She told me that her knowledge about the Hani did not extend beyond the language and festivals. It seemed that her *wenhua zijue* was aroused after she became my major informant. She came to know that her language was a kind of "capital" to realize her "ethnic value." After our second in-depth Interview she told me:

> After I talked with you, sir, I found what I am missing badly. I know very little about my ethnic group. I learned in this long summer vacation that my ethnic knowledge was very shallow. Maybe the senior generations in their 60s and 70s know something more deep. During the vacation, my mom taught me how to do embroidery, but my handcraft was casual and rough, not as delicate as hers. My mother is good at embroidery.
>
> (Noma, Interview, May 30, 2010)

---

[1] Ogbu (1983) defines "community forces" as the products of sociocultural adaptation, which are located within the minority community. One of the major factors determining community forces are ethnic minority groups' histories and self-perceptions.

Noma promised to learn how to count in Hani from her grandfather. She told me, "I must learn counting in Hani. I can learn from my parents when I communicate with them."

In Mammuts, I cannot feel the motivation of knowing more about Naxi culture, though she was very proud of it. I suppose Mammuts had already realized the value of her Naxi identity because of the booming local tourist industry and the reputation of Lijiang as a World Culture Heritage site. For instance, she would introduce herself as a Naxi when she met new people. At the same time, she achieved her *wenhua zijue* from critical thinking. For example, she compared the way of life in Lijiang with that in other places she had visited. She drew a conclusion that the people of Lijiang were "sincere and hospitable." At the same time she acknowledged that, as a Naxi, she could learn much from the Han, the Dai and even foreigners, like Americans and Koreans. She considered the poor English translation in the bus stop sign shameful for Lijiang. She tried to show her Naxi identity and fight against any casual attacks on the Naxi people. In this sense, Mammuts showed "the strongest self-consciousness among the ethnic minorities in Yunnan" (Naxi scholar, Zhou, Interview, October 18, 2010).

7.1.3 Preferential Education Policies

The current preferential policies for ethnic minorities in China provide them not only access to higher education, but also help them complete their studies with various stipends or scholarships. The preferential policies played a critical role in Mammuts' and Noma's decision to apply for YUN, a university of nationalities. For instance, thanks to the preferential policy, Noma was admitted to YUN. Mammuts, although not benefiting from any bonus points in the national matriculation examination, made very positive comments about preferential policies, claiming "students from remote places need chances, too." Mammuts went to a mountain village school with some Korean friends. They taught the children simple words and played games with them. Noma was a typical beneficiary of the national preferential policy for ethnic minorities. She not only gained access to higher education, but also finished her study with the special stipends and scholarships provided by the central and provincial governments. With her "thanksgiving" mentality, she decided to repay the society with the knowledge and skills she learned from her university.

Based on the life histories of the two major informants, I would argue that the beneficiaries of the preferential policies should be screened in a more rational way. The current policies aim to benefit those from certain ethnic groups with small populations and low socioeconomic development. However, some other ethnic groups in need are excluded from the preferential policy. For example, the Naxi students who live in remote and mountainous areas are disadvantaged. It is not fair to exclude all Naxi people from the national preferential policy because there is a dramatic disparity within the Naxi in terms of socioeconomic development. If the ultimate goal of preferential policies is to achieve *Duoyuan Yiti* in a real sense, preferential policies should not only provide easier access to public educational institutions, but they should also promote cultural diversity. Unfortunately, the nationally unified mainstream curriculum portrays ethnic cultures as colorful and exotic. To some extent, these are well-intentioned but culturally exclusive policies that benefit some ethnic groups but exclude others. The policies ignore the cultural heritage of ethnic groups with small populations.

7.1.4 Multilingual Acquisition

Studying English as a third language in a multiethnic university brought the two girls great challenges. These challenges are shared by all EFL learners, no matter whether they are ethnic minority or Han. But ethnic minority students have specific problems. These include a late start in English learning, learning English through Chinese, a curriculum that emphasizes using English to express Chinese culture, and the very tough national tests for English majors. For example, both Mammuts and Noma failed two very important examinations in their secondary and university education. Their failure in the national and local examinations not only made the two informants frustrated but also depressed. As Devine-Eller (2004, p. 11) observes, examination "make(s) each student visible to power as the object of the power; as it does so the power itself becomes invisible." In other word, EMLs will become the indirect subjects of unequal power relationships if they fail in the examinations at various levels. Their legitimacy as participants in their communities of practice will be further challenged. As a result, EMLs have to yield to the dominant language, culture and other norms to become successful within the mainstream education system. In this sense, the dominant majority-oriented English curriculum has created certain degrees of inequality and disempowerment for EMLs in general.

EMLs faced the danger of being assimilated by the dominant Han culture and losing the authenticity of their native languages. As elaborated in the previous chapters, the Hani have no written script, so the only way to pass on the Hani culture is through oral language. As the senior Hani people are passing away, it is hard for the younger generation to learn authentic Hani language. Noma's story is a case in point. The Naxi people have a prestigious written language—Dongba. However, this written form is only used in tourist products now. In the public sphere, Putonghua is accepted as the official language, for the sake of its practical value in education, employment and communication with non-Naxi. The Chinese proficiency of both Mammuts and Noma is also very problematic. They did not perform well in the national entrance examination, in which Chinese is a major subject. At the university, they found their deficiency in Chinese prevented them from understanding Chinese classics in the translation course. This finding conforms Lee's (2001) argument that "the lack of solid Mandarin Chinese language skills puts minority students at a constant academic disadvantage" (p. 41).

7.1.5 Psychological Support

As I have reported through their individual cases, both Mammuts and Noma experienced confusion and frustration after they arrived at YUN. As strangers in a new environment they did not know how to communicate with others and adapt to the new environment. Berry (2003) views this experience as "acculturative stress," as evidenced by symptoms such as uncertainty, anxiety and depression. Later both girls went through a number of difficult times such as the failure in the TEM examination, the loss of a beloved teacher, troubles finding a job and conflicts with their parents on postgraduation employment. All these distresses suggests the importance of establishing a counseling system especially for ethnic minority college students, such as the Hani and Naxi, who usually hold strong religious beliefs and are considered more sensitive to the matter of life and death.

Devine-Eller (2004) once noted that "behavioral or psychological problems might prevent a student from performing as expected on the day of the test, or even from having acquired the necessary skills during the previous year" (p. 15). Chen, Zi and Xi's study of ethnic college students in Yunnan (2007) shows that "these problems are quite common for ethnic minority students who come from poor and remote areas with symptoms of frequent combination of strong self-esteem and inferiority" (p. 167). Likewise, Huang and Yu's study (2009a, b) of the ethnic minority students at YUN reports that twenty one per cent of those surveyed claimed that it would take them 1 or 2 years to adjust to the university life. These findings show the necessity of reviewing the current counseling system at YUN.

The counseling system is an aid provided by YUN since June, 2004. The online counseling website of YUN says that by August 8, 2011, there were 155,763 clicks and 683 posts asking for help. I once inquired of a counselor online why there was less face-to-face consultation but more online postings asking for help. She told me that psychological discomfort is something like a common cold. Everybody may experience trouble like this. The subjects need to learn that counseling is not mysterious. The visitors to the counseling service are not necessarily abnormal. The counseling system needs to be strengthened and publicized. Teachers and administrators should not only pay attention to students' academic progress, but also their psychological health. A mechanism of monitoring college students' psychological complexities should be established.

7.1.6 Identity Issues

In the literature review I mentioned that identity has become a hot topic in the study of second language acquisition since the 1990s. It is generally believed that people develop and embrace new identities while learning new languages (Kramsch 1998; Miller 2000a, b; Kellman 2003; Norton 2004). Researchers try to conceptualize identity from psychological, sociocultural, and poststructuralist perspectives. For

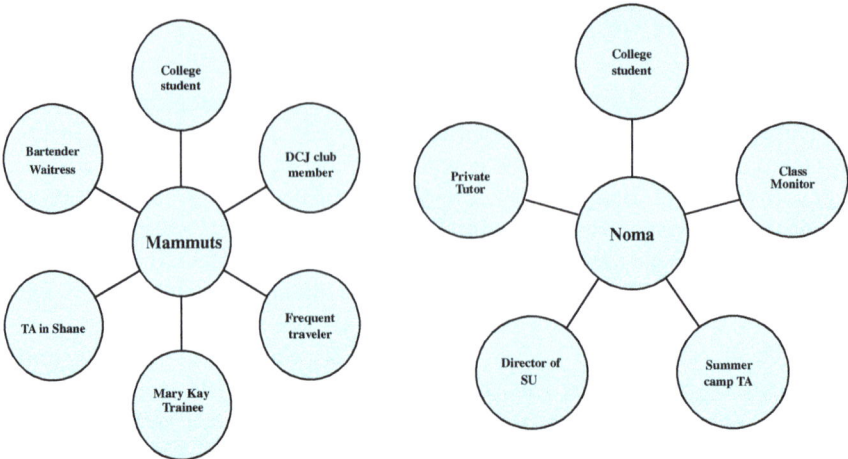

Fig. 7.1 Multiple roles of Mammuts and Noma (Wang 2012)

instance, Gee (2000) summarizes four types of identities according to these attributes: the natural perspective (N-identity), the institutional perspective (I-identity), and the discursive perspective (D-identity) and the affinity perspective (A-identity). Block (2007) talks about seven types of identities ranging from ethnicity to language. Mantero (2007) sees identity in terms of its dynamics and changeability.

As can be seen from Fig. 7.1 Noma and Mammuts played multiple roles inside and outside of their university life. They held multiple identities. In addition to their institutional identity as college students and their natural identity as ethnic minorities, they also adopted several other identities, such as part-time teachers and Student Union members. These multiple roles were connected to create a complex and hybrid identity. Here I would like to discuss some identity issues that arose from this case study.

Both Mammuts and Noma showed very strong traits of their ethnic identities. For instance, both were very pound of their native language, festivals, and values that guided their interpersonal relationships. They also evaluated the behaviors of outsiders according to their own moral standards. For example, Mammuts complained that "the outsiders were not as hospitable as the local Naxi people," while Noma argued that "some Han students cared little about their etiquette while handing something to others." At the same time, Mammuts and Noma both tried to safeguard their ethnic identities and fight against stereotyped perceptions of their groups. For example, Mammuts refuted the female tourist's image of Lijiang, and Noma criticized her ex-schoolmate's unauthentic Hani accent. Though Noma's knowledge of her culture is limited, she displayed her affection toward being a Hani in a few incidents in which she interacted with others or saw them commenting on her people. According to Berry (2003), when different peoples come into contact, acculturation (changing one's habitual patterns because of the others) and enculturation (awareness and affection toward one's own culture) take place at the same time. If Berry is right, then Mammuts and Noma may actually become more conscious of their own ethnic identities through their intercultural experiences, whether or not they decide to display or downplay their own native culture.

At the same time, the two female students showed a very strong identification with the Chinese nation and enjoyment as a citizen of the multiethnic state. It seems that their ethnic identity can coexist with their national identity as Chinese. Their strong patriotic awareness is partially due to years of successful patriotic education as well as the historical relationship between ethnic minority groups and the central government. For example, the ruling class of the Naxi had very strong connections with the central government throughout history. They adopted the Confucian culture and maintained a good relationship with the ruling court of China. From the Yuan to the Qing dynasties, Naxi *Tusi* (the local chiefs) were in favor with the central government. The Naxi *Tusi* not only sent their children to Beijing to receive a Confucian education. They also took part in many ways to safeguard Chinese territory (Zhou 2002). Zhou (2010) argues that "the biggest contribution of the Naxi in history is to maintain the completeness of Chinese territory" (Teacher YNU, Zhou, Interview, October 18, 2010).

At the gate of *Mufu* 木府, *Tusi* Mu's Executive Mansion, there is a couplet reflective of the Naxi rulers' political mindset (See Picture 7.1). It reads "Phoenix scripts each time, bring closer the king's shines; our clouds float free without any crane's lines" (*Fengzhao meilai hongrijin, Heshu budao baiyunxian* 凤诏每来红日近,鹤书不到白云闲).

Picture. 7.1 The *Tusi* Mu's Executive Mansion (Wang 2011)

Picture. 7.2 The Gate of Loyalty and Righteousness (Wang 2011)

In front of *Mufu*, stands a gate engraved with two characters, *Zhongyi* 忠义 (loyalty and righteousness see Picture. 7.2). This shows the loyalty of the Naxi rulers to the central administration. Education also contributed to Naxi students' patriotism. As I mentioned before, Mammuts' high school attached great importance to moral education by a weekly national flag rising and a regular thematic class meeting. Based on the above discussion, it can be seen that for Mammuts there is no conflict between being Naxi and being Chinese.

Likewise, patriotism is also a tradition of the Hani people. Zhang (1996) portrays the Hani as a nation with a "persistent and simple nation-state perception" (p. 30). In history, the Hani people were loyal to the central "imperial system" and complied with the national rules on revenue payment and military service. Now in Mojiang people can still find a stone bridge called "Loyalty Bridge" (*Zhongai Qiao* 忠爱桥), documenting the patriotism of the Hani people (See Picture. 7.3).

Like Mammuts, Noma attributed her patriotism to family education, especially to the role model of her father. As a class cadre and CPC member, Noma also organized some patriotic activities such as visiting the "12.1 Memorial" and "Revolutionary Martyrs Cemetery."[2] Noma's case, like that of Mammuts, implies that there is no conflict between being Hani and Chinese.

---

[2]"12.1 Memorial" and "Revolutionary Martyrs Cemetery" are two landmarks on the Yunnan Normal University campus. They are established to commemorate those who died on December 1, 1945.

7.1 Mammuts and Noma: A Discussion of Contrast

Picture. 7.3 The loyalty bridge (Chen 2015)

7.1.7 Investment and Return

Their parents' perception on education, their child-rearing methods and their commitment to education at any cost allowed the two girls to become university students. It is quite obvious that the parents attached great importance to their children's education. The Naxi people are famous for their excellent performance in education. Naxi children bring home honors by studying well. Mammuts is no exception. She studied very hard because she loved her mother and wanted to be a good daughter. "Study well" was a pet phrase of Mammuts' mother, and she tried her best to save money for her children's education. When Mammuts was a junior secondary school student, her mother told her, "Honey, try your best and get admitted to the secondary technical school, and then you will have a happy life. You don't have to work in the field like me." When China started to expand its higher education enrollment, her mother said, "My dear daughter, you should study hard and prepare for the entrance examination for university enrollment." With her parents' encouragement and support, Mammuts and her elder brother were admitted to university one after another. They became the celebrities in the village with their advanced education.

Noma's success in education is attributed to the joint efforts of her extended family members like her parents, siblings, and two uncles. What I would like to point out here was that Noma was born into a faded landlord family. Her mother was a farmer who received only a junior secondary school education. Without the

Cultural Revolution in the 1970s, she might have become a college student like her two younger brothers. She often mentioned the two younger brothers' life stories to convince Noma that education was a shortcut to a better life. She warned Noma that, without good education, a Hani girl might become a mother at an early age and end up in the fields working all her life. For ethnic minority girls, the family financial condition and the perception of female education pose great threats to receiving education.

As Lee noticed (2001), the "strong sense of belonging together with the special support from their teachers, peers and families" helped Mammuts and Noma "surmount considerable obstacles and succeed in school" (p. 59). At the same time, the two cases display the pervasive influence of Confucian education on the ethnic minority areas. Parents in China throughout history would rather make tremendous sacrifices and suffer any pains necessary to ensure that their children receive a good education. There are no exceptions in the parents of the two informants.

7.2 Reflections on the Multiple Identities of Ethnic Minority Learners

As I have pointed out in the previous chapters, the two major informants hold multiple and hybrid identities. These multiple identities are constructed partly from their cultural heritage and partly from their interaction with the larger society through multilingual education and off-campus engagements. That is to say, their identities can be primordial, situational and constructivist. Different types of identities are not "independent of one another in the larger general identity of a person" (Block 2007, p. 42).

The primordialist approach conceives ethnic identity as something internal that persists through change (Lee 2001). The optimal–situational approach sees identities as fluid and changeable (Lal 1995). For example, some of these identities were born with the informants, such as their natural identities (Gee 2001) as ethnic minorities. Some of their identities were later acquired, such as their institutional identities as students at YUN. Some of their identities were time and space specific, such as that of Noma as a member of the Student Union or of Mammuts as a trainer in Mary Kay. These identities terminated when the girls relocated themselves to other places for certain reasons. Some of these identities were imposed. For instance, when both of them failed in the TEM, the legitimacy of their institutional identities was contested and questioned. They were labeled as "academic losers" in the mainstream system. When they passed the national examination, their legitimacy in their community of practice was regained. Likewise, their identities as "top students" in their hometowns and "good children" at home were also challenged with time and circumstances.

Their multiple identities were not a static set of personality and cultural traits, but part of a dynamic process. Empowerment was gained through integration within and outside of their ethnic communities. This finding supports Lam's argument that trilingual education can be empowering for ethnic minority learners (2007).

Like many multilingual learners in Yunnan, Mammuts and Noma are now facing the danger of losing their ethnic identities, of being assimilated by the dominant Han culture and of being westernized. A challenging issue is that the scope and the quality of their first language are being dramatically minimized. Now their first languages are only used in L1 contexts such as when they communicate with their family and friends from their hometowns whether on the phone or face-to-face. At the same time, the authenticity of their first languages is also problematic. Take Noma for example. Now she cannot count in authentic Hani language but instead uses modern Hani with many loan words from Chinese. Quan (2010) attributed the decline of native language learning to the shortage of *wenhua zijue* (cultural self-consciousness) and the "pressure of being excellent in the mainstream education system." This is very true with the cases of Mammuts and Noma.

The demanding curriculum, assessment procedures and their poor L3 foundation forced them to study hard in order to catch up with the mainstream students. Even though both of them were anxious to maintain their native language and culture, their multicultural awareness did not function well because of the subordinate status of their L1 and because of the dominant mainstream curriculum. In the university guidelines for academic development, there was no emphasis on cultural diversity or on the heritage of ethnic minorities.

The Naxi in general have a very strong ethnic identity due to their brilliant cultural heritage and booming economy, but they are still at risk of being assimilated by the Han. Quan, a senior Naxi sociologist in Yunnan, pointed out (2010a, b):

> It seems most difficult in Lijiang for people to resist assimilation. Even in such a place like Lijiang ancient city, the use of Naxi is diminishing as the result of the mainstream culture and education system. You have to face all kinds of examinations. You have to study Putonghua, written Chinese and English as well. Chinese and English are the priorities. In the Chinese education system if you want to stand out among the others and find a good job, you have to master these skills. Under such pressure, in Lijiang especially in the ancient city, many parents who work in public units start to speak Putonghua with their children. Therefore, I think the *wenhua zijue* is the most important. You have to be proud of your ethnicity first, and then you will have the motivation to learn your native language and other cultures. As a small-sized ethnic minority group, the Naxi are very likely to lose their culture under a dominant education system, with the impact of dominant culture and time trends. The Ji'nuo are a case in point.
>
> (Naxi Scholar, Quan, Interview, July 30, 2010).

It seems to Quan, that the general trend is for ethnic minorities to be assimilated because of the current education system. He argued that if we hope to maintain ethnic diversity the native language should be learned from the very beginning. Actually, this suggestion has been proven functional by the case of Alice, mentioned earlier. She successfully acquired French and at the same time maintained her cultural heritage. She negotiated social, linguistic, gender and class identities in her journey of French acquisition (Kinginger 2004).

In my conceptual framework in Chapter Three, I argued that the identities of multilingual learners are shaped by a power–knowledge relationship between the dominant majority and the subordinate minority. When the power relationship is collaborative, the EMLs will be empowered with various kind of capital and be treated as legitimate participants in various communities of practice. The learners will be proud of their ethnic identities and try their best to excel in the dominant education system. Otherwise, when the power relationship is coercive, EMLs will be disempowered and marginalized.

They will be frustrated and fail further in the dominant education system as Zuengler and Cole (2005) have argued. They may look down upon their native language and culture and be assimilated quickly into the majority. The blind articulation of ethnic identity is difficult when EMLs face the dilemma between modernization and native culture promotion, between demonstrating ethnic authenticity and modernity. Before attempting assimilation, integration, separation or segregation, a cost-effect evaluation is necessary. Actually, the similar dilemma extends to universities of nationalities, which are struggling with being modern or ethnically distinctive. McCarthy (2009) argues (p. 47):

> To the extent minorities modernize, they lose what makes them distinctive, which also constitutes the officially codified identity by which they are bestowed citizenship in the larger Chinese nation. To the extent they do not modernize, they are inferior citizens.

Facing the dilemma of choosing ethnic modernization or authenticity, EMLs may employ different strategies. For example, as an ethnic minority in name, my academic success in the mainstream system was at the cost of maintaining my native language and culture. This assimilationist approach has brought me lifelong pity. As a member of learned and advanced ethnic group, Mammuts took the integrative acculturation strategy and fulfilled her obligations and dreams by navigating through the mainstream education system. Noma, as member of an invisible ethnic group with very strong *wenhua zijue,* tried her best to maintain her ethnic authenticity. She also took a cooperative strategy to achieving her goals.

I conclude that the attitudes, perceptions and beliefs of both policy-makers and policy-takers in the university are quite significant. For example, Lee, a former administrator of the School of Foreign Languages, understood the situation of his students especially the poor academic foundation of ethnic minority students. He acknowledged the English proficiency of most minority students was very problematic, which could be seen from their poor listening skills, oral and written expression. As most of the ethnic students were upgraded from the preparatory division, he initiated many intensive courses before each national examination for English majors. Although the courses were test-oriented, they did help some minority students enhance, if not their overall English proficiency, at least some specific test-taking skills. However, it was also this same dean who set an ambitious goal to build "a first-class discipline at Yunnan, well-known in China." He admitted that the students from the second-choice universities (二本院校), such as YUN, were very poor in their English language foundation. The contradictory perceptions of the minority students made the YUN English curriculum very challenging for these students.

7.2 Reflections on the Multiple Identities of Ethnic Minority Learners

In response to my question on how to strengthen ethnic unity, Lee believed that the university should emphasize equality among minority students but weaken their ethnic consciousness. Lee believed that ethnic equality should outweigh ethnic disparity. Only in this way could ethnic minority students interact with each other peacefully. At the same time, unity, harmony, and progress would be achieved. However, many cadres and scholars with ethnic backgrounds disagreed with this argument. They believed that the ethnic features such as native languages and distinctive lifestyles were a part of their cultural heritage. Ru, a CPC secretary of SFL, argued:

> I think harmony and unity will not conflict with diversity. The emphasis on harmony and unity will not contradict with displaying your personality and developing the excellent heritage of a nationality. If you dissolve the ethnic features, you will have no advantage and features with which you grew up. Now we talk about "people first" 以人为本. This is also applicable to ethnic minority students. "People first" means respecting one's personality but not dissolving his cultural self-consciousness. We don't have to dissolve our heritage. Instead, we should further develop our cultural heritage and take pride in it. I personally don't accept the strategy of dissolution.
> (Administrator YUN, Ru, Interview, October 25, 2010).

Quan criticized overemphasizing the equality as contradicting historical materialism. He suggested looking at ethnic equality from a historical perspective:

> You are right to emphasize the equality of nationalities. However, if you look at the development of the whole of China from a historic perspective, you will find the ethnic minority and the ethnic Han are not equal at all. From the old dynasty till the Republic of China the ethnic minority groups were not treated as people with culture. All the historical literature would describe them in an extremely contemptuous tone. For example, the names of many ethnic groups would contain a Chinese character component meaning "dog". In the long run, some ethnic minority groups were ashamed of speaking their languages. They were ashamed of talking about their culture. They might even not believe they had culture. Instead, they had low self-esteem. In this sense, you will see the imbalanced development of different ethnic groups. Therefore, I think the wording of "equality" should be weighed and considered given the fact that all ethnic groups are not equally developed. Furthermore, you should know why the development is not at balance and know the reasons for the backwardness.
> (Naxi Scholar, Quan, Interview, July 30, 2010).

Quan's point of view on ethnic inequality is in line with Dressman's assumption of the formation of binaries due to historic and cultural inequity (2008). Another Naxi scholar, Guo, disputed the viewpoint of weakening ethnic self-consciousness. Guo (2009) claims that ethnic groups are not a just a "symbol of culture." He argues that the socialist stage is not a time either to integrate or dissolve ethnic groups, but rather a period to seek common progress for all.

Quan and Guo's debates once more highlight the significance of implementing integrative, rather than assimilative, educational policy in China. The ultimate goal of the *Duoyuan Yiti* framework should be ethnic equality with national unity.

To sum up, as I have argued in Chapter Two, the drastic changes in contemporary China call for the development of ethnic minority talents for the purpose of nation building. To meet this requirement, universities of nationalities face new challenges. Like the dilemma of ethnic authenticity versus modernity, universities for the nationalities have to figure out how to maintain their special features while providing all a round development. To address these challenges, more studies on university policies and practices are needed.

7.3 Suggestions for Further Study

This study traced the life histories of two ethnic multilingual learners at a local university of nationalities in Yunnan, China. The study reveals the power relationships that exist and reports on how the informants negotiate their multiple identities within the different communities of practices. However, the unique stories of the specific informants at this particular university do not capture the scenarios of millions of other ethnic multilingual learners in China. For example, English acquisition is very difficult for the two informants in this study but that is not necessarily true for all ethnic minorities. Due to the structures of their native languages, some may have an easier time learning English than learning Chinese, and some may have less difficulty with English pronunciation than Han Chinese students.

Moreover, the composition of bi-ethnic families may bring about different perceptions on the education of their children. The ethnic minority students who have received bilingual education at early stages of schooling and those who gain access to higher education by *Minkaomin* or *Minkaohan* may adopt different learning strategies to address the challenges they meet. EMLs at a mainstream comprehensive university may have different perceptions than EMLs at a university of nationalities. Therefore, further studies on this topic are needed to explore a larger, more diversified ethnic population.

As I mentioned in Chapter Two, there is a rich diversity among EMLs in China. This study involved only two of the 25 officially recognized ethnic groups in Yunnan. A study of other Yunnan minorities, such as the Yi (known for resistance to assimilation), the Dai (a cross-border group) and the Tibetans (an ethnic group inhabiting more than a sixth of China's land) would probably provide different results with respect to identity formation. Furthermore, due to the local and socioeconomic conditions, there is great disparity in terms of the opportunities to receive quality education at the secondary and tertiary levels. For instance, not all ethnic groups in Yunnan are the beneficiaries of preferential admission policies for tertiary education. Within the same ethnic group, the educational levels can also be quite different, given the geographic location and socioeconomic development of a particular ethnic community. In future research, a larger sample is suggested. Another factor worthy of study is the powerful role that Confucianism has played for ethnic minority education throughout Chinese history. The Confucian education has shaped the educational perceptions of both ethnic majority and minority groups.

7.4 Final Remarks

Studies suggest that multilingual learners face constant challenges in acquiring new languages (Cenoz and Jessner 2000; Cenoz et al. 2001; Jordà Safont 2005; Sagin 2006) and shaping new identities (Shen 1989; Ting-Toomy 1999; Kern 2000; Kramsch 1998; Miller 2000a, b; Feere 2003; Kellman 2003; Potowski 2007). There are no exceptions among the major informants in this case study who overcome overwhelming difficulties to excel in the mainstream Chinese education system as ethnic minority learners.

As can be seen from the conceptual framework presented in Fig. 3.3, the cases of two minority students present some scenarios typical of ethnic multilingual education in China. This education is impacted by national and local policies on language, by culture, by ethnicity, by education, by socioeconomic development, and by the curriculum of a local university of nationalities in Yunnan. The case study suggests that the mainstream education system does act as a kind of "political means" (Foucault 1971), along with university policy and practice, to shape the multiple identities of EMLs. The top-down curriculum sets a very high assessment standard for the legitimacy of EMLs in their communities of practice. That is to say, if they cannot integrate with the mainstream and pass the examinations required, then they will be labeled as unqualified English majors and excluded from the mainstream system. However, given the poor English level of most EMLs, it is very difficult for them to pass the TEM-4 and the TEM-8, which are also very hard for majority Han students. In this sense, the YUN curriculum empowers and disempowers EMLs. The curriculum influences their strategies of acculturation (integration, assimilation, separation and marginalization) and enculturation (socialization of native values through interaction). At the same time, the university's strategies of promoting cultural diversity (multiculturalism, segregation and exclusion) may also be impacted by the extent of EMLs' acculturation. Therefore, it is high time to review the current policies concerning ethnic multilingual education.

As I have argued via the conceptual framework, power relationships can be reciprocal. There is still some empowering space (preferential policies and privileged educational opportunities) in the mainstream education system for EMLs to negotiate their identities and build up various kind of capital (linguistic, cultural and social). This capital, in turn, will help them integrate with the dominant culture and achieve social mobility. Take YUN for example. As the only university for the nationalities in Yunnan, it provides EMLs with much better resources for multicultural education (curriculum, library and ethnic scholars).

This study, in contrast to those of Hansen (1999), Lee (2001) and Clothey (2005), examined ethnic multilingual learners through the lens of dynamic sociocultural discourses. I hope this study will offer the EMLs some insight on what they can do as multilingual learners.

With a goal of achieving common prosperity and development for all ethnic groups, China has enacted policies to enhance socioeconomic progress in the minority areas. Ethnic multilingual learners are facing ever-increasing challenges of mastering new languages and forming new identities. At the tertiary level, there exist uneven power relations, represented by the university curriculum. It favors the ethnic majority most. As a result, EMLs have to decide to act as minority "self" or majority "other". They have to decide either to maintain their native language and culture or acquire new "cultural capital" such as Chinese and English, for better life opportunities. Their decisions involve the acculturation strategies adopted by ethnic minorities in Clothey's (2004) and Tsung's (2010) case studies. Whether being active or passive learners, the EMLs have to strive to prove their legitimacy in the mainstream education system. They only can excel by competing with the majority Han and their ethnic peers.

Beyond the storylines of schooling, I intend to provide readers with a snapshot of ethnic multilingual education in China today by addressing a major question: How are the identities of tertiary ethnic minority learners shaped through the process of multilingual acquisition? Additional questions are: What factors contribute to the identity construction of ethnic multilingual learners at the tertiary level in Yunnan? How do the EMLs in this case study negotiate their identities through trilingual education?

This study shows how two ethnic minority girls construct their multiple and hybrid identities through multilingual acquisition. The process of being trilingual provides them with new perceptions about their native language and cultural heritage. In the process of acculturation, they experience the hardships of acquiring new languages and adapting to new environments. Fortunately, without being transformed into "others" at the cost of their cultural heritage, they developed multicultural awareness through multilingual education. The step-by-step building of *wenhua zijue* (cultural self-consciousness) together with the cultural capital developed as tertiary students became resources for them to deal with challenges. These include tensions with language policy, curricula and their parents. A very important identity that they chose to adopt is being Chinese with ethnic characteristics. This choice is due to the result of their negotiation with the dominant culture and their compromising to pursue better life opportunities.

Many factors contribute to their identity construction and reconstruction. Their aspiration to escape poverty and repay family for support become motivations to excel in the mainstream educational system. At this point, the findings are very similar to that of Trueba and Zuo (1997) and Lee (2001). However, their training as English majors also helps them to embrace western learning philosophies such as critical thinking and open-mindedness. Armed with this new perception, they are able to reflect on old practices in the ethnic community and challenge injustices in the mainstream curricula. This finding supports Gao's argument that "English learning exerted influence on learners' identities" in the Chinese EFL context (Gao et al. 2005, p. 39). With their persistent efforts to behave as models in both their ethnic community (by following conventional social and religious practise) and in the larger society (striving to become qualified English majors), they successfully negotiate many facets of their identities in their journey of multilingual acquisition. As Kinginger (2004, p. 204) has argued concerning Alice, their "personal

7.4 Final Remarks

experience, talent and resources help to upgrade their access to cultural capital" and in the end allow them to navigate through the mainstream educational system.

These findings will help policy-makers understand the framework of *Duoyuan Yiti* from a new perspective and better understand the power relationships that exist between the ethnic majority and ethnic minority. Language policy and university curriculum can empower EMLs if the sociocultural discourse is favorable to achieving acculturation and multicultural education. Otherwise, power relationships may disempower EMLs by assimilating and marginalizing them through hegemonic university curriculum and detrimental social practice.

The ethnic diversity of learners requires a new understanding of curriculum, preferential policies and multilingual education at the tertiary level. Although the case study in this book reports the life history of just two trilingual learners at a local university of nationalities, the message is thought-provoking and informative.

The unique stories of the two major informants demonstrate how they struggle to enhance their legitimacy from peripheral to central participants in the university community and to succeed in the mainstream education system. The challenge for higher education reform for multilingual learners is clear. The two informants negotiate their identities and achieve a certain degree of academic success in the process of multilingual education. However, I would like to argue that their academic success is achieved under some critical conditions. From the very beginning of their schooling, they were forced to use Mandarin Chinese as the medium of instruction. They have to be determined to devote time and energy to studying Chinese, English, and their native language. If they had not studied in the curriculum in which Chinese was used as a medium of instruction in their earlier schooling and if they had not acquired adequate Chinese as "cultural capital," they would not have been able to communicate with other nonnative communities. This allowed them access to information in Chinese and helped them obtain better employment opportunities. Without knowing Chinese, they would have been more underprivileged when they entered university, and their disadvantage would have been reproduced at the university. To achieve academic success and social mobility, and by studying in the mainstream educational system, I used an assimilationist strategy of detaching from my ethnic community. My personal story may provide another footnote for the dilemma of ethnic multilingual learners in contemporary China.

I examine the gaps between educational policy and practice in the university setting. I point out that university structure, which contains university history, culture, policy, practice, curriculum and counseling, will play a significant role in the formation of the multiple identities of ethnic minority learners. These identities, either assumed or imposed, are one of the end products of the power–knowledge relationship. This top-down structure, if operated under a collaborative power relationship (Cummins 2009), can still empower ethnic minority learners and can trigger their agency in creating better academic achievement and employment opportunities. They may be able to navigate through the system successfully by making use of the privileged discourse of the state policies for ethnic minority groups.

Throughout its history, YUN has been successful in training ethnic minority cadres and studying minority languages and cultures. As a local university with a diversified ethnic population, YUN should maintain its heritage. The university will never become "first class" if it sacrifices its ethnic features and cultural identity. It is high time for YUN to reset its strategy of development and highlight its advantages in implementing multilingual education. The notion of critical multiculturalism challenges the traditional perception and practice of multilingual education.

Multilingual education based on critical multiculturalism aims to assure that all students have equal opportunities to learn multiple languages at all educational levels. Teachers are expected to understand *Duoyuan Yiti* and help students develop "multicultural awareness" so they can become "cosmopolitan citizens" in the global communities.

To build up "multicultural awareness" and achieve a multilingual education in a positive sense, both the policy-makers and policy-takers should reflect on and clarify the goals, missions and prospects for higher education of ethnic minorities in China. Are we producing ethnic professionals for the twenty-first century? Are universities places to disseminate knowledge or arenas to develop agents for social transformation? Are the current language policies empowering or excluding ethnic multilingual learners? Are the present university curricula sustainable to maintain and develop cultures of all ethnic groups? Are the university practices in minority education building up "capital" for nation-state development under the framework of *Duoyuan Yiti*?

To address the challenging questions mentioned above, I propose to adopt critical multiculturalism as the framework for policy-making and as a guideline for ethnic multilingual education. When multilingual education based on multiculturalism is legitimized, and then a monitoring system will function to ensure its effective implementation.

In terms of language planning and policy-making, I totally agree with Hornberger's (2006, pp. 27–28) point of view:

> For language planners and policy makers in multilingual context, then, the question is not so much how to develop languages as which languages to develop for what purposes, and in particular, how and for what purposes to develop local, threatened languages in relation to global, spreading ones.

Language teachers who are comfortable with the traditional teaching methods and strategies for the homogeneous population have to form new perspectives and learn new skills to cater to the needs of the ever-increasing heterogeneous populations. Above all, educators should abolish the nineteenth century world mindset that diversified students should adapt to an educational system dominated by the monolingual majority. To achieve "critical worldmindedness" (Lo 2009) and "culturally responsive teaching" (Ladson-Billings 1995; Gay 2000), intercultural competence should be introduced into teacher education. Equally important, language teachers need to change their roles from policy-takers to policy-makers at the micro level in the multilingual classroom. In other words, they need to deconstruct their conventional roles and become agents of educational transformation. They should

7.4 Final Remarks

question, review and reform the current teaching practice by embracing the "pedagogy of possible." That is to say, they should "respond to all possibilities and potentialities at the classroom level, thus forging one's own policies that are locally effective and empowering" (Helot and Laoire 2011, p. xvii).

As for EMLs in general, with the power gained from mainstream education, they should stand up and articulate their rights. For example, in educational institutions, they should voice their wishes in developing multicultural curriculum and in creating a multicultural campus. They should appeal for better environments for multilingual education based on multiculturalism. Within their own ethnic groups, they should encourage culture maintenance by enhancing their native languages, and publicizing their heritage. Only with a multicultural awareness and *wenhua zijue* could they build up their economic, cultural, social, and symbolic capital and use appropriate strategies in the process of acculturation.

To sum up, multilingual education for ethnic minorities is not just a pathway to nation-state building. It is also an implementation of the universal values of mutual understanding across difference. Only when the notion of *Duoyuan Yiti* is put into practice, and only when ethnic minority cultures are respected as an indispensable component of Chinese civilization will the "Great revival of the Chinese nation and Chinese civilization" be achieved and will China as an emerging "Big Power" be accepted and appreciated by the world community.

Ethnic minority universities like YUN should never forget the special roles they should play: serving mainly the needs of minority people and their socioeconomic development. Lu Xun, a noted Chinese literature master once argued, "Of the nation, of the world" (*minzude jiushi shijiede* 民族的就是世界的). It means that only when something has the characteristics of a nationality, can it survive in the world. This is still very true given the identity of ethnic minority universities in contemporary China.

At the micro level, the life histories of the two minority students not only tell their individual stories but they also portray YUN and other similar universities. These universities are seeking dramatic development by undertaking higher education reform. I hope this study will shed some light on the development of ethnic minority universities in China and serve as a signpost for sustainable higher education reform. With this in mind, multilingual education based on the notion of multiculturalism will not be a mission impossible but instead a key to ethnic minority development.

References

Berry, J. W. (2003). Conceptual approaches to acculturation. In K. M. Chun, P. B. Organista, & G. Marín (Eds.), *Acculturation: Advances in theory, measurement and applied research* (pp. 17–37). Washington, D.C.: American Psychological Assoc.
Block, D. (2007). *Second language identities*. London: Continuum.
Canagarajah, S. (1999). *Resisting linguistic imperialism in English teaching*. Oxford, England: Oxford University Press.

Cenoz, J., Hufeisen, B., & Jessner, U. (2001). Toward trilingual education. *International Journal of Bilingual Education and Bilingualism, 4*(1), 1–19.

Cenoz, J., & Jessner, U. (Eds.). (2000). *English in Europe: The acquisition of a third language.* Clevedon: Multilingual Matters.

Chen, X., Zi, B., & Xi, R. (2007). *A pedagogical study of the university students' perceptions of nationalities, religion and law.* Kunming: Yunnan Press of Nationalities.

Clothey, R. (2004). *Strangers in a strange place: the experience of ethnic minority students in the Central University for Nationalities in Beijing.* Unpublished PhD dissertation, the University of Pittsburgh.

Clothey, R. (2005). China's policies for minority nationalities in higher education: Negotiating national values and ethnic identities. *Comparative Education Review, 49*(3), 389–428.

Cummins, J. (2009). Pedagogies of choice: Challenging coercive relations of power in classrooms and communities. *International Journal of Bilingual Education and Bilingualism, 12,* 261–272.

Devine-Eller, A. (2004). *Applying Foucault to education.* Unpublished thesis, Rutgers University.

Feere, R. (2003). Bilingual in Puerto Rico. In S. G. Kellman (Eds.), *Switching languages: trans-lingual writers reflect on their craft* (pp. ix–xix). Lincoln: University of Nebraska Press.

Fei, X. T. (2003). Some monologues on culture self-consciousness. *Academic study, 7,* 5–9.

Foucault, M. (1971). *The archaeology of knowledge and the discourse on language* (A. M. S. Smith, Trans.). New York: Pantheon.

Gao, Y. H., Cheng, Y., Zhao, Y., & Zhou, Y. (2005). Self-identity changes and English learning among Chinese undergraduates. *World Englishes, 24*(1), 39–51.

Gay, G. (2000). *Culturally responsive teaching: Theory, research, & practice.* New York: Teachers College Press.

Gee, J. P. (2001). Identity as an analytic lens for research in education. *Review of Research in Education, 25,* 99–125.

Guo, D. L. (2009). Ethnic minority groups are not just a cultural symbol: Review on the theory of weakening cultural self-consciousness. *Ethnic Groups in Yunnan, 2,* 77–79.

Hansen, M. (1999). *Lessons in being Chinese: Minority education and ethnic identity in southwest China.* Seattle, WA: University of Washington Press.

Helot, C. & Laorie, O. (2011). Introduction: From language education policy to pedagogy of the possible. In C. Helot & O. Laorie (Eds.), *Language policy for the multilingual classroom: Pedagogy of the possible* (pp. xi–xxv). Bristo, Buffalo and Toronto: Multilingual Matters.

Hornberger, N. H. (2006). Frameworks and models in language policy and planning. In T. Ricento (Ed.), *An introduction to language policy: Theory and method* (pp. 24–41). Oxford: Blackwell.

Huang, R. Q. (2009). An analysis of the educational status of ethnic minority groups in west China. *Education and Culture Forum, 2,* 22–28.

Jorda, M. P. S. (2005). *Third language learners: Pragmatic production and awareness.* Clevedon, Buffalo: Multilingual Matters.

Kellman, S. G. (2003). Preface. In S. G. Kellman (Eds.), *Switching languages: trans-lingual writers reflect on their craft* (pp. ix–xix). Lincoln: University of Nebraska Press.

Kern, R. (2000). *Literacy and language teaching.* New York: Oxford University Press.

Kinginger, C. (2004). Bilingualism and emotion in the autobiographical works of Nancy Huston. *Journal of Multilingual and Multicultural Development, 25*(2&3), 159–178.

Kramsch, C. (1998). *Language and culture.* Oxford United Kingdom: OPU.

Ladson-Billings, G. J. (1995). Toward A critical race theory of education. *Teachers College Record, 97,* 47–68.

Lal, B. B. (1995). Symbolic interaction theories. *American Behavioral Scientist, 38*(3), 421–441.

Lee, M. B. (2001). *Ethnicity, education and empowerment: How minority students in Southwest China construct identities.* Aldershot, UK: Ashgate Press.

Lei, B. (2002). *A cultural history of the Hani people.* Kunming: Yunnan Press of Nationalities.

Lo Bianco, J. (2009). Dilemmas of efficiency, identity and worldmindedness. In M. Gearon, J. Miller, & A. Kostogriz (Eds.), *culturally and linguistically diverse classrooms* (pp. 113–131). Clevedon, UK: Multilingual Matters.

References

Long, Q. H. (2008). The traditional morality of the Hani and its contemporary significance. In Y. C. Fang & Z. Q. He (Eds.), *The study of Honghe Hani culture* (pp. 30–38). Kunming: Yunnan University Press.

Mantero, M. (2007). Toward ecological pedagogy in language education. In M. Mantero (Ed.), *Identity and second language learning: Culture, inquiry, and dialogic activity in educational contexts* (pp. 1–11). Charlotte, N.C.: IAP.

McCarthy, S. (2009). *Communist multiculturalism: Ethnic revival in Southwest China*. Seattle, WA: University of Washington Press.

Miller, D. (2000a). *Citizenship and national identity*. Cambridge: Polity Press.

Miller, J. (2000b). Language use, identity, and social interaction: Migrant students in Australia. *Research on Language and Social Interaction, 33*(1), 69–100.

Norton, B., & Toohey, K. (2004). Introduction. In B. Norton & K. Toohey (Eds.), *Critical pedagogies and language learning* (pp. 1–17). Cambridge, MA: Cambridge University Press.

Ogbu, J. (1983). Minority status and schooling in plural societies. *Comparative Education Review, 27*(2), 168–190.

Ogbu, J. (1987). Variability in minority school performance: A problem in search of an explanation. *Anthropology and Education Quarterly, 18*, 312–334.

Potowski, K. (2007). *Language and identity in a dual immersion school*. Clevedon, England: Multilingual Matters.

Sagin Simsek, S. C. (2006). *Third language acquisition: Turkish-German bilingual students' acquisition of English word order in a German educational setting*. Munster: Waxmann.

Shen, F. (1989). The classroom and the wider culture: Identity as a key to learning English composition. *College Composition and Communication, 40*, 459–466.

Ting-Toomey, S. (1999). *Communicating across cultures*. New York: Guilford Press.

Tsung, L., & Clarke, M. (2010). Dilemmas of identity, language and culture in higher education in China. *Asia Pacific Journal of Education, 30*(1), 57–69.

Wang, Q. H. (2003). *On the culture of the terraced field*. Kunming: Yunnan University Press.

Wang, G. (2011). Bilingual education in southwest China: A Yingjiang case. *International Journal of Bilingual Education and Bilingualism, 14*(5), 571–587.

Xu, R. J. (2009). Education for ethnic minorities in Yunnan: A new China perspective. *The Journal of Yunnan Provincial School of CCP, 10*(4), 31–33.

Yang, G. C. (2009). The disparity in socioeconomic development for ethnic groups in southwest frontier regions. *Journal of Yunnan Public Administration Academy, 6*, 134–138.

Yi, L. (2008). *Cultural exclusion in China: State education, social mobility and cultural difference*. London and New York: Routledge.

Yu, H. B. (2009a). Naxi intellectuals and ethnic identity. *Diaspora, Indigenous, and Minority Education, 3*(1), 21–31.

Yu, H. B. (2009b). Naxi students' national identity construction and schooling: A case study of Lijiang No.1 Senior Secondary School. *China: An International Journal, 7*(1), 167–175.

Yunnan University of Nationalities. (2010). *A brief introduction to general education courses and foundational courses for science and humanity majors of Yunnan University of Nationalities*, unpublished.

Yunnan University of Nationalities. (2010). *Guidance of YUN Undergraduate Program Training Plan (On trial)*, unpublished.

Zhang, X. W. (1996). The Psychological characteristics of the Hani people. In Z. X. Li & Q. B. Li (Eds.), *The proceeding of the 1st International Conference on Hani culture* (pp. 26–35). Kunming: Yunnan Press of Nationalities.

Zhou, J. H. (2002). *Naxi culture impression*. Beijing: Nationality Press.

Zuengler, J., & Cole, K. M. (2005). Language socialization and L2 learning. In E. Hinkel (Ed.), *Handbook of research in second language teaching and learning* (pp. 301–316). Mahwah, NJ: Lawrence Erlbaum.

Afterword

We approach multilingual education from different perspectives. From a macro-vista, some studies of multilingual education in China focus on language policies and/or educational policies. Such an approach examines institutions and policy making and implementing processes while treating the people affected by these policies as communities and/or statistics (e.g., Beckett & Postiglione 2012; Zhou 2000; Zhou & Hill 2009). From a closer lookout, other studies investigate curricula, pedagogies, schools, and ethnic groups without full attention to how individual students went through all these in class (e.g., Chen 2008; Hansen 1999; Yu 2010; Zhao 2010). From the microlens of ethnographic study and complementing the above two approaches, Dr. Wang Ge has documented two individual minority students' life journeys through multilingual education in schools dominated by the ideology of monolingualism. With theoretical insights, his book gives readers a live picture of two lovely girls, Mammuts and Noma, who experienced pains and enjoyed gains in China's multilingual education.

Whether Han or white, unless they have experienced being a member of a minority group, members of the majority generally don't understand how much more effort minority students have to make and how much more pain they have to go through in order to obtain the same educational achievement as members of the majority do. In this book, Dr. Wang demonstrates to us that the difficulties that Mammuts and Noma underwent are institutional, linguistic, cultural, curricular, and more. The whole system is built with Han bias, values, and expectations in what I call "one-way" cultural flow from the Han mainstream to minority communities (Zhou 2012a). If the Chinese nation is truly one nation with diversity (*Zhonghua minzu duoyuan yiti*), there should be two-way cultural flows, from the mainstream to minority communities and from minority communities to the mainstream, in education. Dr. Wang's study shows that it is far from the two-way flow that we desire. Every step forward that Mammuts and Noma took from primary school to middle school, from middle school to high school, and finally to college ran into a cultural, linguistic, and psychological bumper that painfully jotted both of them. After every such bumper, it took a long while for these two girls to recover academically and psychologically. From the observation of my own fieldwork, I suspected that many other minority students were not as lucky as Mammuts and Noma: they never recovered for moving on and they wished that help had been there.

Multilingual education essentially has to answer this question: What kind of person does it produce? I believe that multilingual education is supposed to cultivate students with multiple identities. Linguistic codes, whether languages or varieties of a language, are dynamically associated with identity construction and identity representation (Zhou 2012b). Mammuts and Noma's study of Putonghua has been connected with the construction of their Chinese identity, which was built along with curricular and extracurricular activities in schools. There is no doubt that both of them strongly identify with the Chinese nation. Successful mastering of a language essentially requires fruitful addition of a companion identity (Zhou 2012b). Conspicuously, Dr. Wang's study does not reveal the identity that Mammuts or Noma should have constructed in learning English as a third language. This is where the curriculum and pedagogy failed Mammuts and Noma as they struggled to take TEM-4 and TEM-8 and had difficulties to pass them. How could one learn a language without a companion identity? On the other hand, mostly at home and sometimes in elementary schools, Mammuts and Noma learned their mother tongues that are expected to connect with their ethnic identities. The findings from Dr. Wang's study indeed confirm that both of the two girls have rather strong ethnic identities, though Noma's proficiency in Hani is weak. Losing a language does not necessarily mean losing its accompanying identity, though successfully learning a language definitely adds an identity. However, policy makers often misunderstand the relationship between language and identity. They promote Putonghua over minority languages, assuming that minority students' ethnic identities would be erased along with their disappearing mother tongues. It is an uphill challenge to convince policy makers that multilingualism and multiple identities are not the enemy of a multiethnic state, not even of the state of one nation with diversity. Multiple identities actually complement each other in enriching an individual's life, a community's life, and a nation's life, and multilingual capacity is a resource for global competitiveness.

I have always been asked, because of my research on minorities in China, whether I am a member of a minority group in China. I reply that I am a Han, but I have minority experience in the United States. Thus, I have both a majority identity and a minority identity. For this reason, I make efforts to understand the challenges that minorities have in school back in China. Dr. Wang's book deepens my understanding of minority educational experience at the personal level. I hope that he will have a Chinese version of the book that shakes up the mindset of Han Chinese on minorities and minority education in China.

Minglang Zhou
University of Maryland
College Park, Maryland, USA

References

Beckett, G. H. & G. a. Postiglione (Eds.) (2012). *China's Assimilationist Language Policy: The Impact on Indigenous/Minority Literacy and Social Harmony*. New York: Routledge.

Chen, Y. B. (2008). *Muslim Uyghur Students in a Chinese Boarding School: Social recapitalization as a response to ethnic integration*. Lanham, MD: Lexington Books.

Hansen, M. H. (1999). *Lessons in Beijing Chinese: Minority education and ethnic identity in Southwest China*. Seattle: Washington University Press.

Yu, H. B. (2010). *Identity and schooling among the Naxi: Becoming Chinese with Naxi Identity*. Lanham, MD: Lexington Books.

Zhao, Z. Z. (2010). *China's Mongols at University: Contesting cultural recognition*. Lanham, MD: Lexington Books.

Zhou, M. (2000). Language policy and illiteracy in ethnic minority communities in China. *Journal of Multilingual and Multicultural Development, 21*(2), 129–148.

Zhou, M. (2012a). Models of nation-state building and indigenous knowledge inheritance. *Journal of Educational Science of Hunan Normal University, 11*(6): 15–20.

Zhou, M. (2012b). Language identity as a process and second language learning. In W. M. Chan, K. N. Chin, S. K. Bhatt & I. Walker (Eds.), *Perspectives on individual characteristics and Foreign Language Education* (pp. 255–272). Boston/ Berlin: De Gruyter Mouton.

Zhou, M. & A. M. Hill (Eds.) (2009). *Affirmative action in China and the U.S.: A dialogue on inequality and minority education*. New York: Palgrave Macmillan.

Appendices

Appendix A: Survey Questions for the Study

This study aims to investigate the construction of tertiary English major students' identities as multilingual learners in Yunnan. Please provide the following information and write an essay of your life history in Chinese about your experience in multilingual acquisition in Yunnan. Your information will be used only for the purpose of my PhD study so the confidentiality of the study is guaranteed. All the names of informants are to be replaced by pseudonyms throughout the dissertation.

Demographic Information and language facts about the informants (Just tick, you can choose more than one answers)

1. Sex: ① M ② F
2. Age: ① 18-20 ② 21-25 ③ others_____
3. How many languages can you speak? 1 2 3 4 5
4. What are those languages that you can speak?
   ① The native ② Chinese ③ English ④ others_____
5. How did you learn these languages?
   ① from parents ② from others in the community
   ③ from teachers ④ self-taught
6. The community you lived in when you were young was a _____.
   ① Monolingual ② bilingual ③ trilingual ④ multilingual
7. What is the sequence of your language learning?
   ①_____ ②_____ ③_____ ④_____
8. What are your family members' ethnicities?
   Father_____ Mother_____ Brother(s) _____Sister(s)_____
9. Can your parents speak their native language? Father _____ Mother_____

10. What is the educational level of your family members?
    Father_____Mother_____   Brother(s) _____Sister(s)_____
11. What do your parents do? Father_____Mother_____
12. What language do you speak in the following situations:
    ① with your father_____ ② with your mother_____
    ③ with your grandparents_____ ④ with brothers and sisters_____
    ⑤ with the local community_____ ⑥ with the Han and other ethnicities
13. Have you received any bilingual education at school? Yes_____No_____
14. What are your self-evaluations of your multilingual proficiency?
    ① good at_____ ② better at_____
    ③ best at_____ ④ worst at_____
15. When did you start your primary school?
    ① at 6 or below ② at 7 ③ at 8 others_____
16. Could you speak Putonghua when you started your primary education?
    ① not at all ② some ③ just a little ④ quite a lot
17. The primary medium of instruction in the earlier years of your primary school was _____.
    ① the local ethnic language ② the local Chinese
    ③ the mixture of ①+② ④ the standard Chinese
18. You started your formal English learning at _____
    ① primary school ② junior secondary ③ senior secondary ④ university
19. So far, I have learned/used my native language_____ years, Chinese_____years, English _____years.
20. Do you family have any religious believes? Would you mind telling me your religious belief?
    ① My grandparents believe in _____ ② My father believes in _____
    ③ My mother believes in _____ ④ I believe in _____

Appendix B: Learning History (See the Sample in the Appendix)

Please write in Chinese an autobiographical narrative of 3–4 critical incidents in your past history as a multilingual learner in Yunnan. Your writing may cover any interesting or critical anecdotes in the junior/senior middle school or university periods. You are expected to write no less than 2000 but no more than 4000 words.

Appendix C: Interview Questions

1. Question for administrators

   1. Professor X (false name), as the head as well as a teacher of the foreign language school I know you have served YUN over two decades, can you tell me the history of this faculty and highlight some events you think are critical?
   2. I know that in this university about 50 percent of the students come from ethnic minority areas, what is the case in the school of foreign languages? What is your impression of minority students in general and what about those in the English department?
   3. Could you tell me something about your policies toward the ethnic minority students of this university?
   4. What would be the outlet/prospect of these English major ethnic minority students?
   5. How are the Chinese and English proficiencies of the ethnic minority students in general? Do you think ethnic minority students encounter any problems in their life and study at YUN? If yes, what are these problems?
   6. Does the school/department take any measure to help those (certain) minority students who are weak in English foundation/proficiency? (Any remedial or transitional courses offered?)
   7. Compared with the syllabus of the sister universities in Yunnan, YUN's syllabus seems distinctive and impressive as English major students are expected to "have a good command of Marxist and Leninist theory in - language and culture and o have a broad understanding of nation-state conditions of China and Sociocultural knowledge about English speaking countries," why do you emphasize these two points in your syllabus?
   8. In a recent faculty meeting, you proposed to build English discipline a "first-class discipline in Yunnan and well-known in China." Can you explain what do you mean by "first-class discipline in Yunnan and well-known in China" and what are the advantages of your faculty to achieve such a great plan?
   9. The stakeholders in China are making every effort to promote the unity and harmony between all ethnicities. If so, what measures have been taken in your faculty to achieve such purposes? Are these measures effective?
   10. What are your overall comments on trilingual education policy and practice in Yunnan?

2. Questions for participant students

   1. What do you think of your life here as an English major student?
   2. Do you feel any difference between you and other Han students in the classroom and daily life?

3. Do you think your experiences of learning Chinese and English have changed your understanding of the values of three languages and the cultures behind them? If yes, can you give some examples?
4. Are you an active English user in your class and daily life? If not, what are the reasons?
5. Are you a member of any study group or societies/associations/clubs/religious group? How do you benefit from being a member of this particular group?
6. You must have registered quite a number of courses offered by the university or your department. What are your comments on these courses?
7. Do you have a religion? What would you say about your religion? Does that have anything to do with your study of English? How much do you know about other religions?
8. What do you know about ethnic minority policies in China? And in YUN?
9. Did your previous bilingual or multilingual experience help you to study English well? If yes, can you give some examples?
10. What is your opinion on the significance of learning Chinese and English well as an ethnic minority learner?
11. Do you have a lot of friends at YUN? What is your standard to make friends? Are most of your friends from the same ethnicity?
12. Have you experienced or observed any problems of being an ethnic minority student in YUN? If so, what are these problems?
13. Who are the most prominent figures in your ethnicity? Do these people have any influence on you?
14. Have you read any books about your ethnicity in your native or other languages?
15. Who do you think have more advantage in English learning in your class, the Han students or the ethnic minority students? Why do you think so?
16. Could you comment on the teaching in your Department?"
17. Do you feel comfortable as an English major student of ethnic background at YUN University? Why and why not?
18. Do you often ask questions in or after class, why/why not?
19. Can you learn anything about your ethnicity and the Chinese nation from the university curriculum and extracurricular activities? If yes, how do you get the information?
20. Are there any courses about civic education, political education, and patriotic education in the university curriculum? Have you selected any of these courses and are these courses useful?
21. What festivals do your family cerebrate? Do you think the celebration of these festivals will influence your understanding of being an ethnic minority at present and in the future? Would you continue to celebrate these festivals? Why?
22. When you think about the *Zhonghua minzu* (Chinese nation), what comes to your mind first? Have you ever talked about this issue with anyone? If yes, what have you talked about?

23. How do you understand the concepts of "Chinese nation" *(zhonghua minzu)* and being an ethnic minority in China?
24. Someone argues that the mastery of three languages will make people lose his/her culture and ethnicity, what is your comment?
25. Any overall comments on your being a university student and learning English here?

3. Questions for informants' parents and friends

   1. Why did you send you child to study English at Yunnan University of Nationalities? Do you still think it is a right decision till now?
   2. Have you noticed any obvious changes in your child since he/she became a university student? What are these changes?
   3. Have you ever argued with your children on any important topics since he/she became a university student? Why did you argue with each other? What did you often argue about?
   4. Are you satisfied with your child's performance as a university student in Kunming, if not, why not?
   5. What kind of career do you expect your kid to engage in the future? Do you have any resources to help him/her to make it happen?

Index

A
Academic, 3
   attainment, 118
   challenges, 117
   competence, 105
   elites, 79
   environment, 75
   excellence, 89
   foundations, 104, 71
   losers, 106, 176
   performance, 88
   preparation, 105
   problems, 107
   progress, 171
   standards, 105
   strength, 17
   success, 183
Acculturation, 30, 162, 172, 181–183. *See also* integration
Acculturative stress, 146, 171
Acquisition, 38. *See also* equality
Agency, 121, 122
Assimilation, xii, 29–30, 52, 77–78, 121, 177–178, 180–181
   cultural assimilation, 121
Assimilationist strategy, 29. *See also* assimilation
Autonomy, 9
   regional autonomy, 9–10, 36

B
Bilingual, 23
   additive bilingualism, 52
   education, 10, 11, 13–14, 19, 21, 23, 36, 132, 180
   productive bilingualism, 52
   subtractive bilingualism, 52

C
Cadre, 21, 69, 85, 132, 133, 137, 148, 157, 167, 174, 179, 184
Campus culture, 82, 118
Capitals, 21, 45, 55, 151, 168
   cultural capital, 46, 51, 85, 158, 160, 183
   economic capital, 45
   linguistic capital, 119, 121, 159
   social capital, 42, 46
   symbolic capital, 46
Chinese literacy, 160. *See also* Chinese proficiency
Chinese proficiency, 6, 20, 41, 72, 74, 85, 89, 102–103, 118, 139–140, 170
Code-switching, 52
Collaborative, 162
Collaborative power relationship, 183
Collaborative strategy, 167
Community of practice, 40–42, 106, 118, 159, 176
Confucian culture, 128, 173
Confucian education, 122, 128, 173, 176, 180
Confucianism, 180
Counseling, 107
   services, 107, 108, 171. *See also* counseling
   system, 108, 166, 171
Critical multiculturalism, 28, 29, 34, 35, 37, 53, 184
Critical thinkers, 33
Critical thinking, 115, 119–121, 166, 182
Cultural awareness, 168. *See also* cultural self-consciousness
Cultural discontinuity, 80
Cultural fusion, 30. *See also* integration
Cultural homogenization, 122
Cultural Revolution, 10, 75, 95, 157
Cultural self-consciousness, xi, 32, 113, 168, 177, 179, 182

Cultural transmission, 128
Culture, 6
　cultural adaptation, 36. *See also* integration, 30
　cultural autonomy, 32
　cultural dilemma, 121
　cultural diversity, 27–28, 30–31, 33, 75, 79, 170, 177, 181
　cultural heritage, 31, 170, 176, 179, 182
　cultural integration, 121
　cultural maintenance, 30
　cultural relevance, 80
　cultural retention, 36
　cultural self-consciousness, 168
　culture discontinuity, 23. *See also* mother tongues
　culture exclusion, 80
　culture shock, 20
Culture Revolution, 176
Curricula, 106. *See also* curriculum
Curriculum, 3
　curriculum reform, 106. *See also* curriculum
　dominant curriculum, 20
　hegemonic curriculum, 105, 159
　multicultural curriculum, 77, 185
　public school curriculum, 14
　university curriculum, 103, 182

D
Discourse, 42
　hegemonic discourse, 117
Discrimination, 9, 21, 27–28
Diversity, 6
　cultural diversity, 27–28, 30–31, 33, 75, 79, 170, 177, 181
　ethnic diversity within national unity, 10, 80, 169, 179, 184, 185
Duoyuan Yiti, 10, 32, 35, 37, 80, 169, 179, 183–185, 189

E
Education, 2
　bilingual education, 10, 11, 13–14, 19, 21, 23, 36, 132, 180
　　bilingual education schools, 10
　Chinese education systems, 6. *See also* education
　educational equality, 33
　educational structures, 118
　elite education, 15
　ethnic multilingual education, 9, 32, 37, 53, 162, 181–182, 184
　higher education, 15
　mass education, 15
　multilingual education policies, 10
　trilingual education, 9, 22, 42, 88, 119, 121, 177, 182
Egalitarianism, 37. *See also* equality
Empower, 119, 121
Empowerment, xii, 30, 34, 42, 51, 54, 117, 119, 120–122, 152, 161, 165, 176, 181
Equality, 9, 13, 33, 36, 51, 83, 179
　ethnic equality, 179
Ethnic, 2
　autonomy, 36
　consciousness, 179
　contacts, 55
　diversity, 10. *See also* diversity
　groups, 21
　identity, 22
　minorities, 3
　　ethnic minority areas, 10
　　ethnic minority communities, 20
　　ethnic minority education, 3. *See also* education, 3
　　ethnic minority groups, 10
　　ethnic minority languages, 6
　　ethnic minority scripts, 10
　　ethnic minority students, 4
　ethnic stability, 35
　ethnic unity, 17, 32, 36, 74, 112, 179

F
Folk songs, 111, 137

H
Habitus, 44, 148, 160
Hegemonic, 183
Hegemony, 44, 45
　cultural hegemony, 42
　linguistic hegemony, 45
Heritage, 121, 166–168, 177, 179, 184, 185
　cultural heritage, 170, 176–177, 179, 182
　culture heritage, 176

I
Identities, 3
　assumed identity, 48
　collective identities, 49
　cultural identity, 50, 184
　ethnic identities, 1, 3, 48
　gender identity, 48
　identity construction, 28, 50. *See also* equality
　identity investment, 50
　identity negotiation, 48–50, 52, 53

Index 201

identity split, 52
imposed identity, 48
language identity, 48
migrant identity, 48
national identity, 48, 113
Naxi identity, 113
negotiable identities, 48
positional identities, 50
racial identity, 48
social class identity, 48
social identities, 50, 121
teacher identity, 50
textual identity, 50
Imagined community, 50
Inequality, 28, 33, 41, 46, 170, 179
Integration, 30, 55, 77, 176
Intercultural, 121
Intercultural communication, 78–79, 88, 105, 146
Investment, 50–52, 158

L
Language, 20
heritage language, 52
language environment, 102
language shift, 103
language transfer, 20
native language, 177. *See also* mother tongues
Learning history, 50
Learning strategies, 180
Legitimacy, 41, 45, 56, 106, 122, 143–144, 159, 166, 170, 176, 181–183
Legitimate participant, xi, 118, 159, 178

M
Mandarin Chinese, 1, 6, 103, 170, 183. *See also* Putonghua
Marginalization, 31, 118
Marginalize, 159
Matriculation examination, 2
Minkaomin, 21
Minority, 9
learners, 21
nationalities, 9
Mother tongues, 21
Multicultural, 3
critical multiculturalism, 28, 29
multicultural awareness, 33, 182, 184, 185
multicultural education, vii, xi, 6, 28, 32–37, 42, 57, 77, 79–83, 106, 160, 165, 181, 183
Multiculturalism, xii, 27–29, 31, 34, 37, 53, 79, 181, 184–185

Multilingual, 3
multicultural awareness, 3, 33, 74, 177, 182, 184, 185
multilingual acquisition, 119
multilingual competencies, 9, 14
multilingual learners, 6, 7

N
Native, 21
language, 21. *See also* mother tongues

O
Open-mindedness, 119, 120, 182

P
Paradigm, 47
post-structuralist paradigm, 50
Patriotic, 47, 112, 113. *See also* patriotism
Patriotism, 17, 36, 69, 72, 98, 112–113, 174
Policy, 2
affirmative action policy, 21
assimilationist policies, 29, 77. *See also* assimilation
bilingual education policies, 13
coercive policy, 21
collaborative policy, 19
ethnic minority policies, 35
multicultural policy, 27, 28
multilingual education policy, 23
national language policies, 3
nationality policy, 9
national policies, 10, 158
"positive discrimination" policy, 21
preferential policies, 18, 89, 110, 117, 149, 150, 158, 169
state policy, 150
trilingual education policy, 19
trilingual policies, 11, 118
Post-structuralism, 41, 47
Power, 18
coercive power, 42
coercive power relationship, 42, 118–119, 122
collaborative power, 42
cooperative power relationship, xii, 122, 183
disempower, 183
disempowerment, 54, 117, 165, 170
empower, 119, 178, 181, 183
empowering, 138
empowerment, 152, 161, 165
Preparatory division, 71, 104, 134, 178
Preparatory program, 71, 158
Psychological, 20, 107

care, 107. *See also* counseling
consultant, 108
health, 107, 145, 171
obstacles, 107. *See also* counseling
problems, 20, 23, 93, 101, 107, 144, 171
Putonghua, 2, 13–14, 19–21, 45, 95, 102–103, 119, 132, 139, 143, 159, 170, 177, 190

R
Resistance, 21, 42, 43, 48, 50, 118, 147, 166, 167, 180

S
Self-esteem, 136, 137. *See also* counseling
low self-esteem, 41, 107, 136, 144, 179
Separation, 31, 178, 181
Suzhi, 73, 146

T
Total school environment, 34–35, 37, 106, 108
Trilingualism, 10, 19, 21
trilingual education, 19, 22, 42, 88, 119, 121, 177, 182

U
University structure, 34, 183

W
Wenhua zijue, xi, 168, 169, 177, 178, 182, 185. *See also* cultural self-consciousness

Y
Yunnan Institute of Nationalities, 69. *See also* Yunnan University of Nationalities
Yunnan University of Nationalities, vii, xi, 15, 69, 134

Lightning Source UK Ltd.
Milton Keynes UK
UKHW02f1306240518
323149UK00002B/17/P